CAMINO DE SANTIAGO:
CAMINO FRANCÉS

About the Author

Sanford 'Sandy' Brown is a community activist, long-distance walker and ordained minister from a small town near Seattle, Washington. Inspired by *The Pilgrimage* by Paulo Coelho, he first trekked the Camino de Santiago in 2008 and since then has walked over 14,000km on pilgrim trails in Spain, Switzerland and Italy. He records his pilgrim adventures in his popular blog at https://caminoist.org.

Sandy earned his undergraduate degree in medieval history at the University of Washington in Seattle, his MDiv at Garrett Theological Seminary, which honored him in 2006 as Distinguished Alumnus, and in 1997 earned a doctorate from Princeton Theological Seminary in gender, sexuality and spirituality. In his spare time he enjoys yoga, sailing and piano. He has two grown sons and his wife, Theresa Elliott, is a yoga master teacher.

Other Cicerone guides by the author
The Way of St Francis: From Florence to Assisi and Rome
Walking the Via Francigena: Lausanne to Lucca
Walking the Via Francigena: Lucca to Rome

CAMINO DE SANTIAGO: CAMINO FRANCÉS

INCLUDES FINISTERRE FINISH

by The Reverend Sandy Brown

JUNIPER HOUSE, MURLEY MOSS,
OXENHOLME ROAD, KENDAL, CUMBRIA LA9 7RL
www.cicerone.co.uk

© Sandy Brown 2020
First edition 2020
ISBN: 978 1 78631 004 0
Reprinted 2022 (with updates)

Printed in China on responsibly sourced paper on behalf of Latitude Press Ltd.
A catalogue record for this book is available from the British Library.
All photographs are by the author unless otherwise stated.

Route mapping by Lovell Johns www.lovelljohns.com
Contains OpenStreetMap.org data © OpenStreetMap
contributors, CC-BY-SA. NASA relief data courtesy of ESRI

Dedication

To my wife, Theresa: the easiest, smoothest, lightest-footed, most carefree and fun pilgrim with whom I've ever had the pleasure to share a path.

Updates to this Guide

While every effort is made by our authors to ensure the accuracy of guidebooks as they go to print, changes can occur during the lifetime of an edition. Any updates that we know of for this guide will be on the Cicerone website (www.cicerone.co.uk/1004/updates), so please check before planning your trip. We also advise that you check information about such things as transport, accommodation and shops locally. Even rights of way can be altered over time.

The route maps in this guide are derived from publicly available data, databases and crowd-sourced data. As such they have not been through the detailed checking procedures that would generally be applied to a published map from an official mapping agency, although naturally we have reviewed them closely in the light of local knowledge as part of the preparation of this guide.

We are always grateful for information about any discrepancies between a guidebook and the facts on the ground, sent by email to updates@cicerone.co.uk or by post to Cicerone, Juniper House, Murley Moss, Oxenholme Road, Kendal, LA9 7RL.

Register your book: To sign up to receive free updates, special offers and GPX files where available, register your book at www.cicerone.co.uk.

Front cover: A pilgrim walks among green fields on the Camino de Santiago. Photo by Alberto Roth Albarca (Getty Images)

CONTENTS

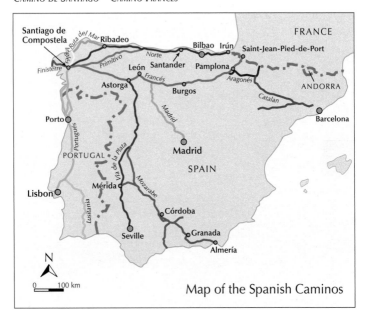

Map of the Spanish Caminos

Acknowledgements

A talented team of co-contributors put together everything good in this book – Roxanne Brown Nieblas's accommodation listings, Rod Hoekstra's photographs, Mike Wells's descriptions of several routes – while any error, omission or head-scratcher belongs to me. It was Joe Williams and Jonathan Williams of Cicerone who pushed to make a new-generation guidebook, following in the trailblazing footsteps of Cicerone author Alison Raju, a true Camino pioneer. Siân Jenkins, Andrea Grimshaw, Georgia Laval, Clare Crooke, Caroline Draper and the rest of the Cicerone team did the artful work of coaxing it onto the printed page. David Gitlitz and Linda Kay Davidson's landmark tome, *The Pilgrimage Road to Santiago*, was a trusted source along with several others. The inspiration to take on this project comes from happy memories of pilgrim friendships formed over 14 pilgrimage walks. Sebastian, Martin, Jacqueline and Andreas were my frequent and favorite companions until I first walked with my wife, Theresa Elliott, in 2014.

Symbols used on maps

〰	main route	**11.1** distance marker		🎯	lighthouse
⌁	alternative route	3.2 alt distance marker		🏰	castle
〰	main route (alternative stage)	= footbridge		☀	viewpoint
Ⓢ	start point	≍ bridge		★	point of interest
Ⓕ	finish point	■ building		🗼	transmitter station
ⓈⒻ	start/finish point	■◉ bus stop/bus station		▲	summit
ⓈⒻ	alternative start/finish point	■◉ railway station		⬩•⬩	international boundary

Facilities

- 🏠 Accommodation
  - 🏠 ❽ albergue
  - 🏠 ❺ albergue/hostal
  - 🏠 ❷ hotel or hotel/pension
  - 🏠 ❷ casa rural
  - ▲ 🏠 ❽ camping

- 🍽 Catering
  - 🍺 bar
  - 🍴 restaurant
  - ☕ café

- 🛒 supermarket/groceries
- 🥖 bakery
- 🔩 vending machine
- 🚻 public toilets
- 🏧 ATM
- ✉ post office
- 💧 drinking water tap
- 🪑 rest area
- ⊕ pharmacy
- Ⓗ hospital
- ⊕ medical clinic
- ℹ tourist/pilgrim information
- ✚ church/cathedral/monastery
- 🧺 laundrette

Relief
in meters

Relief band
2800–3000
2600–2800
2400–2600
2200–2400
2000–2200
1800–2000
1600–1800
1400–1600
1200–1400
1000–1200
800–1000
600–800
400–600
200–400
0–200

MAP SCALES
Route maps at 1:100,000
Town maps at 1:12,500 unless
otherwise stated (see scale bar)

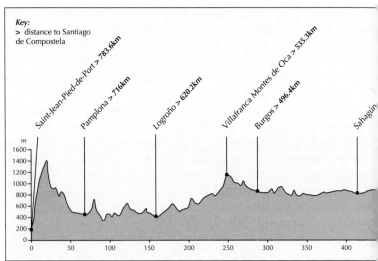

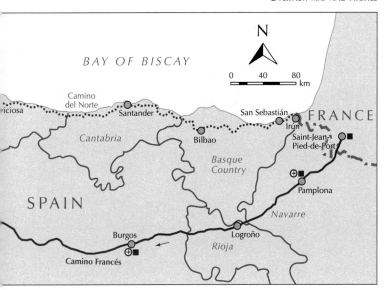

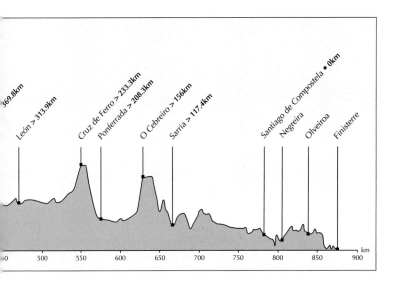

ROUTE SUMMARY TABLE

Section	Overview	Places	Distance	Time	Page
Section 1	**Saint-Jean-Pied-de-Port to Pamplona:** Steep Pyrenees then gentle foothills leading to Pamplona	Saint-Jean-Pied-de-Port – Roncesvalles – Zubiri – Pamplona	68km	3 or more walking days	51
Section 2	**Pamplona to Burgos:** Low ridges and broad valleys through vineyards and grain fields until a mountainous crossing	Pamplona – Puente la Reina – Estella – Los Arcos – Logroño – Nájera – Santo Domingo de la Calzada – Belorado – San Juan de Ortega – Burgos	220km	9 or more walking days	73
Section 3	**Burgos to León:** The broad and flat Meseta with little shade and few services	Burgos – Hontanas – Boadilla del Camino – Carrión de los Condes – Terradillos de los Templarios – Bercianos del Real Camino or Calzadilla de los Hermanillos – Mansilla de las Mulas – León	183km	7 or more walking days	127
Section 4	**León to Sarria:** The fertile Bierzo region between climbs to Cruz de Ferro and Alto do Poio	León – Hospital de Órbigo – Astorga – Foncebadón – Ponferrada – Villafranca del Bierzo – La Faba – Triacastela – Sarria	196km	8 or more walking days	165
Section 5	**Sarria to Santiago de Compostela:** Forests, dairy farms and eucalyptus plantations in undulating countryside	Sarria – Portomarín – Palas de Rei – Arzúa – O Pedrouzo – Santiago de Compostela	117km	5 or more walking days	217
Section 6*	**Santiago de Compostela to Finisterre or Muxía:** Galician farmlands opening out to the dramatic Costa da Morte	Santiago de Compostela – Negreira – Olveiroa – Finisterre – Muxía	91 or 87km	3 or more walking days	253

* Additional stages beyond Santiago to the Atlantic coast

Most camino waymarks are variations of a scallop shell or a yellow arrow or both

GENERAL INTRODUCTION

Façade of the Cathedral of Santiago de Compostela

To walk on the Camino de Santiago is to set sail on a river of time. Every ancient church tower, every proud castle, every silent ruin, every rusting, ringing bell has a story to tell the passing pilgrim. These landmarks are the rugged and rounded boulders in the river, silently testifying to the hands that long ago placed them here. The river itself is the thousand-year stream of pilgrims – men, women, children even – who set out toward the far west of Spain to start a new chapter, to remember a lost loved one, to release a burden, to lift a prayer, or to savor an adventure. Pilgrims over this wide estuary of many channels have hardened under their feet a firm path in the soil that beckons the traveler of today to join the procession and be forever changed.

Of the Camino's many tributaries, the Camino Francés is its most legendary, its most traveled and most revered. The 'French Way' begins on the French slopes of the Pyrenees Mountains, where nervous and excited pilgrims receive a stamp on their pilgrim passports in redroofed Saint-Jean-Pied-de-Port. After an early morning start they walk – or cycle or ride on horseback – up, down and through the green mountains and foothills to Pamplona. Their feet, hardening with the miles under them, carry them across the Alto del Perdón ridge into the wide valleys of fields and vineyards in western Navarre and La Rioja. Days later, on a windswept hilltop overlooking historic Burgos they pause to peer out over the vast Meseta, the vacant

A family sets out from Nájera on an early Camino morning (Stage 9)

farmland plain leading to historic and energetic León, where images of pilgrims like them from hundreds of years before gaze down from the tall glass walls of its Gothic cathedral. Two days later pilgrims are climbing to the Iron Cross – Cruz de Ferro – where they can pass by unmoved or leave a burden or a token or a tear. Then the yellow arrows point them through the Bierzo valley of vineyards and castles and wines before they pass across the Serra do Courel mountain threshold at O Cebreiro into emerald Galicia and its crowning city, Santiago de Compostela. Damp with sweat and sore of foot, there will be songs and dancing, tears and smiles at this end point, and afterward laughter and joy if the smoking *botafumeiro* swings above

them at pilgrim mass. Soon they continue to the coast or they head to home, spirits soaring with hard-earned memories of walking and wonder.

The Camino is both a maker and storehouse of memories. Camino families and friendships form and imprint themselves on the heart. Vistas and sunsets color the mind. The pulsing rhythm of a million steps beats like a drum in the bones. The taste of wine recalls the vineyards of jade and purple. The smell of bread evokes the green or golden fields of grain. The cross atop a tower at home recalls the brick towers in Spain where storks make their nests. The memories may fade over time, but the Camino always owns a deep place inside every pilgrim's heart.

WHAT MAKES THE CAMINO FRANCÉS SPECIAL?

When someone says, 'I'm going to walk the Camino,' they mean the Camino Francés – the main one, the big one, the first one to return after a hiatus of centuries. Other walks hold treasures, too, but this walk is incomparable. Its fame may be because of the allure of Santiago, although as wonderful and historic as that Galician capital is, most experienced pilgrims will tell you it is the journey itself that is the star. The unique blend of ordeals, experiences and traditions make it more than a trip. They make it truly a pilgrimage.

A pilgrimage is a journey of meaning, a passage toward transformation that seeks something deeper than a mere hike. As Phil Cousineau wrote in *The Art of Pilgrimage*, 'What matters most on your journey is how deeply you see, how attentively you hear, how richly the encounters are felt in your heart and soul.' By its nature, the Camino Francés touches a person deep inside.

For one thing, the Camino Francés is *a journey fraught with difficulty: an ordeal.* 'The ordeal is the central, magical stage of any journey,' wrote anthropologist Joseph Campbell. Any pilgrim who arrives at Praza do Obradoiro in Santiago de Compostela on the Francés has overcome adversity. She has experienced thirst, hunger, blisters, tendonitis, illness, injuries, hangovers, loneliness or emotional challenges, not to mention wind, sun, rain or snow. He has walked over hills and mountains, crossed rivers, eaten strange foods – and all of this without his usual circle of family and friends.

The Camino Francés *includes the carrying of a burden and the burden's release.* At Cruz de Ferro, a tall iron cross near the highest point of the walk, pilgrims may leave a stone or other small token that represents a burden from which they seek release. Many pilgrims imbue this moment with great meaning and find in it a release from grieving, loss or failure. They time their arrival at sunrise as a symbol of the new life they hope to receive after letting go of the weight.

The Camino offers an experience of awe. Pilgrims arriving in Santiago may or may not be impressed by the contents of the silver reliquary said to hold St James's bones. Either way, Santiago Peregrino greets them at the cathedral tower and in the altarpiece statue that receives every hug or prayer, no matter how ambivalent. If they are still unconvinced, they may be impressed by the hand-shaped imprint on the stone of the Santiago sculpture at the Portico of Glory, an imprint carved out one gentle touch at a time by millions of nameless and forgotten pilgrims before them who wanted to do more than just look. And if all of that leaves them untouched, at the noontime pilgrim mass when the smoking *botafumeiro* censer swings from the ceiling, every heart finally is transformed at the sight of the crowd of joyful adult children armed with a sea of shimmering smartphone cameras. Along the way, amazing and historic churches emblazoned with golden altarpieces adorn the walk even as Nature offers its testimony in the unexpected colors of sunrise, the waving fields of grain, and the precious purple blossoms on mountain carpets of heather.

The Camino Francés *offers a temporary identity and a transformation.* From

17

the moment of the first stamp on her *credencial* and the donning of her scallop shell medallion, a person becomes a pilgrim. A pilgrim receives certain benefits – the kindness of others in a thousand '*buen caminos*,' entrance to places non-pilgrims aren't allowed – and has certain responsibilities: an attitude of reverence, gratitude, kindness toward others. The transformation happens along the way. Some say the first third of the Camino Francés is a renovation of the body as it adjusts to the physical challenge. The second third is transformation of the mind as the emotions confront the monotony (or beauty) of the vast plains of the Meseta. The final third is renewal of the spirit or soul as pilgrims consider their purpose in life while they near their journey's end. The *compostela* certificate releases the pilgrim back to the world with a changed identity and renewed purpose.

When it's all finished, a pilgrim typically helps someone else make the walk. This may be as simple as giving a scallop shell to a prospective pilgrim or sharing Camino photos with a community group or church. It may mean returning to the Camino as a *hospitalero* (a host in a pilgrim hostel) or contributing to a local confraternity of Santiago pilgrims. For many, the best part of the Camino de Santiago is maintaining the rich relationships built with new-found pilgrim friends whose lives, like the Camino itself, made an indelible imprint on the heart.

HISTORY OF THE CAMINO DE SANTIAGO

Tradition holds that after the death and resurrection of Jesus his apostles spread out across the world to tell his story. James, one of the most beloved disciples

A bicycle in Castrojeríz advertises a quiet place of reflection, Stage 14 (photo: Rod Hoekstra)

and first to be martyred, spread the gospel in the Roman province of Hispania, modern-day Spain and Portugal. Over the following centuries a tradition developed that each apostle was buried in the region he had evangelized, although in many cases no one knew the exact location.

Around 813, depending on the storyteller, either a monk named Pelayo or a simple shepherd boy saw a star that seemed to rest above an elaborate marble sarcophagus, overgrown and forgotten near the Church of San Fiz de Solovio in northwest Spain. Alerted to the discovery, the local bishop, Teodomir, immediately claimed the remains to be those of James the Great, Apostle of Jesus Christ.

Pilgrimage to the site soon began, along with the slow process of transformation of the little town itself. Saint James in Latin is *Santo Iacomus*, which soon morphed in local languages to *Sant'Iago*. The name Compostela refers either to the stars that led to the tomb (Latin: *campus stellae* – 'field of stars') or perhaps the burial mound itself (*compositum* or *composita tella* – burial or burial mound), where the tomb was found.

The economic and strategic benefits of Christian pilgrims and their purses led to promotion of the Camino de Santiago throughout Europe, a strategy planned in part to fill the lands left vacant in the ongoing expulsion of the Moors. The legend developed that at the 844 Battle of Clavijo (now seen as a mythical rather than historical battle) Santiago Matamoros ('killer of Moors') appeared on a white stallion, leading the charge against the Iberian Muslims.

With the expulsion of Muslims from across northern Spain in the 10th and 11th centuries, activist kings like Alfonso VI of León and visionary monks like Santo Domingo de la Calzada helped create an infrastructure of bridges, roads and hospitals to serve the pilgrims and encourage permanent settlement by French religious travelers and others, lending names to the new towns like Villafranca (French-town) Montes de Oca and Villafranca del Bierzo. This new route – the Camino Francés – was the most direct from other points in Western Europe and soon after the reconquest (Reconquista) of this part of Spain became the primary route to Santiago.

In 1100 activist Santiago Bishop Diego Gelmírez convinced his friend Pope Calixtus II to commission the creation of the *Liber Sancti Jacobi* (Book of St James), in part a sort of pilgrim guidebook, and to craft its introduction and commendation to pilgrims. The resulting book, called the *Codex Calixtinus* to honor the Pope, includes a detailed itinerary documenting the route. By the 12th century, over 500,000 pilgrims per year would make the journey to and from Santiago de Compostela, making it Christendom's premier medieval pilgrimage destination outside Rome and Jerusalem.

Healing properties were attached to veneration of relics like those of Santiago. In some cases, criminals were required to journey to Santiago as penance for their crimes. Others traveled in order to receive remission of sins from the Church. Typically, before setting off from home Santiago pilgrims would secure a credential letter from their priest, confirming their identity as pilgrims and asking for protection and hospitality on their journey. They would brave heat and cold, rain and snow, bandits and wolves, to arrive at the holy apostle's tomb. Then, bearing a symbolic scallop shell acquired in Santiago, they would repeat the journey in reverse to return home.

By the 16th century, due in part to the Reformation in Northern Europe and England, interest in the pilgrimage to Santiago began to wane. After a 1589 raid on nearby A Coruña by the Englishman Sir Francis Drake, Santiago's holy relics were hidden by the cathedral staff who feared Drake would carry them to England. They hid the bones so well it was not until 1879 that they were rediscovered beneath the cathedral. Some believe this 300-year absence of the actual relics led to the demise of the Santiago pilgrimage. It was gone but not forgotten – its regeneration would wait for the end of WWII.

In 1948, Spanish historians published a magisterial study of the Santiago pilgrimage, drawing on sources from throughout Western Europe to describe the grandeur of the Camino Francés that had by then been dormant for centuries. In 1969, historian Father Elías Valiña Sampedro, priest at O Cebreiro, published the first usable guidebook and, using surplus yellow paint from the Galician highway authority, marked the entire route from Saint-Jean-Pied-de-Port to Santiago, painting the now-iconic yellow arrows to guide pilgrims along the way. In October 1987 the Camino de Santiago was designated the first European Cultural Itinerary by the Council of Europe. In 1991 some 10,000 pilgrims walked the route and by 2018 over 300,000 pilgrims appeared at the Cathedral of Santiago de Compostela to request their *compostela* completion certificates. The Camino de Santiago was back and had become the most popular walking pilgrimage in the world.

DO I HAVE TO BE RELIGIOUS TO WALK THE CAMINO?

People come from all over the world with a variety of motivations – exercise, contemplation, recreation – as well as for religious purposes. On the Camino no one is ever forced to say, believe or do something that doesn't fit with their own religious or spiritual perspective.

Many do have a religious motivation behind their walk. Each year in July and August busloads of Spanish Catholic youth groups fill the last 100km of the Camino, earning their *compostelas* as part of their religious education. Sermons (in Spanish, of course) by Catholic priests at pilgrim masses in churches along the way are laden with teaching about the religious ideals of a *camino*. A modern Catholic pilgrim even today can earn a plenary indulgence – remission of punishment for past sins – by completing the pilgrimage under certain circumstances.

Although the completion certificate is issued by the Cathedral of Santiago and its application includes an inquiry about motivations, there is no religious litmus test to receive a *compostela*, and everyone is always welcome for each public activity along the way.

PLANNING YOUR WALK

Night falls on the white stucco buildings of central Saint-Jean-Pied-de-Port (photo: Rod Hoekstra)

While modern pilgrims need not worry about hungry wolves or scruffy bandits, it is still important to prepare and to plan for the challenges and opportunities along the way. Included below is some basic background information that will help you begin your preparations.

WHERE TO BEGIN?

The Camino de Santiago has no mandatory starting point, except that a *compostela* certificate is awarded only to those who have walked the last 100km or more, or who have biked or ridden on horseback the last 200km or more before Santiago. So, any town farther than those distances is a valid starting

point. Four major tributaries in France funnel people onto the Camino Francés route, with pilgrims on the Paris, Vezelay and Le Puy routes joining at Saint-Jean-Pied-de-Port, while pilgrims from the Arles route join at Puente la Reina. Here are a few popular places to begin:

Saint-Jean-Pied-de-Port: To most, doing 'the whole Camino' means beginning in this charming town on the French side of the Pyrenees. While there are some good arguments for not starting here – arrival is fairly complicated and departure means climbing over the tall Pyrenees Mountains – it has been the launching point for famous Camino authors like Paulo Coelho, Shirley MacLaine, Hape Kerkeling and many

21

Looking up toward perfection in the dome at Burgos Cathedral

more. About 12% of all pilgrims walk from here to Santiago, covering the distance of 784km in 4–5 weeks.

Pamplona or Roncesvalles: The famous bull-running Basque city is the first major transportation hub along the Camino Francés route. A walk from Pamplona to Santiago covers 716km in around 29 days. Two days' walk and 43km east of Pamplona is the Monastery of Roncesvalles, traditionally the first overnight in Spain and a starting point that eliminates the need to surmount the Pyrenees. About 4% of all Santiago pilgrims will begin in Pamplona or Roncesvalles.

Burgos: The lovely city of Burgos is one of the 'big three' cities on the Camino Francés along with Pamplona and León. Burgos also has train, bus and air connections, making it another reasonable starting point. People who begin at Burgos are immediately plunged into the Meseta, which depending on weather and attitude can be warm and beautiful or hot and boring. The distance to Santiago from Burgos is about 497km, covered in around 21 days. Only 1% of all Santiago pilgrims begin here, most likely due to its setting at the threshold of the Meseta rather than any lack of charm or accessibility.

León or Astorga: A start at León puts pilgrims within two days' walk of the Montes de León and some of the Camino's most beautiful scenery. León has good bus and train connections as well as a small airport, and is 314km or 13 or so days from Santiago. Two days after León and at the foot of the Montes de León is Astorga, a charming town reachable by train and bus that is 54km and two days closer to Santiago. Around 6% of all Santiago pilgrims will begin in one of these two towns.

Ponferrada: On the opposite side of the Montes de León sits Ponferrada with its lovely Knights Templar castle amid the Bierzo wine region. This mid-sized city also has good train and bus connections, and a start here allows a day of relaxed walking through vineyards before the climb to O Cebreiro. Ponferrada is the fifth most common starting point on the Francés and the trip is 208km, manageable in about 9 days.

O Cebreiro: Many Spaniards arrive at O Cebreiro by private bus service since public transport is poor to this mountaintop village near the last peak before Santiago. Still, this is the fourth most common starting place and a beginning here means 156km and around 6–7 days to Santiago.

Sarria: Number one among starting points for all *caminos* is the Galician town of Sarria, about 117km and 5 days' walk to Santiago. In high season the town is awash with groups of young Spaniards who seek to hike the minimum 100km to receive a *compostela* certificate with their youth groups and schools. The Camino

atmosphere does begin to change here, particularly in July and August, and the solitude and beauty of the earlier stages is lost to jostling and noisy clumps of short-term pilgrims serviced by vans. However, for anyone with just a week to spare, Sarria is a handy beginning, and other, less-traveled parts of the Camino can wait until time allows.

WHERE TO END?

For most, Santiago is the final destination and the airport, train and bus service make return from here very easy. Some people opt to walk another 3–4 days or to bus the remaining 90km to the Atlantic Ocean at Spain's Costa da Morte, finishing at Finisterre or its slightly smaller neighbor, Muxía. Many believe Finisterre is the original, pre-Christian end for the walk, and indeed Celtic sites and Roman settlements at nearby Dugium confirm the area was

The museum at the Basilica of San Isidoro in León offers views of some of the oldest frescoes in Spain

a focus for these two cultures. The Finisterre/Muxía route after Santiago is like a 'Y,' with the first two days traveling up the stalk and the final day choosing either the Finisterre or Muxía branch. An extra day of walking allows a pilgrim to connect the ends of the branches by walking from Finisterre to Muxía or the reverse. Both towns are dramatic oceanfront end points but walking first to Finisterre allows pilgrims to enjoy the many kilometers of silent forest after Hospital and then relax in the picturesque, seaside towns of Cee and Corcubión – something that would be missed by walking first to Muxía. This guidebook offers pilgrims the full range of options by describing endings at Finisterre and Muxía as well as connecting the two in a final, day-long coastal walk.

WHEN TO WALK?

The Camino Francés is a four-season pilgrim route, although pilgrims in deep winter or high summer can expect some extremes of temperatures and conditions.

Winter (Nov–Feb): Cold temperatures and snow are wintertime possibilities on any of the three mountain passes – the Pyrenees, the Montes de León and O Cebreiro. Dangerous conditions close the Route Napoléon over the Pyrenees, moving pilgrims to the lower Valcarlos Route. Overnight options are reduced in winter since many albergues close due to lower pilgrim traffic. Shorter days mean some morning hours are spent waiting for the sun to come up and then dealing with sundown before the day's walk is complete. If the temperature is

too warm for snow it may be replaced by rainfall, which increases in winter.

Spring (Mar–Jun): The grain fields of the Meseta are glorious in their array of greens, brought on in part by heavier springtime rains. Conversely, the leaves in the vineyards are barer in the spring. The way is populated but not really overcrowded, and moderate temperatures make spring a comfortable option.

Summer: July and August are high season on the Camino with the largest crowds in these months. The hot sun on the Meseta can make it hard to appreciate the array of beautiful, golden fields of grain. After Sarria the Camino is filled with school-aged youths who sometimes set a chattier mood and have less interest in the international flavor of Camino friendships developed over the previous kilometers. Beds can be scarce in these months and reservations are necessary, particularly after O Cebreiro.

Autumn (Sept–Oct): Although the weather is mild, with the schools back in session, this shoulder season finds fewer pilgrims competing for beds. Vineyards and orchards are often ripe with fruit, while the reddish-brown furrows of the Meseta await their spring plantings. Rain is more common and trampling among fallen leaves in forest stretches has its unique charm.

Holy Years: In any year that St James's feast day – July 25 – lands on a Sunday the Church offers additional incentives to make the walk, filling the route's infrastructure to overflowing. Popes visit Santiago in Holy Years and Spain's royals arrive to celebrate the holiday. Pilgrim numbers swell all year long, and crowds fill the plazas of Santiago to enjoy the festivities. Holy

Year pilgrims should make reservations early. The next Holy Years are 2022, 2027, 2032, 2038 and 2049.

WHERE TO STAY?

Accommodations along the Camino Francés range from spartan to posh, which opens this pilgrimage to most any budget or taste.

Albergues

These pilgrim hostels (pronounced 'al-*bear*-gaze' and sometimes called *refugios*) come in a variety of types and generally offer the lowest prices for pilgrims, save outdoor camping. Expect a bare mattress, a wool blanket and something between four and 100 beds per room. **Municipal albergues** are owned and operated by the local government, are cheapest and have the fewest facilities available. They seldom accept reservations and often have no website for information. **Parochial albergues** are church-owned and often ask for a donation (*donativo*) rather than specifying an overnight cost. These sometimes include a religious service as part of the package and, like municipal hostels, often are hard to find on the Internet. Religious albergues sometimes have a common meal that pilgrims help prepare. **Private albergues** are owned by individuals or families and often have at least a few private rooms, although usually still with shared bathrooms. They commonly accept reservations and have more services available, like coin-operated washing machines. **Xunta albergues** are exclusive to Galicia and are owned and operated by the Galician government as part of its plan to encourage pilgrimage in the region. Sometimes they feature unique and interesting architecture, while at other times they are housed in converted schoolhouses from the Franco era. They do not accept reservations and most always have a kitchen available for pilgrim cooking. **Association albergues** are run by pilgrim associations from various countries and often feel like private albergues but with an even friendlier vibe since they are staffed by volunteers.

A valid pilgrim credential and international passport or official identification are most always required for entry. Albergues typically allow only one night's stay and have a mandatory departure time in the morning, allowing staff members to clean the facility. The large dormitory rooms of municipal and parochial albergues sometimes resound with the snores of sleeping pilgrims, so if night-time snuffling, wheezing or bleating of fellow sleepers bothers you, it's best to bring a pair of earplugs or rent a private room.

Hotels, hostals and pensiónes

Hotels have a front desk along with private rooms with bathrooms. **Hostals** are usually family-operated hotels, generally with private rooms and bathrooms and sometimes linked to a family-run restaurant. **Pensiónes** ('pensions' in English) often have private rooms but with a shared bathroom. Most allow reservations and levels of service vary, with hotels offering the most and *pensiónes* the least.

Habitaciónes

These are, as the name suggests, literally 'rooms.' A *habitación* may be a single room in a private home or a room in a *pensión*. Sometimes these are advertised simply by a sign on the path. All generally include linens and access to a shared bathroom.

A faded sign beckons pilgrims before Palas de Rei, Stage 29 (photo: Rod Hoekstra)

Coffee, beer and bocadillos are offered in a café at Viloria de Rioja on Stage 10 (photo: Rod Hoekstra)

Casas rurales

Literally a 'rural house,' *casas rurales* are rental homes, sometimes of several bedrooms, bathrooms and a kitchen. Pilgrim groups or families sometimes rent a *casa rural* to enjoy group life and cook group meals.

Camping on the Camino

Campgrounds are sprinkled along the way, and some albergues have spacious lawns they make available for pilgrims with tents. If you don't mind the extra weight of a tent, sleeping outdoors on an albergue lawn in the summer can be a pleasant alternative. Because of the environmental impact of large numbers of pilgrims, camping in the wild is strongly discouraged. Of course, a tent should never be set up without permission of the property owner and camping on public land in a non-designated area without permission is illegal in Spain.

The Camino Francés has a vast network of restaurants, grocery stores, food kiosks and food vans. Often lodging will come with breakfast or even dinner included. Sometimes a shared kitchen allows you to cook your own meals.

Breakfast and dinner in the albergue

Seasoned pilgrims love the communal dinners offered as part of the package at certain albergues along the trail. Some private albergues offer a sit-down dinner at an extra cost, while some have only a shared kitchen, and others have no cooking facilities at all. A simple breakfast of toast, butter, jam and coffee is most always available in albergues. If pilgrims opt to cook in a group kitchen, one of the first post-walk tasks is to find a local grocery store for supplies.

27

'Second breakfast' and lunch on the road

Since bar-cafés and restaurants usually abound along each day's itinerary, many pilgrims do not pack much additional food and instead stop mid-morning and again at midday for a second breakfast and lunch. Pilgrims who prefer a more varied menu purchase food the day before to toss in their pack and eat along the way.

The pilgrim menu

Restaurants often advertise a *menú del peregrino* – a one-price, two- or three-course dinner including wine or water – costing €8–15 per person. This will include a soup or pasta first course, a second course of meat and fries/chips, and a simple dessert of ice cream, fruit or flan to finish. The simplicity and low cost make this a common choice for pilgrims, and often pilgrims fill restaurants for an early evening pilgrim meal, with Spanish diners following later in the evening.

Exploring local delicacies

Adventurous pilgrims and those looking for a more varied diet can ask for local specialties by going to the printed menu. Look for the village and town descriptions in this guide for advice on what to ask for in many villages along the way.

HOW MANY DAYS SHOULD I ALLOW FOR THE WALK?

Although holiday schedules often pinch the time available to walk, it's always best to allow a comfortable number of days so you won't feel rushed. To walk the 784km from Saint-Jean to Santiago at a walking pace of 20–25km per day requires 32–39 days, in theory. After adding in rest days and remembering that overnight lodging is not always available at exactly 20 or 25km intervals, it's best to stretch that another 3–4 days. Many pilgrims plan their rest days to coincide with overnights in some of the Camino's more interesting cities, like Pamplona, Logroño, Burgos, León and Santiago itself. Of course, a walk to the ocean at Finisterre or Muxía adds 3–4 walking days to the total. This guide is based on a 32-day itinerary from Saint-Jean-Pied-de-Port to Santiago de Compostela with extensions of 3–4 days beyond to Finisterre or Muxía. Check Appendix A for a helpful route planner that lays out itineraries based on 20 and 30km daily averages and provides room to plan your own itinerary.

HOW DO I PLAN MY DAILY STAGES?

Popular pilgrim guidebooks often have the unintended side effect of grouping pilgrim readers at predetermined stage endings, making for overcrowding at traditional end points. To avoid this disadvantage it's wise to diverge from guidebook recommendations – including those of this book – and instead overnight partway through a stage. This can be done by walking an extra few kilometers or walking a few less, going off-beat, as it were, to avoid normal pilgrim haunts. Appendix A's planning grid is a helpful tool to sketch out your daily stages based on distances between each town and your own personal walking pace.

SHOULD I MAKE RESERVATIONS AHEAD?

It's completely normal to worry about whether you'll have a bed at the end of the day. So why not book the entire walk in advance? Well, remember that if you suffer an injury, make a friend, experience bad weather, or simply find an interesting place to linger, a month of reservations could all be made in vain. In high season after O Cebreiro always make reservations so you can be assured a bed. The least expensive accommodations – municipal and parochial albergues – do not allow reservations, so in high season you'll need to arrive soon after opening, usually in the early afternoon, to ensure you secure a bed.

The festivals in Santiago during Holy Years squeeze the capacity of pilgrim accommodations. In those years (2022, 2027, 2032, 2038 and 2049) it's wise to make your reservations further in advance, particularly in Santiago where Holy Year beds are reserved months ahead.

HOW MUCH MONEY SHOULD I BUDGET?

Food in Spain is fairly economical. A budget of €12/day for the evening *menú del peregrino* and another €15 for breakfast and lunch (for which there are seldom pilgrim discounts) is more than ample. Staying in a kitchen-equipped albergue and cooking for yourself can keep expenses down. An overnight at a municipal albergue or a *donativo* (donation) night at a parochial albergue will cost €10 or below. This allows a minimum daily cost of around €20–30. Some pilgrims relish the challenge of keeping costs at rock bottom and can manage a month on the Camino Francés for under €1000. Even adding airfare, that makes for an extraordinarily inexpensive month of travel in a foreign country. Add a private room and a preference for eating

On the way to Belorado, Stage 10

out and costs increase quickly. The average double room is €50/night, and every non-pilgrim meal at a restaurant or café would add another €30 or more to the daily total.

HOW DO I GET TO AND FROM THE CAMINO?

Pilgrims from the UK and northern Europe will find many options for flying in and out of their starting city. For pilgrims arriving from outside Europe, it is common to plan a round-trip flight to and from a hub city serving both the arrival airport and Santiago's airport (SCQ). Hub cities generally are London, Paris, Madrid, Barcelona, Frankfurt, and Amsterdam. Rail connections from France are easier if you are beginning your *camino* at Saint-Jean, while starting points in Spain work best with connections through Spanish train and bus stations.

Getting to Saint-Jean-Pied-de-Port
The nearest airport to Saint-Jean is Biarritz (BIQ) and the train to Saint-Jean runs from nearby Bayonne. Connect the two with a direct taxi or city bus transfer from BIQ to nearby Gare de Bayonne train station (Route 'Ligne 14,' half-hourly departures, www.chronoplus.eu) and then enjoy the pleasant train ride to Saint-Jean on the spur rail line from Bayonne (www.sncf.com, €14, 1hr). Alternately, direct trains to Bayonne from Paris (Montparnasse) or Paris CDG airport via Bordeaux open other hub options for flights to Europe and rail connections to Saint-Jean.

Spanish train connections from Madrid or Barcelona to Saint-Jean can be complicated, requiring several changeovers, including a mandatory transfer at the Spanish/French border. People who travel from these two largest Spanish cities generally take a plane, bus or train to Pamplona and then a bus to Saint-Jean (www.alsa.com, 1hr 45min).

Getting to Pamplona or Roncesvalles
Pamplona's small airport (PNA) receives arrivals from Frankfurt year-round as well as seasonally from Madrid and Barcelona. Buses (www.alsa.com) from Madrid, Madrid Barajas airport or Barcelona are available, as is the train from Madrid (Atocha) and Barcelona to the Pamplona station which is about 3km northwest of central Pamplona (www.renfe.com). An inexpensive bus runs from Pamplona's bus station to Roncesvalles (look for Líneas Roncesvalles at www.autocaresartieda.com; same-day ticket purchase only, no reservations, 1hr 10min).

Getting to Burgos
The small Burgos airport (RGS) receives arrivals only from Barcelona at present. Buses to Burgos from Madrid and Barcelona are available (www.alsa.com), as are trains through Burgos-Rosa de Lima station (www.renfe.com), although the 7km distance from the station to central Burgos is an inconvenience.

Getting to León, Astorga or Ponferrada
León's bus and train stations are just a short walk from the city center. Buses (www.alsa.com) and trains (www.renfe.com) arrive from Madrid and Barcelona as well as most other Spanish cities. Leon's tiny airport (LEN) offers flights only from Barcelona at present. Astorga

Flying buttresses support the tall arched roof of León's cathedral (Stage 20)

and Ponferrada can easily be reached by train or bus from León.

Getting to Sarria

Sarria has no commercial airport but is served by train from Madrid, Barcelona and Santiago de Compostela, although the twice-daily departures from Santiago are in the evening and stretch to 4 hours (www.renfe.com). A brutal 10-hour bus ride is available from Madrid (www.alsa.com), but a 2-hour ride from Santiago's bus station is much more pleasant (www.monbus.es/en), so the train from Madrid or Barcelona or bus from Santiago make the most sense.

Leaving Santiago

The return from Santiago de Compostela offers many options. Trains leave Santiago's 1873 station at regular intervals each day heading to Madrid's Chamartín station and other destinations

throughout Europe (www.renfe.com). Buses leave the station on Clara Campoamor street many times each day to many destinations (www.alsa.com). Both the train and bus stations are within easy walking distance for pilgrims. Santiago's Lavacolla airport (SCQ) has direct flights to many European cities. The airport bus from Praza Galicia or the bus station costs around €3 and departs about every 30 minutes (www.empresa-freire.com/en).

HOW DO I SECURE MY CREDENCIAL AND COMPOSTELA?

Pilgrims must carry an official *credencial* (pilgrim 'passport') authorized by the Cathedral of Santiago to stay in many pilgrim lodgings and to receive a *compostela* completion certificate. Approved pilgrim *credenciales* are available either from the national confraternity in your country of residence or for a small fee of €3–5 at an albergue or pilgrim information center along the Camino. The major English-speaking confraternities are:

- **Australia and New Zealand:** Australian Friends of the Camino, www.afotc.org
- **Canada:** Canadian Company of Pilgrims, www.santiago.ca
- **Ireland:** The Camino Society of Ireland, www.caminosociety.com
- **South Africa:** Confraternity of St James South Africa, www.csjofsa.za.org
- **United Kingdom:** Confraternity of St James, www.csj.org.uk
- **United States:** American Pilgrims on the Camino, https://americanpilgrims.org

A *credencial* includes the pilgrim's name, home country and starting place and has 20 or more blank squares for stamps. When checking into an overnight lodging on the Camino the pilgrim secures a *sello* (stamp), and handwritten or stamped date, affixed in one of the blank squares. Starting at Sarria, pilgrims need to secure two stamps per day to confirm they have walked the requisite 100km (200km for bikers and horse riders) to receive their *compostela*. A second daily stamp can easily be secured from cafés or from many churches along the way.

At the pilgrim office in Santiago (Rúa Carretas, no.33, https://oficinadel peregrino.com/en) pilgrims can present their completed *credencial* and receive a *compostela* with their name translated into its Latin equivalent. For a small fee the office sells cardboard tubes to protect your *compostela* on your trip home and also an additional certificate that documents the distance walked.

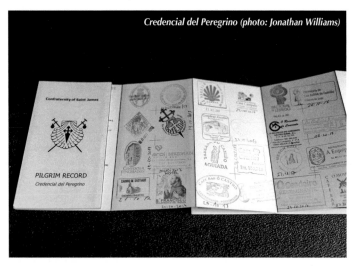

Credencial del Peregrino (photo: Jonathan Williams)

TIPS FOR MAKING THE MOST OF YOUR WALK

The vast sweep of the Meseta (photo: Rod Hoekstra)

TOPOGRAPHY OF THE CAMINO

The Camino Francés crosses three mountain ranges with elevations of over 1200m (3900ft) as well as smaller mountains and ridges. Every uphill climb also involves a steep downhill walk, which can be just as demanding. Even the long, flat Meseta includes elevation variations, such as the Alto de Mostelares after Castrojeríz, a quick but steep climb of 150m.

Pilgrims should prepare for these topographic zones of the Camino Francés:

Pyrenees Mountains and foothills in the Arga River valley (Saint-Jean to Pamplona): This mountainous region, running from the French Basque slopes of the Pyrenees over the pass to the Spanish Basque foothills, is walked primarily on dirt paths and occasionally farming roads, gradually leading downhill along the Arga (Arre) River. Vast forests cover much of this territory until the rolling fields and vineyards that begin after Pamplona.

Western Navarre to Montes de Oca (Pamplona to Burgos): The vineyards and grain fields stretch out for miles here, but elevations range from around 400 to 1150m. This is hilly country, gradually building up to a final ascent over the Montes de Oca before descending to Burgos.

The Meseta (Burgos to Astorga): Best called 'High Meseta,' since elevations are in the 800m range. The area is flat-ish, although almost every day

33

Springtime on the way to Villar de Mazarife, Stage 20 (photo: Rod Hoekstra)

requires some gentle elevation change. This is grain country, with mostly dryland farming. Occasionally the days are walked on asphalt, but most commonly on gravel paths along country roads or on gravel farming tracks.

Montes de León to Galicia (Astorga to O Cebreiro): The climb to Cruz de Ferro is a long and sustained uphill march, and the descent to Molinaseca is steepest of any downhill on the Camino. The uphill section just after Las Herrerías and before O Cebreiro is quite steep, while much of the official section before it is on pavement.

Galicia (O Cebreiro to Santiago): Emerald-green Galicia is a land of rolling hills with a daily series of 100m undulating dips and rises. Galicia has done a good job of interspersing asphalt with gravel trails under trees or alongside quiet pastures.

Costa da Morte (Santiago to Finisterre/Muxía): Galicia's undulations persist after Santiago to the coast, although the sudden quiet of this less-developed itinerary and the endurance absorbed over many pilgrim miles makes it feel gentler. A few steep downhill walks lead to the area's beautiful beaches.

PREPARING FOR THE CLIMATES OF NORTHERN SPAIN

While many people think of Spain as having a warm and dry climate, northern Spain's location off the North Atlantic Ocean and Cantabrian Sea and its major mountain ranges and high plains give the Camino Francés a wide climatic variation. On the same day during the summer it can be hot on the Meseta, chilly atop Cruz de Ferro and rainy and cool in Galicia. Here are some general guidelines for how to prepare:

Spring and fall/autumn: Expect sun and occasionally warm temperatures on the Meseta, but plan for cold nights in the mountains with dependable rain in Galicia. Warm layers of clothing and good rain gear are a must. Cold albergue nights atop mountain ridges, like Foncebadón and O Cebreiro, can make a light sleeping bag a welcome addition to the kit.

Summer: Hot temperatures in the Meseta are balanced with cool nights in the mountains, so a light jacket is still essential. Intensely sunny days make it important to wear sunscreen and to wear protective clothing, such as long-sleeve shirts. Rain is less common, but still likely in Galicia. Some pilgrims rely on albergue blankets for cold nights in the mountains and skip packing a sleeping bag.

Winter: Bring the best rain gear you can afford if you want to stay dry in Galicia's damp coastal areas, and prepare for snow at higher elevations with warm clothes and well-soled boots. Smart pilgrims will bring detachable micro-spikes for snowy and icy mountain trails. Albergues keep bills low by providing minimal heat, so a good sleeping bag is a must. The roughly 42°N latitude of the Camino Francés allows only 9 hours of daylight at winter solstice.

The following weather charts show the average conditions each month in six Camino locations:

Average precipitation

Month	Saint-Jean		Pamplona		Burgos		León		Santiago		Finisterre	
	mm	inches	mm	inches	mm	inches	mm	inches	mm	inches	mm	inches
Jan	105	4.1	57	2.2	44	1.7	50	2.0	210	8.3	96	3.8
Feb	96	3.8	50	2.0	35	1.4	34	1.3	167	6.6	67	2.6
Mar	111	4.4	54	2.1	34	1.3	32	1.3	146	5.7	92	3.6
Apr	105	4.1	74	2.9	61	2.4	45	1.8	146	5.7	51	2.0
May	88	3.5	60	2.4	63	2.5	56	2.2	135	5.3	55	2.2
Jun	80	3.1	46	1.8	41	1.6	31	1.2	72	2.8	38	1.5
Jul	69	2.7	33	1.3	23	0.9	19	0.7	43	1.7	19	0.7
Aug	81	3.2	38	1.5	23	0.9	23	0.9	57	2.2	41	1.6
Sept	107	4.2	44	1.7	38	1.5	39	1.5	107	4.2	57	2.2
Oct	160	6.3	68	2.7	60	2.4	61	2.4	226	8.9	76	3.0
Nov	154	6.1	75	3.0	60	2.4	59	2.3	217	8.5	127	5.0
Dec	121	4.8	72	2.8	63	2.5	66	2.6	261	10.3	124	4.9
Total	1277	50	671	26	545	21	515	20	1787	70	843	33

Average temperature highs/lows

Month	Saint-Jean		Pamplona		Burgos		León		Santiago		Finisterre	
	C°	F°	C°	F°	C°	F°	C°	F°	C°	F°	C°	F°
Jan	11/3	52/37	9/1	48/35	7/-1	45/31	7/-1	45/34	11/4	52/39	12/8	54/46
Feb	11/4	52/39	11/2	52/35	9/-1	48/31	10/0	49/35	13/4	55/39	13/7	55/45
Mar	15/6	59/43	15/4	58/39	13/1	55/34	13/2	56/39	15/5	59/42	15/9	58/48
Apr	15/8	59/46	16/5	62/42	14/3	58/37	15/3	59/42	16/6	61/43	16/10	62/49
May	18/11	64/52	21/9	69/47	18/6	65/43	19/7	65/48	19/9	65/47	18/11	64/52
Jun	21/13	70/55	25/12	77/53	24/9	75/49	24/10	75/54	22/11	72/52	21/13	70/56
Jul	23/16	73/61	28/14	83/58	28/12	82/53	27/12	81/58	24/13	76/55	22/15	72/59
Aug	23/16	73/61	28/15	83/58	28/12	82/53	27/12	80/57	25/13	76/56	23/15	73/60
Sept	22/14	72/57	25/12	76/54	23/9	74/48	23/10	73/53	23/12	73/53	21/15	70/59
Oct	18/10	64/50	19/9	67/48	17/6	63/43	17/7	62/47	18/10	65/49	19/13	66/55
Nov	14/7	57/45	13/5	56/41	11/2	52/36	11/3	52/40	14/7	57/44	15/11	60/51
Dec	11/5	52/41	10/2	49/36	8/0	46/32	8/0	46/36	12/5	53/41	13/9	56/47

UNDERSTANDING LOCAL CULTURES

Modern Spain is a rich and diverse tapestry, and the 800km itinerary of the Camino Francés crosses several of Spain's many cultures and languages. During the rule of 20th-century Spanish dictator Francisco Franco most of these subcultures were brutally repressed, and it is only recently they've been allowed to express their uniquenesses. Today's Spain consists of 17 autonomous regions (*comunidades autónomas*) that are loosely knit together as a single country, with various regions occasionally tugging for independence from the federation and all of them happily celebrating their local customs and history.

The province of Navarre (from Saint-Jean to Logroño)

Here many residents proudly speak the Basque language, a pre-Latin tongue whose source has mystified scholars. The Basque Country spans the Pyrenees into France and Spain, and its residents will happily recount their triumph over mighty French King Charlemagne's friend Roland in the 778 Battle of Roncesvalles. Signs and place names throughout Navarre are spelled out in Basque first, then Castilian. The region's gastronomy features hearty stews, fine wines and rich cheeses.

Castile-León

The most 'Spanish' of the autonomous regions is Castile-León, itself a federation which emerged from among the

A spontaneous folk dance erupts in Pamplona's Plaza del Castillo, Stage 3 (photo: Rod Hoekstra)

smaller kingdoms that repelled Muslim influences in the reconquest of the Iberian Peninsula 500–1000 years ago. Careful listeners will recognize the Castilian-Spanish pronunciation in this region, where the 'th-' sound replaces the letters c, z and final d of Spanish words. Castile-León suffers from depopulation in its rural areas, as villages in the vast agricultural lands have emptied young people into urban population centers. Even so, the rich lands of Castile-León retain the most diverse architectural monuments. Beyond the stunning Gothic cathedrals in Burgos and León are dozens of examples of plateresque (meaning 'like silverwork'), Mozarabic (by Christians during the Moorish period) and Mudéjar (Muslim-influenced) styles. The Meseta is a treasure trove of these historic Spanish designs since many towns have been too poor to be touched by much modernization. For more about the different architectural styles you may encounter, see 'Architecture along the Camino' box.

Galicia

Northwest Spain has its own unique culture – *gallego* – and pilgrims will sometimes puzzle at *hórreos*, the elevated grain-storage structures unique to this area. Galicia was the last of the Spanish regions to convert to Christianity, and it retains strong ties to its Celtic roots, evident in ruins of *castro* fortress cities, striking dolmen tombs, and delicately balanced *pedras de abalar* (balancing stones). Summer solstice celebrations in a Galician village may include fire jumpers leaping over bonfire flames and witch characters prancing about on parade. Other times of the year, head to Punta da Barca at Muxía and cure your ailments by walking nine times around the Pedra dos Cadrís as Galician Celts have done for centuries.

ARCHITECTURE ALONG THE CAMINO

The regions covered by the Camino feature a variety of architectural styles, displaying the area's rich and complex history as part of mainland Europe. Here are a few:

Romanesque is based on Roman architectural techniques and originated in 11th century Europe as a result of significant monastic expansion. It is characterized by barrel-vaulted semi-circular stone arches and thick outer walls with small windows. Romanesque decoration is often simple and based on geometric shapes.

Gothic architecture is a pan-European style that originated in 12th century France and grew out of Romanesque architecture. With high ceilings, steep craggy spires and intricate decorative features, Gothic buildings are characterized by pointed arches that allowed them to be built higher than previous structures and feature more windows, creating spacious interiors.

Baroque is an extravagant and highly ornate style that originated in 17th century Italy before flourishing worldwide, creating dramatic structures with high contrasts of colour and detail.

Rococo combines the elegant French architectural style of *rocaille* with the extravagance of Italian Baroque (*barocco*). This ornamental design is characterized by elaborate yet delicately crafted curves, curls and scrolls, and often features natural motifs including shells and plants.

Byzantine refers to the style of the eastern half of the Roman Empire and the Eastern Orthodox Church. This style features more domes and smooth arches than the high, pointed structures of western European styles.

A few notes on the specific features of religious buildings referred to within this guide:

A **portal** is an arched opening in a religious building that usually includes tableaus of intricately carved sculptures, and often surround the doors into the building and different sections within.

An **apse** is a semi-circular end of a church that usually contains or sits just behind the altar and is covered by a semi-dome.

Retablo or **altarpiece** refers to artwork behind the altar, which can be spectacular ceiling-reaching wonders in cathedrals. Usually depicting the lives of significant religious figures, they often incorporate a combination of painting and sculpture.

TRAINING FOR YOUR WALK

While you don't have to be an athlete to have a successful walk on the Camino Francés, the daily routine of walking for hours tests any pilgrim's physical stamina. Before arriving in Spain it's best to have undertaken an exercise regimen to strengthen the walking muscles of the legs and feet so they're ready to endure the challenge. This generally requires a few weeks of long walks or runs in advance of the walk itself. Walking long distances can be difficult for someone who is overweight, so cardio exercise and diet revisions are helpful before a walk.

A training regimen also gives time to test out which shoe and sock combination works best to prevent the bane of all pilgrims – blisters – which lead to a premature finish for too many walkers. Walking in crisp, new hiking shoes with new, untested socks is a recipe for disaster, so test yourself and your gear by training over increasing distances in the very gear you plan to use – boots, socks, poles and backpack.

WHAT AND HOW TO PACK

The gear list below is based on spending most overnights in albergues and

carrying your own gear rather than using a baggage transfer service. Some say a fully loaded pack (including water and food) should weigh in at 10% or less of body weight, so the pilgrim's biggest planning challenge is choosing what to carry and what to leave behind.

Backpack: Your rucksack is your most important choice. It should have a rigid frame with ventilation for your back and a nicely padded waist strap for comfort. Ask for help to fit yourself in the right size and consider something with a volume of 35–50 liters.

Clothes: Bring two to three maximum of any item. Always steer clear of cotton, which is heavy and slow-drying, and look instead for synthetic or wool fabrics. Plan ahead to layer your clothes so you're well prepared for cold temperatures, which can occur at night at higher elevations even in summer. Bring non-cotton undergarments, at least two short-sleeve technical (poly

Backpacks gathered outside a café (photo: Rod Hoekstra)

or wool) t-shirts, one long-sleeve t-shirt, one pair of walking shorts and one pair of quick-dry long pants. Test your socks in advance as part of your training and bring along three pairs, including the same quantity of sock liners if you use them (see 'Blister prevention and treatment' below). Duplicate items give you something to wear in your lodging while your clothes are washing and drying. Take a jacket suitable for the season to serve as your warm layer and a water-resistant and breathable wind/rain jacket to put on top. In cold weather start with a long-sleeve t-shirt, add your lightweight jacket and top it off with your wind/rain jacket to stay warm. In cold-weather seasons a knit cap/woolly hat and warm pair of gloves can come in handy.

Rain gear: When it comes to dealing with rain, there are two distinct tribes: some pilgrims favour a poncho which covers both themselves and their pack, others prefer a rain jacket and separate pack-cover. Still others swear by trekking umbrellas. Choose your tribe and prepare your debate points.

Sun gear: A tube of sunscreen is a must, as well as a hat or other covering for your head and neck. The westward

Galician farmers stored their drying grain in hórreos like this one near Castromaior (Stage 29)

In rural areas watch for signs that confirm water is safe to drink: 'agua potable'

direction of the Camino means sun coverage is most important on your left side.

Bedding: To keep weight to a minimum, many people gamble and bring along only a sleeping bag liner, which works as a personal linen sheet and, when paired with a woolen albergue blanket is fine for warmth on most overnights. Remember, however, that not all albergues have blankets available, so on cool nights in the mountains even in summer a lightweight sleeping bag can be most welcome.

Two pairs of shoes: Only experience will help you decide whether boots, hiking shoes, trainers or hiking sandals are best for your own feet. All seasoned pilgrims will share free advice, but every pilgrim's feet are different. Your unique feet and your experience in training will decide for you. In general, there are only a few places on the Camino Francés where steep downhill terrain makes a true hiking boot necessary, and soles with a good cushion and good traction are important no matter the shoes' upper. Trainers and sandals work great on dry days but can be miserable when wet. Whatever you choose for your feet while walking, bring along a pair of camp shoes suitable for afternoons and evenings once your day's walk is complete. Some pilgrims bring along a pair of very light flip-flops as footgear for albergue bathrooms.

Hydration system: A reusable water bottle or a water bladder system is essential. The Camino Francés does include a few places where water sources are 10–15km apart, so make sure you have enough capacity for 4–5 hours to cover those stretches. In very hot weather you'll need 2–3 liters for that distance.

Basic first-aid: Cuts, scrapes and aches are the most common injuries, so adequate bandages, sterilizing pads and pain relievers should find their way into your pack.

Blister kit: A small plastic bag with tiny scissors, paper surgical tape and sterilizing pads works well. Blister prevention ointments include Vaseline®, deer fat, Body Glide® or HikeGoo™.

Toiletries: Toothbrush, toothpaste, shampoo, soap, etc. Since international flights limit the volume of liquids allowed in hand luggage, many people buy their toiletry items after they arrive.

Hiking towel: Some albergues are starting to supply pilgrims with clean towels at extra cost; however most often it's wise to carry a lightweight, quick-drying hiking towel if you're staying in albergues.

Smartphone/camera and charger: A modern smartphone usually includes an excellent camera function, so a separate camera is necessary only for camera buffs. A charger with plug adapter is important, of course. Pilgrims who bring a multi-outlet Euro plug or multi-plug USB charger are much appreciated in albergues where electrical outlets are scarce.

Documents: Keep your passport, pilgrim credential, tickets and any other documents in a waterproof document envelope. Take photos of the fronts and backs of your documents and credit cards and bring printed copies, email them to yourself or bring them along on a thumb drive in case the originals get lost.

Cash and cards: Most pilgrims withdraw cash from ATMs when they get there, rather than bringing euros with them from home. Bring along at least two debit cards and a credit card for emergencies. Check your international bank fees in advance since they can vary

widely. Note that many albergues, stores and smaller restaurants do not accept cards, so you will want adequate cash for each day's needs.

Toilet paper and a few plastic bags: When nature calls sometimes a bathroom is not nearby, so a partial roll of toilet paper kept dry inside a plastic bag can be a lifesaver. Additional plastic bags allow you to carry out your used tissue and dispose of it properly. Always remember to bury or at least cover over what you've left behind so you leave no trace.

Trekking poles: If you use trekking poles (see 'Walking sticks and trekking poles' below) be advised that at some airports collapsible poles are allowed through airport security only as checked luggage.

Miscellaneous: Zippered mesh bags are helpful for keeping your items organized inside your pack. Some like to bring along a small clothesline and clothespins for drying just-washed items as well as earplugs for a restful sleep. Last but not least, many pilgrims fasten a scallop shell onto their rucksack to identify themselves as pilgrims. If you don't have one handy, you can easily purchase one along the way.

BAGGAGE AND STORAGE SERVICES

Medieval pilgrims had horses, donkeys and wagons to accompany them. Today, pilgrims can arrange online or by phone for pickup and delivery of their bags by one of many baggage services, typically costing around €4–6 per stage. Some will use Correos, the Spanish postal service, to ship bags ahead to Santiago so their non-Camino necessities will be waiting for them there. Baggage services include:

Poppies fill in the margins along farm roads in La Rioja (Stage 9)

- Caminofácil (Francés plus Finisterre and Muxía, https://caminofacil.net)
- Correos (the Spanish national postage service carries bags to most every stop between Saint-Jean and Finisterre with storage available in Santiago, www.elcaminoconcorreos.com/en)
- JacoTrans (a network of drivers across Spain carries bags between Saint-Jean and Santiago, www.jacotrans.es/en)
- Casa Ivar in Santiago (private baggage storage facility in Santiago costing €15–25 for 60 days depending on size, www.casaivar.com). This service will pick bags up for you at the Santiago post office and hold them until you arrive.

Most accommodations have a shelf where baggage service contact info and baggage tags can be found, usually near where bags are claimed in the afternoon. Remember never to leave valuables in your transported bags, and make sure you have specified the correct destination.

The use of trekking poles has become popular among hikers, particularly for those with hip, knee or ankle issues. They are also helpful for balance in mud or on uneven terrain and can help in steep up- or downhill situations. By some estimates as many as 90% of long-distance hikers use trekking poles. On the downside, trekking poles with metal tips can damage paths, sidewalks and roads and can be awkward in tight spaces or when reaching in packs for gear so fit rubber tips. The best hiking sticks telescope into a size small enough to fit into a backpack. Wooden walking sticks are available in stores and kiosks all along the route.

HEALTH AND WELL-BEING

Personal safety

Recent studies have shown Spain to be one of the safest countries in the world for hikers. Even so, solo walkers should understand it's always safer to walk in a group than to walk alone, and with the quantity of pilgrims on the Camino Francés it's generally easy to find a walking partner or compatible pilgrim group.

Remember these emergency numbers just in case:
- 112 medical emergencies
- 091 police (national)
- 061 health emergencies requiring an ambulance
- 080 firefighters
- 092 police (local)

Safeguarding your valuables
While assaults are rare, burglaries and theft are not uncommon. Thieves look for electronics, identity documents and cash, so keep an eye on these items. While many albergues are now providing lockers it's always a good idea to keep hard-to-replace items like passports and credit/debit cards with you at all times.

Blister prevention and treatment
Nothing ends a *camino* faster than painful and infected blisters. The best blister strategy is prevention, which means testing out blister prevention strategies before you begin. Start by making certain your boots, shoes or sandals fit well. Test these by taking consecutive, day-long walks before you leave home. Some pilgrims buy shoes a half-size larger than normal to accommodate the foot swelling that often occurs after walking long distances.

Many pilgrims cover blister-prone areas with paper surgical or other tape to keep trouble spots from rubbing against socks and shoes. You may want to use a blister prevention ointment that softens the skin and lubricates potential trouble areas. Rub the product you've chosen into the skin of your feet just before putting on your socks. Consider wearing silk sock liners to allow the foot to slide around inside the

The last statue on the way to Cape Finisterre, Stage 35A (photo: Mike Wells)

sock, reducing the formation of blisters. Experienced pilgrims will also suggest changing or airing out socks regularly during the day since perspiration makes the skin soft and susceptible to blisters. Once you're on the trail and experience a hot spot, don't tough it out. Treat it immediately by covering it over with a bandage, tape, blister-covering (such as Compeed) or gel.

If you develop a blister, carefully drain it while keeping the roof intact. After puncturing the blister with a sterile scissor or sharp blade, squeeze out the moisture and wipe it down well with an alcohol pad or other disinfectant. Once it's dry, place a clean bandage on the surface and keep it there for 12–24 hours as the lower skin hardens. If the region of a blister becomes red and painful or if pus appears, see a doctor immediately.

Finding medical help

Injuries do occur on the Camino – most often severe and infected blisters, plus bruises, cuts, scrapes, and also tendonitis and joint injuries caused by repetitive motion. Fortunately, medical attention is most always available. Ask your *hospitalero* (pilgrim host) or desk clerk for information about finding the nearest medical clinic. Spain has a national medical system that makes healthcare low-cost or free to its citizens while people from outside the country will be asked to pay cash for their medical care and prescriptions. Bring cash to a clinic appointment so you can pay whatever the generally small fee will be. Hospitalization can be expensive, so check whether your health insurance includes international coverage.

Bedbugs

These annoying insects are rarer than pilgrim lore would have you believe. Even so, it's wise to have a strategy for dealing with them. Some pilgrims treat their backpacks and the outside of sleeping bags with permethrin (a synthetic derivative of chrysanthemums) to discourage these unwanted hitchhikers. Others carry a small bottle of lavender oil spray, a known insect repellent, to treat their bed. When you arrive, inspect the seams of your mattress for the small, black specks that are evidence of a bedbug infestation and if you find them notify your *hospitalero* or hotel clerk. If you suspect you've been bitten during the night, check to see if the bites are pink and form a zigzag pattern or line. If so, contact your host and ask for help. Instead of continuing on, the safest and most courteous next step is to throw all of your garments and kit into a hot clothes dryer and let them spin on the hottest cycle for a full hour, killing the pests which otherwise can remain in your things and spread to your next lodging and even your own home.

Self-care

Whether it's time constraints, peer pressure or a personal achievement goal, it's easy to push your body too hard and then find yourself sick or injured. Nothing beats eating right, resting when you're tired, and getting a good night's sleep. There's no shame in taking time off from walking or shortening the daily distance goal. If you skip ahead by public transport, you may be relieved to discover you are not the only pilgrim on the bus. Be kind to yourself. Listen to your body and be gentle as you coax and nourish it toward the goal.

PILGRIM ETIQUETTE

At meals, in overnights and along the trail the Camino is an ever-flowing river of personalities and cultures, a social scene that presents all varieties of human interaction. The Camino has developed a sort of 'pilgrim code' that smooths out these interactions and helps everyone to have a better time.

Walk your own camino – Others will have advice for you, but *your camino* belongs to you. So, sleep in late. Take the bus. Wear make-up if it feels right to you. Bring a hairdryer if you like or walk with a pack that's too heavy. It's your *camino*.

Leave no trace – A few steps off the trail can mean finding small clusters of toilet tissue used in bathroom breaks. It's better for everyone if you carry out your waste paper or carefully cover it.

Mind your tips – The click-clack-click of metal tips on pavement comes from pilgrims who don't change out their metal tips with rubber ones when walking on hard surfaces. Hiking poles can be clumsy in the tight confines of a grocery store or on a narrow path and an unaware pilgrim can scratch or poke a fellow walker.

Respect the need for solitude – The sudden 24-hour-a-day community can be overwhelming, so allow partners and friends some quiet time during the day.

Albergue life is fun and demanding – Most people aren't used to sleeping with 3–100 strangers, so the friendly community of albergue life is balanced with some challenges.

- It's said that 45% of adults snore intermittently and 25% are chronic snorers, so the only real answers to albergue snoring are either earplugs or a change in attitude.

- Instead of awakening sleeping pilgrims in an early morning departure, it's best to pack the night before, and of course always avoid crinkly plastic bags and tempting light switches that disturb sleepers.

- Remember, **the *hospitalero* is your friend**. They know the neighborhood and can tell you about laundry machines, groceries, restaurants, bus services, and much more.

- Keep in mind that **donativo does not mean free**. Parochial and association albergues depend on pilgrim generosity to cover their costs for food, heat, lights, water, garbage and such. Consider beginning with a donation of €10/night for a bed and about that much for dinner, too.

- Since bedbugs are known to hide in the seams of backpacks, **don't put your backpack on your bed**. It's easy to place the rucksack on the floor or hang it from the bedstead. Some pilgrims place their packs in a large garbage sack to keep bugs away.

- **Clean up after yourself** in the bathroom and kitchen just like your parents told you, since other pilgrims use those spaces after you.

- Most importantly, **make friends**. An albergue is an international experience that becomes even more pleasant with a cheerful greeting to a stranger. The person you greeted over an albergue breakfast 500km ago may be the same one who hugs you and cries with you as you arrive at the Cathedral of Santiago.

HOW TO USE THIS GUIDE

This guide is part of a two-volume set. The Camino Francés map booklet offers detailed, stage-by-stage maps of the route as well as over 120 town and village maps that help the reader to find the exact location of albergues and other sites important to pilgrims. The small size allows pilgrims to keep this slim book in an accessible pocket to help orient them throughout the day.

This volume, the guidebook, offers tips, directions and background information for each day, plus a listing of over 500 overnight lodgings. Here are some of the features of each stage description:

Stage beginning and end: While the walk is divided into 32 stages of approximately 25km each as a sample itinerary, Appendix A provides a helpful planning grid recommended for determining your own stages. For clarity on distance calculations, specific start and end points for each stage are specified. These points are often the central town or city square, a cathedral or important church, or when lacking such major landmarks sometimes the town's municipal albergue.

Distance and duration statistics: Original GPS tracks from the authors' own walks were edited to remove extraneous data and the resulting tracks form the basis of all distance calculations. The distance shown is a straight-line ideal walk that does not include coffee breaks, lunches or other wanderings of a typical pilgrim day. Durations – by which is meant walking time – are calculated using a formula based on a 4km/

hr pace with 7.5min added for each 100m of vertical ascent. They do not include lunch or rest breaks.

Cumulative ascents and descents: These figures tabulate cumulative uphill and downhill components of each stage. Elevation data is based on GPS coordinates and corrected using NASA SRTM data provided by www.gpsvisualizer. com.

Difficulty ratings: Each stage is given one of four subjective difficulty ratings: easy, moderate, moderately hard or hard. Factors like length, duration, steepness and frequency of available services are considered in determining the rating.

Percentage paved: Hard surfaces like asphalt/tarmac and concrete are harder on your feet than gravel roads and dirt trails, so the percentage on hard (paved) surfaces is included for each stage.

Albergues: The location of albergues along the way and their distance in kilometers from the stage start are provided for at-a-glance planning. Since all distances were rounded to the nearest 0.1km, slight variations between stage totals and cumulative intermediary distances naturally occur.

Stage overview: These brief descriptions are intended to give a flavor of the route and to offer helpful tips.

Walking directions: Since the Camino Francés is extremely well marked, walking directions in this guidebook are minimal and are intended to provide a flavor of unique terrain as well as information about interesting features.

Distances, municipal information and infrastructure symbols: There are entries for key villages, towns and cities ('municipalities') along the route. The distance between them is shown, as well as between minor landmarks mentioned in the route description. For each municipality the distance remaining to Santiago (or Finisterre and Muxía) is given. Villages, towns and cities are identified by population and elevation and then marked with a set of 10 symbols to identify their infrastructure. See Figure 1 for an example.

Town and monument descriptions: The Camino Francés is full of sites and monuments whose unique stories and meanings are often not evident to the pilgrim walker. In these instances, a brief description is offered to give background and meaning to the walk.

Elevation profiles: The GPS tracks that form the basis for distance calculations and maps were used to create elevation profiles. The elevation axis of some profiles has been adjusted to allow all the profiles to fit more neatly on the page, and variant overlays to the main route profiles are sometimes not shown at scale.

Accommodation listings: The Camino Francés offers over 1100 unique accommodations to pilgrims, making it impossible to show all listings in a book of this size. Instead, this book includes all 550 public and private albergues on the Camino Francés plus campgrounds and, when they are on the trail and in areas without an albergue, a few *pensiónes* and *casas rurales* as well. Likewise, hotel information is excluded

except in cases where they are either of special interest, are in a key location or are the sole lodging in a village. Non-albergue accommodation options are shown in the map booklet for the purpose of location only; search booking sites for more information and reservations. All prices given in this guide are accurate as at 2022.

Accommodations are grouped into the following categories, each with its own symbol:

🔺 Albergue with dormitory rooms only

🔺 Albergue with dormitory and private rooms, including some features of a *hostal* or *pensión*

🔺 Hotel (usually with 24-hour front desk and private bathrooms), *hostal* (family-run hotel), or *pensión* (hotel with some shared bathrooms)

🔺 *Casa rural* rental home with kitchen and multiple bedrooms and bathrooms

▲ Campground for tent-camping pilgrims

A full accommodation listing is available at the Cicerone Press website (www.cicerone.co.uk).

Accommodation infrastructure listing: Each accommodation listing includes helpful information about the facilities and services available. See Figure 2 for an example and list of symbols. Some albergues also have private

Figure 1: Example of stage description and municipal information

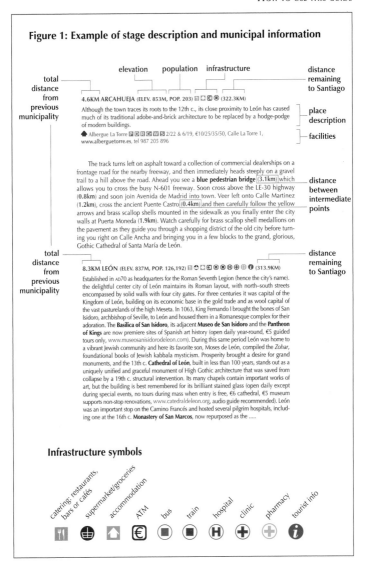

total distance from previous municipality

elevation   population   infrastructure

distance remaining to Santiago

4.6KM ARCAHUEJA (ELEV. 853M, POP. 203) ▯🏙🏠€◉ (322.3KM)

place description

Although the town traces its roots to the 12th c., its close proximity to León has caused much of its traditional adobe-and-brick architecture to be replaced by a hodge-podge of modern buildings.

facilities

🔺 Albergue La Torre ▯🄿🄳🅁🄶🅆🅂 2/22 & 6/19, €10/25/35/50, Calle La Torre 1, www.alberguetorre.es, tel 987 205 896

The track turns left on asphalt toward a collection of commercial dealerships on a frontage road for the nearby freeway, and then immediately heads steeply on a gravel trail to a hill above the road. Ahead you see a **blue pedestrian bridge** ⟨3.1km⟩ which allows you to cross the busy N-601 freeway. Soon cross above the LE-30 highway (**0.8km**) and soon join Avenida de Madrid into town. Veer left onto Calle Martinez (**1.2km**), cross the ancient Puente Castro ⟨0.4km⟩ and then carefully follow the yellow arrows and brass scallop shells mounted in the sidewalk as you finally enter the city walls at Puerta Moneda (**1.9km**). Watch carefully for brass scallop shell medallions on the pavement as they guide you through a shopping district of the old city before turning you right on Calle Ancha and bringing you in a few blocks to the grand, glorious, Gothic Cathedral of Santa María de León.

distance between intermediate points

total distance from previous municipality

distance remaining to Santiago

8.3KM LEÓN (ELEV. 837M, POP. 126,192) ▯🏙🏠€◉◉◉⊕➕🅸 (313.9KM)

Established in AD70 as headquarters for the Roman Seventh Legion (hence the city's name), the delightful center city of León maintains its Roman layout, with north-south streets encompassed by solid walls with four city gates. For three centuries it was capital of the Kingdom of León, building on its economic base in the gold trade and as wool capital of the vast pasturelands of the high Meseta. In 1063, King Fernando I brought the bones of San Isidoro, archbishop of Seville, to León and housed them in a Romanesque complex for their adoration. The **Basílica of San Isidoro**, its adjacent **Museo de San Isidoro** and the **Pantheon of Kings** are now premiere sites of Spanish art history (open daily year-round, €5 guided tours only, www.museosanisidorodeleon.com). During this same period León was home to a vibrant Jewish community and here its favorite son, Moses de León, compiled the *Zohar*, foundational books of Jewish kabbala mysticism. Prosperity brought a desire for grand monuments, and the 13th c. **Cathedral of León**, built in less than 100 years, stands out as a uniquely unified and graceful monument of High Gothic architecture that was saved from collapse by a 19th c. structural intervention. Its many chapels contain important works of art, but the building is best remembered for its brilliant stained glass (open daily except during special events, no tours during mass when entry is free, €6 cathedral, €5 museum supports non-stop renovations, www.catedraldeleon.org, audio guide recommended). León was an important stop on the Camino Francés and hosted several pilgrim hospitals, including one at the 16th c. **Monastery of San Marcos**, now repurposed as the .....

Infrastructure symbols

catering: restaurants, bars or cafés   supermarket/groceries   accommodation   ATM   bus   train   hospital   clinic   pharmacy   tourist info

🍴 🌐 🏠 € ◼ ◼ 🅷 ➕ ➕ 🅘

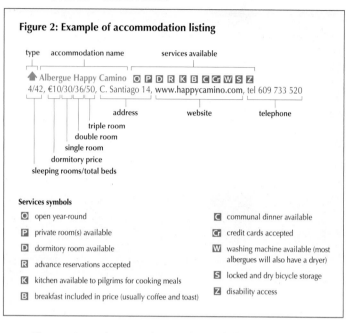

Figure 2: Example of accommodation listing

Services symbols

- **O** open year-round
- **P** private room(s) available
- **D** dormitory room available
- **R** advance reservations accepted
- **K** kitchen available to pilgrims for cooking meals
- **B** breakfast included in price (usually coffee and toast)

- **C** communal dinner available
- **G** credit cards accepted
- **W** washing machine available (most albergues will also have a dryer)
- **S** locked and dry bicycle storage
- **Z** disability access

rooms, like a pension. In these cases the rooms/beds for the albergue are listed first, followed by those for the pension. For example, in '3/13 & 7/16' the '3/13' refers to the rooms/beds in the albergue and '7/16' refers to the rooms/beds in the pension.

GPX TRACKS AND ACCOMMODATION DOWNLOAD

GPX tracks for the routes in this guidebook are available to download free at www.cicerone.co.uk/1004/GPX. GPX files are provided in good faith, but neither the author nor the publisher accepts responsibility for their accuracy.

Watch the book's webpage (www.cicerone.co.uk/1004/updates) for ongoing updates so you have the very latest information before you make your walk.

A fuller list of accommodation along the Camino Francés is available to download at www.cicerone.co.uk/1004/downloads.

SECTION 1:
SAINT-JEAN-PIED-DE-PORT
TO PAMPLONA

Night-time stroll on the Rue de la Citadelle in Saint-Jean-Pied-de-Port (photo:

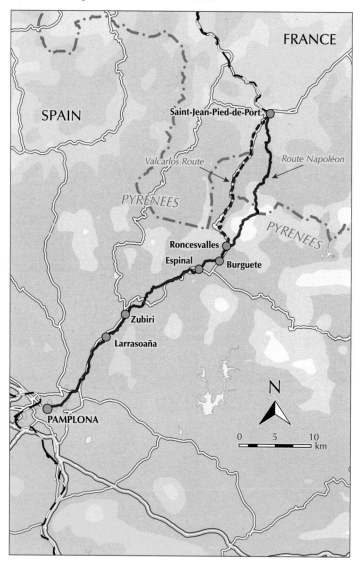

SECTION 1:
SAINT-JEAN-PIED-DE-PORT TO PAMPLONA

Pilgrims enjoy a quiet trail on the path near Burguete, Stage 2

The first three-day stretch of the Camino Francés is a transit across the Pyrenees Mountains, a sometimes-rugged passage of forests and river valleys with a long history of conquests and pilgrim travel.

Since prehistoric times trekkers have used the Ibañeta Pass up the Nive d'Arnéguy valley to enter Spain, a route famously traveled by the conqueror Charlemagne and his French troops in the ninth century. Nine centuries later Napoléon Bonaparte sought the element of surprise by using the more circumspect, higher and more challenging Roman alternative which now bears his name. Because of its spectacular clear-weather views, the steeper Route Napoléon is preferred by most in summer, while thanks to its lower elevations

the Ibañeta Pass through Valcarlos is the foul-weather choice. The two options converge near the monastery of Roncesvalles before the track descends through forested foothills along the Arga River drainage toward legendary Pamplona.

The local Basque people, resident here for many centuries, give this region its unique flavor. While they also speak French or Spanish, many residents are fluent in the ancient Euskara tongue, and they view the Basque Country (Euskal Herria) as their homeland, not France or Spain. Town names are often in Spanish or French plus Euskara and type fonts on signs are often shown in the Harri folk font derived from centuries-old tombstones in local Basque cemeteries. Alpine-like white stucco homes with steep roofs fill the villages, while regional cuisine features hearty meats and stews, fish grilled over hot coals, *tolosa* bean dishes, Idiazábal sheep's cheese, *txakoli* wine and sweet Basque apple cider.

The Camino's pathway through this region is relatively sparse of pilgrims, although the numbers increase at Roncesvalles, Pamplona and then just afterward at Puente la Reina, where pilgrims who've crossed the Somport Pass of the Camino Aragonés join the stream.

PLANNING

1   Winter walkers are required to cross the Pyrenees on the Valcarlos Route over the Ibañeta Pass. On shoulder seasons, watch weather forecasts to see if a Route Napoléon crossing is allowed. Always confirm your plans at the pilgrim office in Saint-Jean-Pied-de-Port.

2   Many pilgrims ease into a Route Napoléon crossing with an intermediate stay at Refuge Orisson or Albergue Borda, 8km up the hill.

3   Because of its historic significance and ease of accommodation, most pilgrims who start in France will overnight at Roncesvalles. A second overnight is common at Zubiri or Larrasoaña, with a third night in Pamplona or just afterward at Cizur Menor.

4   Pilgrims will find Pamplona a hectic and preoccupied place during the Running of the Bulls (July 6–14), when the world converges on its grand festivities. Otherwise, it's well worth an afternoon, evening or a full rest day spent enjoying the lively city's food and wine and catching an impromptu outdoor folk dance with the locals in Plaza del Castillo.

WHAT NOT TO MISS

Some albergues, like Beilari in Saint-Jean and Refuge Orisson, help pilgrims get acquainted over the shared evening meal. Nationalities of all pilgrims staying at its albergue are announced at the nightly Roncesvalles Pilgrim Mass where priests offer a pilgrim blessing. Pamplona's vibrancy is on display in its pedestrian-filled streets each evening, and a pause or overnight in this Navarran capital is worth the extra time. Pamplona Cathedral houses remains of the royalty of Navarre and the adjacent diocesan museum has many important pieces from Pamplona and the surrounding countryside.

STAGE 1
Saint-Jean-Pied-de-Port to Roncesvalles

Start	Pilgrim office, 39 Rue de la Citadelle, Saint-Jean-Pied-de-Port
Finish	Roncesvalles, Church of Santiago
Distance	24.7km (23.8)km via Valcarlos variant)
Total ascent	1565m (1485m via variant)
Total descent	795m (715m via variant)
Difficulty	Hard (moderately hard via variant)
Duration	8¼hr (7¾hr via variant)
Percentage paved	58% (72% via variant)
Albergues	Gîte Huntto 5.3; Orisson 7.7; Roncesvalles 24.7 (accommodation on variant: Arnéguy 8.6; Valcarlos 11.0)

Famously difficult for its exhausting climb and seemingly endless descent, the stage can be broken up with an overnight at Refuge Orisson or Albergue Borda. Plan food carefully, since Orisson and a food van at the summit are the only food options along the way. Unsurpassed mountain views are constant on clear days, but on cloudy or rainy days the climb, coupled with a sloppy trail, can turn the stage into a slog. The lower and less-steep variant through Valcarlos is mandatory in winter and also offers a pleasant walk with a quick downhill from the Ibañeta Pass into Roncesvalles.

SAINT-JEAN-PIED-DE-PORT (ELEV. 190M, POP. 1580) 🏨⊕🏧Ⓒ◎◉⊕⊕ⓘ (783.6KM)

This charming, red-roofed, medieval village serves proudly as a sub-regional capital, tourist destination, and pilgrimage starting point. The original town on a nearby site, Saint-Jean-le-Vieux, was destroyed in 1177 by Richard the Lionheart and historians point to a 12th c. deed by King Sancho VII (Sancho the Strong) of Navarre as the official founding of Saint-Jean-Pied-de-Port at its current location. The name derives from its two patron saints, John the Baptist and John the Evangelist, and its position at the *pied* (foot) of the *port* (mountain pass). As gateway to two of the most easily passable transits over the Pyrenees – the Puerto de Ibañeta (Valcarlos Route) and the Route Napoléon – the town has served alternately as a military stronghold, invasion point, pilgrim staging location, and recreational hub for modern vacationers.

The **Porte St-Jacques** (St James Gate) in the upper village is a UNESCO World Heritage Site, celebrating the town's historic role as confluence-point for Europe-Santiago pilgrimage itineraries and starting point for the Camino Francés route to Santiago de

Compostela. The town's oldest buildings stand below, between there and the banks of the Nive River which is crossed on the Roman bridge, the **Pont d'Eyheraberry**. Its oldest church, **Notre-Dame-du-Bout-du-Pont**, near the **Porte d'Espagne** (Spanish Gate), was built by Sancho the Strong to commemorate his military victory over the Moors in 1212. The walled **citadel** above town was heavily fortified against Spanish invasion beginning in the 17th c., allowing its garrison of 500 French troops to storm down the valley in case of a Spanish invasion. In the early 20th c. the French military abandoned the fortress, which now houses a school.

Saint-Jean is best enjoyed in a slow walk among shops along the scenic **Rue de la Citadelle**, the old town's main street. A short climb to the citadel and a stroll with an ice cream cone along the banks of the Nive River make for a charming afternoon. At dinner enjoy a glass of the celebrated red and rosé wines of the Irouléguy grape or the beloved local apple ciders first noted by Sancho the Great in 1084. Other local specialties include the *fromage de brebis* cheese, trout omelets and Bayonne ham.

Note that the phone numbers in the following accommodation list require the French prefix (+33).

🏠 Beilari **D R B C S** 4/14, €40/-/-/-, 40 Rue de la Citadelle, www.beilari.info/en, tel 559 372 468

🏠 Gîte Bidean **P D R C S** -/12, €17/-/45/-, 11 Rue d'Espagne, www.facebook.com/SaintJeanPiedDePort, tel 670 296 666

🏠 Gîte communal Ospitalia **O P D B W S Z** 3/32, €12/30/30/-, 55 Rue de la Citadelle, www.st-jean-pied-de-port.fr, tel 617 103 189

🏠 Gîte de la Porte Saint-Jacques **D R K B S** 2/6, €25/-/-/-, 51 Rue de la Citadelle, tel 630 997 561

🏠 Gîte Le Lièvre et La Tortue **P D R Cr C W S Z** 2/9, €21/62/62/-, 30 Rue de la Citadelle, www.facebook.com/giteleliervreetlatortue, tel 663 629 235

🏠 Le Chemin Vers L'Etoile **O P D R Cr B C W S Z** 5/46, €20/23/46/-, 21 Rue d'Espagne, www.pelerinage-saint-jacques-compostelle.com/en/gite, tel 559 372 071

🏠 Refuge Accueil Paroissial (Maison Kaserna) **D R B C W S** 2/14, €23/-/-/-, 43 Rue d'Espagne, www.saintjeanpieddeport-paysbasque-tourisme.com, tel 559 376 517

🏠 Gîte Compostelle **P D R K S** 2/8 & 7/16, €18/50/50/75, 6 Route d'Arneguy, tel 621 371 831

🏠 Gîte Izaxulo **P D R W S** 2/14 & 3/6, €21/72/77/-, 2 Avenue Renaud, www.en-pays-basque.fr/hebergement/gite-izaxulo, tel 684 331 205

🏠 Gîte Makila **P D R Cr B W S** 3/25 & 2/4, €25/-/65/-, 35 Rue de la Citadelle, http://makila-saintjean.com/fr, tel 663 101 346

🏠 Gîte Ultreia **P D R Cr K B W S** 1/7 & 3/8, €23/51/56/75, 8 Rue de la Citadelle, www.ultreia64.fr, tel 680 884 622

🛏 Zuharpeta 🅟 🄳 🅁 🄶 🅂 1/23 & 4/8, €18/-/48/-, 5 Rue Zuharpeta,
www.en-pays-basque.fr/hebergement/gite-zuharpeta, tel 559 373 588

▲ Camping Municipal Plaza Berri 🅆 🅂 53/160, €11/-/-/-, daily pass, 7 Avenue du Fronton,
www.saintjeanpieddeport-paysbasque-tourisme.com, tel 559 371 119, bungalow and tent
camping available

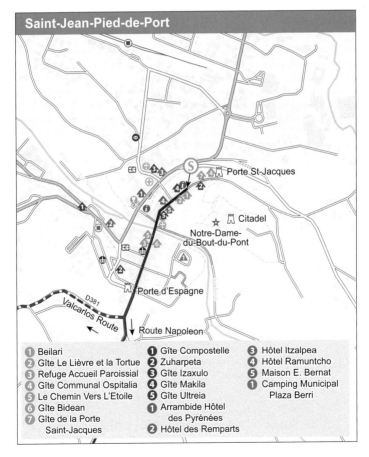

Saint-Jean-Pied-de-Port

1 Beilari
2 Gîte Le Lièvre et la Tortue
3 Refuge Accueil Paroissial
4 Gîte Communal Ospitalia
5 Le Chemin Vers L'Etoile
6 Gîte Bidean
7 Gîte de la Porte
   Saint-Jacques

1 Gîte Compostelle
2 Zuharpeta
3 Gîte Izaxulo
4 Gîte Makila
5 Gîte Ultreia
1 Arrambide Hôtel
   des Pyrénées
2 Hôtel des Remparts

3 Hôtel Itzalpea
4 Hôtel Ramuntcho
5 Maison E. Bernat
1 Camping Municipal
   Plaza Berri

A pilgrim pauses with an ice cream cone on the Nive River bridge in Saint-Jean-Pied-de-Port (photo: Rod Hoekstra)

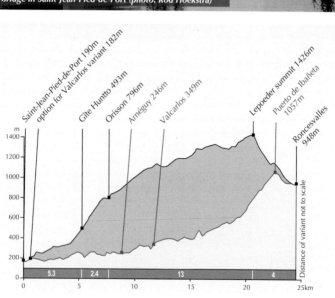

Route Napoléon

From the pilgrim office, follow Rue de la Citadelle downhill as it crosses the river and continue to the Porte d'Espagne (Spanish Gate). Pass the blue 'route-condition' sign, making certain it reads 'Ouvert,' which confirms the way is open across the high pass (if marked 'Fermé' turn right toward Valcarlos, the only safe route – see below) and go straight ahead up the asphalt road which quickly becomes steep. Follow signs to Refuge Orisson, passing a few private gîtes among hayfields and pastures. ⛰ Gîte Zazpiak Bat 🅿 🄳 🅁 🄺 🄱 🅆 🅂 6/18, €27/-/-/-, 13b Rue du Maréchal Harispe, www.gite-zazpiak-bat.com, tel 675 783 623 ⛰ La Coquille Napoléon 🅿 🄳 🅁 🅆 🅂 1/10 & 2/4, €18/-/55/-, Route Napoléon, http://lacoquillenapoleon.simplesite.com, tel 662 259 940 ⛰ Gîte Antton 🅿 🄳 🅁 🄺 🄱 🄲 🅂 1/6 & 2/4, €38/-/-/-, Route Napoléon, www.gite-antton.fr/en, tel 665 195 073. After a time, note the white, horizontal buildings on the ridge above, which comprise

5.3KM GÎTE HUNTTO (ELEV. 493M, POP. 0) 🛏 (778.3KM)

⛰ Ferme Ithurburia Huntto 🅿 🄳 🅁 🄶 🄺 🅆 🅂 5/17 & 5/10, €20/-/74/74, Route Napoléon, tel 559 371 117

A few hundred meters past Huntto turn left onto a two-track footpath that climbs very steeply on jagged gravel. After several switchbacks the path returns to the asphalt road at **Gîte Kayola (1.3km)**, an overflow facility for **Refuge Orisson**, just above (**0.8km**, café). Not long afterward is Albergue Borda.

2.4KM ORISSON (ELEV. 796M, POP. 0) 🛏 🍴 (775.9KM)

⛰ Refuge Orisson 🄳 🅁 🄱 🄲 🅆 4/28, €40/-/-/-, Chemin de Compostelle RD428, www.refuge-orisson.com, tel 559 491 303

⛰ Auberge Borda 🅿 🄳 🅁 🄱 🄲 🅆 🅂 🆉 3/12, €42/50/100/-, Route Napoléon, www.facebook.com/AubergeBordaPaysBasque, tel 661 929 743, 9 km from Saint-Jean-Pied-de-Port

After Orisson continue uphill less steeply on asphalt, surrounded by pastures of sheep, cattle and horses. Soon the turn-off for the **Virgin statue (3.8km)** is marked on the left. Continue upward past a food truck (**3.5km**), if luck, fate or grace provides, and come to the low stone memorial called **Cross Thibault (0.2km)**. After the cross the way turns off the asphalt, following a single-track path of red dirt and jagged gravel, crossing into Spain near the **Roland Fountain (0.7km)** and climbing now more steeply to the **Bentarte summit (0.4km)**. Continue on undulating road to **Refugio Izandorre (2.6km)**, a stone hut prior to

Griffon vultures keep a watchful eye over pilgrims as they near the Lepoeder summit (photo: Rod Hoekstra)

13.0KM LEPOEDER SUMMIT (ELEV. 1426M, POP. 0) (NO SERVICES) (762.9KM)

The highest point of the Route Napoléon, the Lepoeder Pass holds considerable history. Ruins of a first c. Roman tower celebrating the conquest of Aquitaine can be seen today atop nearby Mount Urkulu, once standing guard over the Via Traiana Roman road. Napoléon's armies used the pass on their way to Spain, and during WWII pilots and soldiers crossed the pass to escape Nazi rule in Vichy France.

Now begin the long downhill, mostly through thick forest. After crossing the Arranosin brook on a wooden bridge (**3.8km**) come to the back side of the **Roncesvalles** complex. Climb between the stone buildings onto a wide stone walkway, passing through arches, by the church, museum and hotel and onward to the albergue.

4.0KM RONCESVALLES/ORREAGA (ELEV. 948M, POP. 30) 🏨 🛏 ◉ 🏧 ❶ (758.9KM)

At the mountain doorway to Spain, Roncesvalles (Basque: Orreaga) has been an important and influential pilgrim hostel virtually since the beginning of the Camino Francés. Due to continual bad weather, the original pilgrim hospital at the Ibañeta Pass was moved in 1132 to the more protected vale where it currently resides. For centuries, monks, after appropriate religious services, tended to the health and well-being of every pilgrim man, woman and child. Important buildings include the elegant **Real Colegiata church**, consecrated in 1219 and restored in the 1940s. This Gothic masterpiece houses the **Virgin of Roncesvalles**, a 13th c. wood and silver statue from Toulouse, sheltered under an ornate silver baldachin canopy. The **Chapter House** holds the tomb of Sancho VII and the nearby museum houses religious relics and articles relating to Roland and Charlemagne. The tower of the 13th c. **Chapel of Santiago** holds a bell rung in the evening for centuries to help guide pilgrims down the mountainside to a safe harbor among the monks. A pilgrim mass is shared each evening (Mon–Fri, 8pm; weekends and holidays 6pm). Tour of the monastery complex available after mass.

These and all following phone numbers require the '+34' prefix for Spain, unless otherwise indicated.

🏠 Albergue de Roncesvalles-Orreaga Ⓞ Ⓓ Ⓡ Ⓚ Ⓦ Ⓢ 3/183, €14/-/-/-, Calle Única, www.alberguederoncesvalles.com, tel 948 760 000

🏠 Casa Sabina Hostería Ⓞ Ⓟ Ⓡ Ⓒ Ⓢ 4/8, €-/54/63/-, Carretera de Francia, http://casasabina.roncesvalles.es, tel 948 760 012

🏠 La Posada Hotel Ⓟ Ⓡ Ⓒ Ⓢ 20/55, €-/73/85/100, Carretera de Francia, http://laposada.roncesvalles.es, tel 948 790 322

🏠 Hotel Casa Beneficiados Ⓟ Ⓡ Ⓒ Ⓢ 16/32, €-/59/77/97, Calle Nstra Señora de Roncesvalles 14, www.hotelroncesvalles.com, tel 948 760 105

Valcarlos variant (mandatory in winter and during inclement weather)

Leave Saint-Jean-Pied-de-Port by the Porte d'Espagne gate then turn right at the option (**0.5km**) on Route D301 out of town through **Uhart-Cize**. Join the D933 main road and after **house 33** (**1.3km**) fork right on a quiet country road crossing the Arnéguy River. Follow this frequently turning, well-waymarked route that undulates along a series of country lanes, crossing the unmarked Franco-Spanish border just before a large shopping center at **Venta Peio** (**5.4km**, supermarket). Then follow the winding track through woods to

8.6KM ARNÉGUY/ARNEGI (ELEV. 246M, POP. 234) 🔢 ⊕ 🛏 ⊚ (774.2KM)

The presence of this village on the Arnéguy River is attested to since 1284, although most of its buildings are 17th c. or later, including the Église de l'Assomption (17th–19th c.). In WWII the town demarcated the extreme southern border of occupied France.

🏠 Hôtel Le Clementenia Ⓟ Ⓡ Ⓒ Ⓢ 5/10, €-/78/70/-, Le Bourge D933, www.leclementenia.com, tel 524 341 006

Ascend gently along the side of the Luzaide valley and pass through the hamlets of **Bachoa** (**0.8km**) and **Ondarolle** (**1.5km**). Turn right on a steep path down to the river and cross a narrow bridge back into Spain. Climb very steeply into

2.9KM VALCARLOS/LUZAIDE (ELEV. 349M, POP. 390) 🔢 ⊕ 🛏 🅒 ⊚ ⊕ (771.3KM)

The epic poem 'Song of Roland' records the Battle of Roncesvalles in 778, most likely here at Valcarlos where the great French King Charlemagne's friend, Roland, was defeated by the Basque army. Notwithstanding the defeat, Charlemagne's name is imprinted in the town's French and Spanish moniker ('Valcarlos' means Valley of Charles or 'Carlos' the Great). On July 25, 1813, some 11,000 English and Portuguese soldiers were subdued by 40,000 soldiers of Napoléon's army, resulting in over 600 dead. The modern town remembers its ancient roots in prominent families' coats of arms on the white stucco façades of their homes.

🔼 Albergue de Luzaide/Valcarlos Municipal Ⓞ Ⓓ Ⓡ Ⓚ Ⓑ Ⓦ Ⓢ 2/24, €10/-/-/-, Plaza Santiago, http://luzaide-valcarlos.net, tel 948 790 117

Leave the village along the N-135 main road, ascending gently through forest, then **fork left** (**2.7km**) onto a narrow road and drop to pass through tiny **Gainekoleta** (**0.8km**). Cross the river and fork right on a riverside path, eventually climbing to reach the N-135 again (**1.1km**). At a **gravel trail** (**2.0km**) branch left and climb very steeply through forest into the Pyrenees. Briefly rejoin the main road at the **Guardian House** (**2.7km**), then continue up through the forest to reach the top of

10.7KM PUERTO DE IBAÑETA (ELEV. 1057M, POP. 0) (NO SERVICES) (760.6KM)

Puerto de Ibañeta, one of the lowest crossing points of the Pyrenees, is closely linked to the 778 defeat of Charlemagne's rear guard. A 1967 memorial stone commemorates Roland who died in the battle. The pass was the original site of the monastic pilgrim hospital moved across the pass to today's Roncesvalles. The modern chapel of San Salvador and the summit cross replace historic buildings long since fallen into ruin.

Continue on the forest trail, now downhill and parallel with the main road, to emerge beside the large complex of monastic buildings in **Roncesvalles** (see Roncesvalles info above).

Interior view of the 13th c. Real Colegiata church at Roncesvalles monastery (photo: Rod Hoekstra)

STAGE 2
Roncesvalles to Zubiri

Start	Roncesvalles, Church of Santiago
Finish	Zubiri, Plaza Mayor
Distance	21.8km
Total ascent	535m
Total descent	960m
Difficulty	Moderately hard, due to long downhill stretches on loose rock
Duration	6¼hr
Percentage paved	19%
Albergues	Burguete 2.9; Espinal 6.5; Viscarret 11.7; Linzoain 13.7; Zubiri 21.8
Note	Food establishments open at Roncesvalles no earlier than 7am, so if you plan to leave earlier either buy food the night before or wait until Burguete for breakfast.

The brief challenge of a couple of 100m climbs is overshadowed by the long and sometimes steep descents on this mostly downhill stage. Concrete paths are often available to make for better footing, but they can be slippery when wet. Overall, however, a pleasant, wooded stage with occasional views and frequent village cafés for refueling and rest.

From the church at **Roncesvalles**, look for the famously photographed 'Santiago de Compostela 790' sign and pick up a pathway to its right. Follow this gentle path under trees, through the **Sorginaritzaga Forest** ('Oakwood of Witches – where nine witches were burned at the stake in the 16th c.) and along pastures to the town of **Burguete**.

2.9KM BURGUETE/AURITZ (ELEV. 894M, POP. 243) ⅡⅡ ⊕ ◰ Ⓒ ◉ ⊕ ⊕ (756.0KM)

Two streams flank the main road through this town of graceful 16th–18th c. homes emblazoned with family coats of arms. Ernest Hemingway lodged here between binges while fishing local streams in 1924–25 and describes the town in his novel *The Sun Also Rises*. The 16th c. **San Nicolás de Bari church** was destroyed several times over the centuries by fire (including one set by the French in 1794) and was most recently reconstructed in the 20th c.

🔺 Albergue Lorentx Aterpea Ⓞ Ⓓ Ⓡ Ⓖ Ⓚ Ⓦ Ⓢ 7/42, €15/-/-/-, Calle San Nicolás 56, www.lorentxaterpea.com, tel 623 286 129

Burguete's San Nicolás de Bari church was destroyed and rebuilt many times in French-Spanish wars

Continue along Burguete's main road to the bank (ATM) and turn right, downhill toward a wooden bridge after which the path becomes a gravel road. The pastures and barns along the way provide complimentary smells of livestock, which will become a familiar scent on the Camino in the days and weeks ahead. Continue on stone bridges over a series of rivulets as the way becomes a gravel path alongside pastures and woods in a lush river valley en route to

3.6KM ESPINAL/AURIZBERRI (ELEV. 867M, POP. 243) 🈕 ⊕ 🝗 🅒 ⊛ ⊕ ⊕ (752.4KM)

A town of stately homes located along its central main street, Espinal was founded in 1269 by King Teobaldo II. Its striking San Bartolomeo church, built in 1961, includes some Renaissance pieces inside. While the core of its economy is agriculture, the town has long cared for pilgrims on the road to Santiago. Trout and wild *beltza* mushrooms are prized in its gastronomy.

🛆 Albergue Irugoienea 🄿 🄳 🅁 🄲 🅦 🅂 2/21 & 3/7, €12/45/45/60, Calle Oihanilun 2, www.irugoienea.com/albergue, tel 622 606 196

🛆 Hostal Rural Haizea 🄾 🄿 🄳 🅁 🄲 🄱 🅦 🅂 2/21 & 12/24, €15/65/65/80, Carretera Pamplona-Roncesvalles, www.hostalhaizea.com, tel 948 760 379, electric bicycle rental possible

Partway through town turn left on an asphalt road that soon becomes a single, gravel track and climbs atop the nearby hill (950m). On the other side arrive at the **Alto Mezkiritz** (**1.9km**, elev. 923m), where you cross the N-135 before continuing downhill on a path under birch trees. Soon a sidewalk with flagstones appears to ease the descent. After a few hundred meters the path once again meets the main highway before continuing back into the woods for another climb, now on a path of stamped concrete. After meeting the highway again, memorably cross the tiny **Sorabil Creek** on concrete pylons before reaching

5.2KM VISCARRET/BIZKARRETA (ELEV. 781M, POP. 98) ⏸ ⊕ ⬙ ⬤ (747.2KM)

Although never a large town, the 12th c. *Codex Calixtinus* places Viscarret as the end of the stage that begins at Saint-Jean-Pied-de-Port. Interior columns of the 13th c. **San Bartolomeo church** embody the transition from Romanesque to Gothic architecture.

🛏 Amatxi Elsa **P** **R** **G** **K** **W** **S** 5/10, €-/50/60/-, Calle San Pedro 14, tel 948 760 391

🛏 Casa Batit **O** **P** **R** **K** **W** 2/6, €-/25/30/-, Calle San Pedro 47, tel 616 068 347

🛏 La Posada Nueva **P** **R** **W** **S** 8/18, €-/35/50/75, Calle San Pedro 2, www.laposadanueva.net, tel 948 760 173

   Having wound through town, return to the stamped concrete pathway at first along the road. After a small cemetery and rest stop the path becomes a gravel trail once again before crossing the highway into

2.0KM LINZOAIN/LINTZOAIN (ELEV. 735M, POP. 74) ⏸ ⬙ ⬤ (745.3KM)

The tiny village's medieval roots are seen in the 13th c. Romanesque **San Saturnino church**, but most interesting are the town's homes, with lintels bearing dates from the 17th and 18th c.

🛏 Posada El Camino **O** **P** **R** **G** **K** **W** **S** 4/12, €-/20/40/55, Calle Camino de Santiago 46, www.posadaelcamino.com, tel 622 688 535

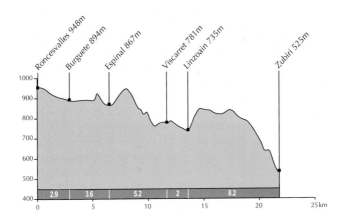

Continue on a concrete trail steeply up the longest ascent of the day toward **El Fuerte** (847m). Finally, the trail begins an undulation through the woods, summiting on **Mount Karrobide** (850m). Exercise extreme caution on the slippery descent on shale and bedrock. Soon you see microwave towers ahead, which mark **Alto Erro** (**4.5km**, 801m), situated on the highway with its food van and lawn. A medieval inn, on the Pamplona side of the pass, hosted weary travelers and pilgrims for centuries. Its sparse remains are now a lowly cattle pen. Continue a long downhill on a wide gravel track, noting the black smokestack of the Zubiri factory below. After 3km of steep and sometimes slippery shale, arrive at the welcoming white walls and red tile roofs of **Zubiri**. Cross the stone bridge over the Arga River to enter town.

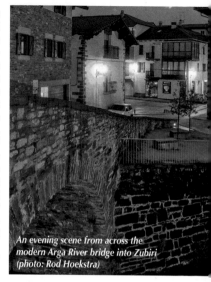

An evening scene from across the modern Arga River bridge into Zubiri (photo: Rod Hoekstra)

8.2KM ZUBIRI (ELEV. 525M, POP. 435) 🏠⛲🏪◉⊕ (737.1KM)

The bridge of Zubiri (in Basque, 'Town of the Bridge') is a modern take on the historic 12th c. bridge over the Arga. It is said that cows that walk three times around the bridge are protected from rabies. The modern town and its major services face the N-135 highway a few blocks from the bridge and the **magnesium factory** outside town is its largest landmark and economic engine.

🛏 Albergue Río Arga ⓞⓟⒹⓇⓀ ⒷⓌⓈⓏ 2/8, €15/20/40/-, Calle Río Arga 7, www.alberguerioarga.com, tel 680 104 471

🛏 Albergue Segunda Etapa ⒹⓇⒷⓌⓈ 2/12, €15/-/-/-, Avenida de Roncesvalles 22, http://alberguesegundaetapa.com, tel 697 186 560

🛏 Albergue Suseia ⓟⒹⓇⒼⓌⓈⓏ 4/20, €16/21/42/-, Calle Murelu 12, www.facebook.com/AlbergueSuseia, tel 679 667 603

🛏 Municipal Albergue Zubiri ⒹⓌⓈ 6/46, €8/-/-/-, Avenida Zubiri, tel 628 324 186

🛏 Albergue El Palo de Avellano ⓟⒹⓇⒼⒷⒸⓌⓈ 5/47 & 3/8, €18/-/62/-, Avenida Roncesvalles 16, http://elpalodeavellano.com, tel 666 499 175

🛏 Albergue Zaldiko ⓟⒹⓇⒼⓌⓈ 3/24 & 4/8, €14/22/44/66, Calle Puente de la Rabia 1, http://alberguezaldiko.com, tel 609 736 420

STAGE 3
Zubiri to Pamplona

Start	Zubiri, Plaza Mayor
Finish	Pamplona Cathedral
Distance	21.1km
Total ascent	690m
Total descent	755m
Difficulty	Moderate, due to long downhill stretches
Duration	6hr
Percentage paved	48%
Albergues	Ilárraz–Urdániz 3.0; Larrasoaña 5.7; Zuriaín 9.5; Zabaldika 12.7; Trinidad de Arre 16.5; Villava 17.8; Pamplona 21.1

The trail follows the Arga (Arre) River valley and plays cat and mouse with the N-135 highway as it winds its way on sometimes overgrown paths through woods and farms to historic and scenic Pamplona, capital of the Navarran region. Watch carefully for provisions and stock up at vending machines since the only convenient bar/café between Zubiri and Trinidad de Arre is at Zuriaín.

From **Zubiri**, return across the bridge and turn right heading to Larrasoaña on a single-track gravel path that crosses a creek and soon becomes a flagstone walkway. At the top of the first rise you see the massive magnesium factory and smokestack. Walk past the factory's vast mounds of gray slag and come to the tiny village of **Ilárraz** (Ilarratz) and its neighbor across the river, **Urdániz** (Urdaitz).

3.0KM URDÁNIZ (ELEV. 551M, POP. 19, 98) ⬆ (734.1KM)

Between the two towns is the 12th c. Ermita de Santa Lucia o de La Abadia, where a stolen altar revealed precious mural paintings. Pilgrim Neil Le Roux is restoring the building with help from passersby (www.facebook.com/theabbey.es).

🏠 Albergue Acá y Allá 🅳 🆁 🅶 🅺 🅱 🅦 🆂 3/6, €15/-/-/-, Calle San Miguel 18, http://alojamientosacayalla.com/urdaniz, tel 615 257 666

Re-enter the woods with their dense undergrowth over low hills. Soon you will come to the sign for **Larrasoaña**, a right turn off the track and just over a bridge.

2.7KM LARRASOAÑA (ELEV. 502M, POP. 138) ▥ ⊕ ☖ ◉ (731.5KM)

Two pilgrim hospitals and an 11th c. Augustinian monastery served medieval pilgrims through Larrasoaña, although their remains are now long gone. Still standing are the 14th c. **Puente (Bridge) de los Bandidos**, whose name suggests it had become notorious as a hangout of thieves and ruffians; and the **Clavería de Roncesvalles**, a monastery warehouse (currently a private home) across from the town's church. The town has a fine collection of 14th and 16th c. homes built for its former wealthy class.

🛖 Albergue Municipal de Larrasoaña **D K S** 2/32, €9/-/-/-, Calle San Nicolás 21, www.facebook.com/alberguemunicipallarrasoana, tel 626 718 417

🛖 Albergue San Nicolás **D R Gf K C W S** 8/20, €14/-/-/-, Calle Sorandi 5, https://alberguesannicolas.com, tel 619 559 225

🛖 Asteia Hostel **D R Gf W S** 2/12, €15/-/-/-, Casa Errotabidea 24, www.asteiahostel.com/en, tel 948 060 411

The trail now rises above the river to **Akerreta** (**0.7km**, 536m), its Parish of the Transfiguration and hotel (🛖 Hotel Akerreta **P R Gf B S** 11/22, €-/82/105/-, Calle la Transfiguración 11, http://hotelakerreta.com, tel 948 304 572. Shown in movie *The Way*), before descending again to accompany the Arga until it crosses the river at **Zuriaín** with its welcome pilgrim café.

3.9KM ZURIAÍN (ELEV. 474M, POP. 31) 🏨 ⛲ (727.6KM)

After its busy pilgrim bar, the tiny hamlet of Zuriaín's most notable site is the painted crucifixion scene over the door of its 16th–17th c. church.

🔼 Albergue La Parada de Zuriaín 🅿 🅳 🆁 🆆 🆂 2/7 & 3/6, €9/-/30/-, Calle Landa 8, www.facebook.com/mariajose.gomaraalonso.5, tel 616 038 685

Circling behind the Zuriaín café, the path meets the highway and follows it for about 600m before branching off onto a smaller road which leads back to the river's west bank. Entering the woods again, the path comes to the tiny village of Irotz (**2.2km**) with its porched San Pedro church, then continues along the road to cross the river once again. After the bridge the path turns left and straddles the bank between the park and the highway, arriving soon in lower

3.2KM ZABALDIKA (ELEV. 474M, POP. 29) ⛲ ◉ (724.4KM)

Since the Middle Ages this tiny village has divided itself between two centers – one around the plain 12th c. church in the upper town and one below, along the Camino trail.

🔼 Albergue Zabaldika 🅳 🅺 🅲 🆆 🆂 3/18, €Donation, Calle San Esteban de Arriba 8A, www.facebook.com/ZabaldikaCaminoSantiago, tel 948 330 918, breakfast with donation

The path now descends to a wide concrete pedestrian road, a welcome relief from the narrow, overgrown pathways along the hillsides. After a few hundred meters on the concrete walkway, continue under the N-135 highway to a roadside **rest area** with a fountain and restroom (**0.7km**) before climbing a steep path on the tall hillside above the narrowing valley. From here you can see the beginnings of Pamplona's urbanization, and beyond, the ridge of Alto del Perdón with its signature wind turbines. Pass the

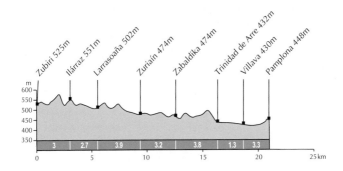

Santa Mariña church (0.7km), then descend and cross the N-135 **underpass** (1.1km) to an old roadbed that continues down the valley above highway traffic. At a right turn you suddenly cross a Romanesque bridge over the Ulzama River and leave the countryside behind as **Trinidad de Arre**, the first suburb of Pamplona, greets you.

3.8KM TRINIDAD DE ARRE (ELEV. 432M, POP. 10,217)  (720.6KM)

Situated at a narrow river passage between two hills, the medieval village of Arre was surmounted by a castle that controlled this strategic position on the Roman road to Roncesvalles. The town's Romanesque bridge funneled pilgrims directly into the welcoming archway of its medieval pilgrim hospital, today one of the best preserved in all of Spain. The dam below the bridge served millworks for grain and felt.

🔺 Albergue de la Trinidad de Arre **O D R K W S** 4/34, €10/-/-/-, Puente del Peregrino 24, **www.facebook.com/pg/suseiarre**, tel 691 619 028

Continue straight for the next hour on urban streets filled with shops and cafés through **Villava** (Atarrabia) and then **Burlada** (2.5km), a medieval village/suburb.

1.3KM VILLAVA–BURLADA (ELEV. 430M, POP. 29,084) (719.3KM)

🔺 Albergue Municipal **O P D R C K W S** 5/54 & 2/10, €14/-/-/-, Calle Pedro de Atarrabia 17–19, **www.aterpevillava.org**, tel 948 517 731, two family rooms available

A tower of Pamplona's Cathedral of Santa María la Real stands among colorful homes (photo: Rod Hoekstra)

Watch for blue/yellow directional signs painted onto the sidewalk as you make your way first through suburban streets then verdant parks. Finally, cross a three-arched stone bridge near the site of a medieval leprosarium and veer to the right into a grassy moat between **Pamplona**'s medieval walls. At the Portal de Francia gate ascend into town and find yourself in the city's crowded and often noisy streets with the cathedral a few blocks to the left.

3.3KM PAMPLONA/IRUÑA (ELEV. 448M, POP. 195,853)
🍴 ⊕ 🏧 🄲 ⊛ ⊛ Ⓗ ⊕ ⊕ 🄸 (716.0KM)

Known worldwide for its testosterone- and liquor-fueled Running of the Bulls (annually July 6–14), legends say Pamplona (Basque: Iruña) was Christianized by disciples of Santiago and later the Saints Saturnino and Fermín. Overcoming occupations by Charlemagne from the north and Moors from the south, the kings of Navarre created a diverse city which by the 12th c. hosted Basque, French, Jewish, Gascon and Mudéjar *barrios* (quarters), each with its own laws, language and internal city walls. In 1422 King Carlos III united the *barrios*, forming the basis of the modern city. Meantime, Pamplona was a key stop on the Camino Francés and hosted several pilgrim hospitals, most of them near the **Cathedral of Santa María la Real** (€3 entry for pilgrims. The current cathedral building was begun in 1394 after its 12th c. predecessor collapsed, and boasts the second largest church bell in Spain in its left tower. Kings of Navarre were crowned at the main altar in front of the 12th c. Virgen del Sagrario, a wooden image now nearly completely covered in silver. Pamplona is famed for its artful ironworking, seen here in elaborate chapel screens. The **Cloister** and the **Diocesan Museum** are worthy tour stops, as is the pilgrim-friendly **Church of San Cernín**, which includes among its many chapels one dedicated to its 15th c. La Virgen del Camino. The **Church of San Lorenzo** holds the San Fermín statue which is paraded around the city during its bull festivities and displays a finger of the saint. The elegant façade of the 15th c. *ayuntamiento* (town hall) overlooks the starting point of the annual bull run and a few blocks away is the **Plaza de Toros bullring** where bull festivities conclude. The **Museum of Navarre** hosts a collection of ancient to modern local art and stands next to the handy **food market of Santo Domingo**. Head in early evening down **Calle de la Estafeta** for *pinchos* (like tapas), watch for spontaneous folk dancing breaking out in squares like **Plaza del Castillo**, and take a photo in front of the bronze bulls and runners of the **Monumento al Encierro**. On the way out of town, pass the battlements of the **Ciudadela** fortress and the leafy green campus of Opus Dei's **University of Navarra** (*sello* for pilgrims). For a city tour guide, ask for Francisco at www.novotur.com.

🛏 Albergue Jesús y María 🄾 🄳 🄳 🅁 🄺 🅆 🅂 4/112, €10/-/-/-, Calle Compañía 4, www.facebook.com/alberguejesusymaria, tel 948 222 644, reservations only from Oct-Apr

🛏 Albergue Pamplona-Iruñako Aterpea 🄾 🄿 🄳 🅁 🄶 🄺 🄱 🅆 🅂 🅉 2/22, €16/20/40/-, Calle de Carmen 18, www.alberguedepamplona.info, tel 948 044 637

🛏 Albergue Plaza Catedral 🄾 🄿 🄳 🅁 🄶 🄺 🄱 🅆 🅂 🅉 4/42, €16/-/56/63, Calle Navarrería 35, www.albergueplazacatedral.com/en, tel 948 591 336

🔺 Albergue Xarma Hostel **O P D R G K B W S Z** 4/18, €15/32/42/-, Avenida Baja Navarra 23, tel 948 046 449

🔺 Casa Ibarrola **D R G K B W S** 1/20, €18/-/-/-, Calle Carmen 31, www.casaibarrola.com, tel 692 208 463

🔺 Casa Paderborn **D W S** 5/26, €7/-/-/-, Calle Playa de Caparroso 6, www.jakobusfreunde-paderborn.com/unser-verein-2/casa-paderborn, tel 948 217 712

🔺 Aloha Hostel **O P D R G K B W S** 3/18 & 2/4, €22/30/46/-, Calle Sangüesa 2, www.alohahostel.es, tel 648 289 403

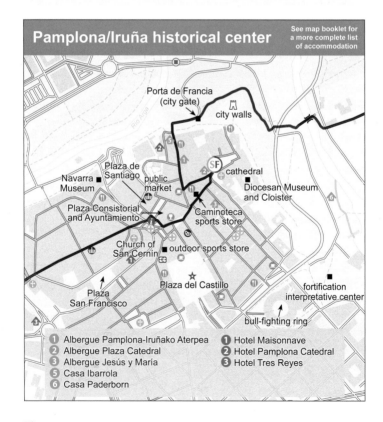

Pamplona/Iruña historical center

See map booklet for a more complete list of accommodation

- ① Albergue Pamplona-Iruñako Aterpea
- ② Albergue Plaza Catedral
- ③ Albergue Jesús y María
- ⑤ Casa Ibarrola
- ⑥ Casa Paderborn

- ① Hotel Maisonnave
- ② Hotel Pamplona Catedral
- ③ Hotel Tres Reyes

Pilgrims walk amid springtime green near Cirueña (photo: Rod Hoekstra)

SECTION 2:
PAMPLONA TO BURGOS

SECTION 2:
PAMPLONA TO BURGOS

Two memorable mountain ridges stand like bookends to this section of the walk – the Alto del Perdón after Pamplona and the Sierra de Atapuerca before Burgos. In-between is one of the most delightful and memorable stretches of the Camino Francés, filled with natural beauty and echoing with history.

After Pamplona and the Alto del Perdón, western Navarre feels more arid than the lush Arga valley behind it. In these wide valleys, quiet and simple agricultural towns like Puente la Reina, Estella and Los Arcos hold surprises of medieval architecture and art. Take a few extra moments to enjoy the wonders of Eunate

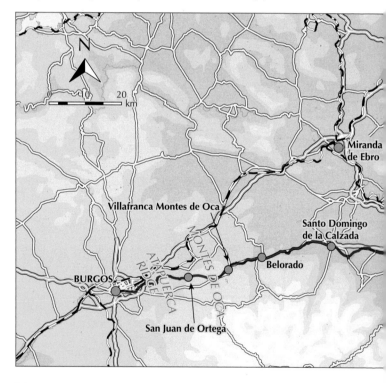

and step inside the cool and colorful confines of Santa María de la Asunción in Los Arcos, to admire sculptures on the Romanesque portal of San Miguel in Estella or wonder at the graceful arches of the bridge at Puente la Reina. A sip of the latest vintage at the wine fountain of Irache is a must, just before witnessing the natural beauty of the distant Sierra de Lokiz of the Cantabrian Mountains that serve as silent sentinels on the walk to Villamayor de Monjardín.

The wonders continue into La Rioja, capital of Spanish wine regions and home to historic cities like Logroño, Navarrete, Nájera and Santo Domingo de la Calzada. Memories of the Camino are strong here, and each of these Riojan towns holds notable shrines important to Spanish and pilgrim history. After Nájera the terrain spreads out, like a foretaste of the Meseta, until it's interrupted by the forested slopes of the Montes de Oca. The sky widens again in the Atapuerca valley, home to one of Europe's most important anthropological discoveries, much of which can be viewed later in Burgos, a city of

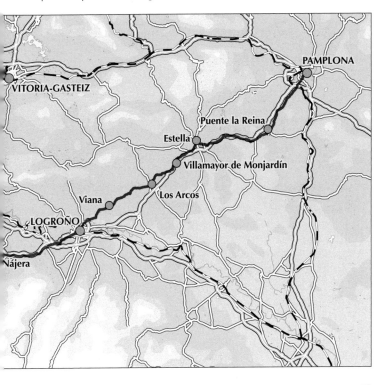

surprising beauty capped by a glorious baroque Gothic cathedral.

Look for white asparagus in Navarre, along with *piquillo* peppers, Idiazábal and Roncal cheeses, and the Pacharán Navarro liqueur after dinner. In La Rioja, look for *patatasa la Riojana* – potatoes cooked with chorizo. When in Burgos, ask for *morcilla de Burgos* (blood sausage) or roast lamb (*cordero asado*).

And there is so much more. A walk through this storied region offers some of the best of the Camino de Santiago. Savor your steps through the abundant expanse of beauty and history.

PLANNING

Three times in this section pilgrims have partial day options, none of which adds much time to the day's journey: 1) on Stage 4, the 3km optional walk from Muruzábal to the enchanting and mysterious Chapel of Eunate provides a tranquil pause at what some people find to be the most authentic medieval holy place of the Camino Francés; 2) on Stage 6, choose whether to walk through Luquin or Villamayor de Monjardín after Irache, both of which have equal merit, although the latter offers the better scenery; 3) on Stage 8, decide whether to take the recommended short detour to enjoy the services of Ventosa on the dry stretch before Nájera.

WHAT NOT TO MISS

Los Arcos features the most elaborate parish church on the Camino, but it can only be appreciated when the lights are on during Mass or in low-light photography. The portal of Estella's San Miguel church holds an excellent example of 10th-century Romanesque sculpture. Bring a small cup just after Estella to enjoy a drink from the famous wine fountain at Irache. In Viana look for the grave of César Borja, dashing warrior and ladies' man, and promise yourself to read his complicated and fascinating story when you get home. Logroño's Calle Laurel is famous around the world for its crowded and exuberant tapas culture. A few steps off the path in Navarrete is the finest of golden altarpieces that should not be missed. Nájera holds the cave where a king followed a hawk to a Gothic statue of the Virgin, a site best explored after an outdoor riverside lunch by the bridge. Don't miss the unforgettable evening view from the Citadel in Burgos, and of course a tour of the interior of the spectacular Burgos Cathedral.

STAGE 4

Pamplona to Puente la Reina

Start	Pamplona Cathedral
Finish	Puente la Reina, Plaza Mena
Distance	24.4km (27.6km including Eunate option)
Total ascent	530m (565m including Eunate option)
Total descent	630m (670m including Eunate option)
Difficulty	Moderately hard, due to steep ups and downs
Duration	7hr (8hr including Eunate option)
Percentage paved	43%
Albergues	Cizur Menor 5.1; Zariquiegui 11.3; Uterga 17.2; Muruzábal 19.9; Obanos 21.7; Puente la Reina 24.4

Today's apex at Alto del Perdón offers some of the most dramatic views on the entire Camino Francés. The effects of steep uphills and downhills are cushioned somewhat by towns with ample services at regular intervals along the way. An optional jaunt to the beautiful and mysterious Chapel of Eunate adds a worthwhile 3.2km to the day's total.

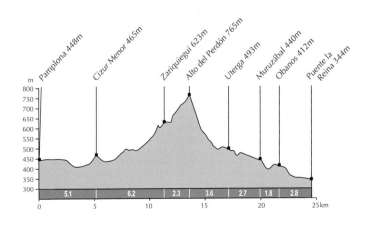

The iconic steel sculpture at Alto del Perdón depicts pilgrims throughout the ages (photo: Rod Hoekstra)

From the cathedral in **Pamplona**, make your way down Calle Curia to pick up the stainless steel medallion waymarks in the pavement, which point you through the Plaza Consistorial, out the Calle Mayor, and into the verdant parks that surround the **Ciudadela fortress** (**1.4km**). Turn right and enter modern, multi-storied neighborhoods before joining a roadside bike trail through the University of Navarra (**1.5km**). The bike trail becomes a pink sidewalk, crosses train tracks, and then reaches the valley floor below the village of

5.1KM CIZUR MENOR/ZIZUR TXIKIA (ELEV. 465M, POP. 2402) 🅗 🛆 ◉ ⊕
(710.9KM)

The Monasterio de San Juan de Jerusalem, part of the Crusade-era Order of Hospitallers, was established here in 1135 to serve pilgrims. All that remains of the pilgrim hospital is the 12th c. **Church of San Miguel Archangel** which retains its classic, Romanesque barrel-vaulted nave.

🔺 Albergue la Orden de Malta 🅓🅚 1/27, €7/-/-/-, Calle Irunbidea 6A, tel 616 651 330

🔺 Albergue Roncal 🅓🅡🅚🅦🅢 5/51, €13/-/-/-, Paseo Belzeta 1, www.elalberguedemaribel.com, tel 670 323 271

The path continues under plane trees and past tennis courts as a valley of wheat fields opens before the long ascent to Alto del Perdón, easily identifiable as a narrow space between rows of wind generators on the ridge ahead. The occasional park bench under shade offers a welcome relief before the cafés of

6.2KM ZARIQUIEGUI/ZARIKIEGI (ELEV. 623M, POP. 173) 🍴 ⊕ 🏠 (704.7KM)

This medieval village was decimated by the Plague in 1348, but by the 15th and 16th c. became the site of several large villas whose 17th c. coats of arms surmount their entry portals. The 13th c. **Church of San Andrés** includes a 14th c. carved statue of the Virgin Mary. On the exit from the village, watch for the **Fuentes Reniega**, where legend says the Devil tempted a thirsty pilgrim with water before Santiago rescued him with a drink from his own scallop shell.

🔼 Albergue San Andrés ⓞⒹⓇⓀⓌⓈ 2/18, €10/-/-/-, Calle Camino de Santiago 4, www.alberguezariquiegui.com, tel 948 353 876

After the village the path begins flat then climbs quite steeply. Looking back, you can now see Pamplona spread out behind as the whooshing sound of the wind generators and the almost constant breeze fill your ears. The food van from Puente la Reina's Albergue Santiago Apóstol may await you at the top.

2.3KM ALTO DEL PERDÓN/ERRENIEGA (ELEV. 765M, POP. 0) (NO SERVICES) (702.4KM)

In medieval times this high passage was home to the Basilica of Our Lady of Perdón with its pilgrim hospital, although their remains are long gone. When Energia Hidroelectrica de Navarra built its line of 40 wind turbines in 1994 it commissioned the iconic steel pilgrim statue at the summit, which represents a line of pilgrims stretching from the first medieval pilgrims on the left past pilgrim caregivers and merchants to modern pilgrims on the far right – all crowned by stars above.

Both the pilgrim sculpture and the spectacular views on both sides of this storied ridge make pilgrims want to pause and enjoy the moment before very carefully walking down the steep slope on the ridge's opposite side. After reaching the valley floor the white gravel path begins to rise gently until it reaches the town of

3.6KM UTERGA (ELEV. 493M, POP. 163) ⊞ ◱ (698.8KM)

Uterga was once home to six medieval hermitages, although traces are gone of all but the **San Nicolás**, near the cemetery. The main retablo of the 16th–18th c. **La Asunción church** includes fine Renaissance reliefs along with a Santiago Peregrino.

🔺 Albergue Casa Baztán Ⓞ Ⓟ Ⓓ Ⓡ Ⓖ Ⓚ Ⓑ Ⓦ Ⓢ Ⓩ 1/24, €12/-/40/60, Calle Mayor 46, tel 689 357 550

🔺 Albergue Camino del Perdón Ⓟ Ⓓ Ⓡ Ⓖ Ⓦ Ⓢ 1/16 & 5/10, €15/-/60/80, Calle Mayor 61, www.caminodelperdon.es, tel 948 344 598, additional private rooms at Calle Iruzpeguia 20

Note the small rest area with picnic benches and a white statue of the Virgin Mary. A well-groomed path leads the short distance to

2.7KM MURUZÁBAL (ELEV. 440M, POP. 257) ⊞ ◱ ◉ ⊕ (696.1KM)

Belying its minor village appearance, Muruzábal's **San Esteban church** contains a noteworthy early 16th c. retablo with vivid Hispano-Flemish portrayals of favored saints, including Santiago, Andrés and many others. Look in the village also for its 16th c. palace and three medieval hermitages.

🔺 Albergue Mendizabal Ⓞ Ⓟ Ⓓ Ⓡ Ⓖ Ⓚ Ⓑ Ⓦ Ⓢ 1/6 & 4/12, €13/18/36/54, Calle Mayor 7, www.alberguemendizabal.com, tel 678 010 119

🔺 El Jardín de Muruzábal Ⓟ Ⓓ Ⓡ Ⓖ Ⓒ Ⓦ Ⓢ 1/14 & 3/9, €10/40/50/55, Calle Monteviejo 21, www.eljardindemuruzabal.com, tel 696 688 399, swimming pool, ask for Alicia (the owner)

There is now the option of keeping your day short by following the markings to **Obanos**, or taking a detour to Eunate.

Optional 3.2km extension to Eunate
Divert left at the *ayuntamiento* (town hall) in Muruzábal and walk across fields to serene **Eunate**.

The small octagonal **Iglesia de Santa María de Eunate** is believed to be a 12th-century Crusader construction based on the octagonal Church of the Holy Sepulchre in Jerusalem. The elegant building is perfectly symmetrical except for the semi-circular apse on one side and staircase that reaches toward the crowning belfry which served as a watchtower and lantern to guide pilgrims walking the Camino Aragonés. The building is surrounded by an octagonal colonnade of 33 semi-circular arches held up by pillars with richly carved capitals. The two portals are decorated with fanciful – albeit now deteriorated – carvings of humans, animals and monsters. Inside, the high vault is formed by powerful ridges and pierced by skylights. Interior acoustics make it an enchanting place to hear music. The Virgin of Eunate statue was reinstated here in 1997, maintained by a volunteer confraternity. Note that the church closes at midday for siesta year-round.

Pass Eunate's service building and join a small path that follows the trajectory of the road, heading back to the main Camino track just below **Obanos**. A steep climb brings you to the tiny town with its prominent, single-tower church.

1.8KM OBANOS (ELEV. 412M, POP. 923) 🚻 ⊕ 🛏 🄲 ⊚ ⊕ (694.3KM)

Here the Camino Francés merges with another main pilgrim route, the Camino Aragonés, which crosses the Pyrenees at Somport Pass to the south. On the Sunday following the Feast of Corpus Christi in even years the town hosts *El Misterio de Obanos*, a play about the life of pilgrim Saint Felicia and her brother, Saint Guillermo. While the two were returning from a pilgrimage to Santiago she decided to become a nun, which angered her brother so much that he killed her. The guilt-wracked man sought forgiveness through a second pilgrimage to Santiago. On his return he settled in Obanos and his skull can be found, encased in silver, in the **San Juan Bautista church**. When his body was exhumed centuries later a silver Santiago pilgrim medallion was found among his bones. The 1911 church includes a 14th c. stone portal, a beloved statue of the seated White Virgin and a 16th c. crucifix with a heavily muscled Christ.

🔼 Albergue Atseden Hostel 🄳 🅁 🄶 🄺 🄱 🅆 🅂 1/12, €13/-/-/-, Calle Santa Felicia 9, www.atsedenhostel.com, tel 646 924 912

🔼 Albergue Usda 🄳 🅆 🅂 3/42, €9/-/-/-, Calle San Lorenzo 6, tel 676 560 927

Head downhill, crossing a road and then reaching a small river at the valley's floor before climbing into **Puente la Reina**, with the tall tower of its Parish of Santiago church on the Calle Mayor just before Plaza Mena.

2.8KM PUENTE LA REINA/GARES (ELEV. 344M, POP. 2807) 🚻 ⊕ 🛏 🄲 ⊚ ⊕ ⊕ (691.6KM)

Since the Arga River is too deep to ford, independent ferrymen served or swindled pilgrims who tried to cross it. This led the Queen of Navarre in the 11th c. to order the building of a graceful bridge spanning the river, which ultimately gave the town its Spanish name (literally 'Bridge of the Queen,' although in Basque still 'Gares'). Knights

Templar hosted one of the town's several medieval pilgrim hospitals, theirs at the current site of the **Padres Reparadores monastery** at the entry to town. Pilgrim services were then, as now, clustered along the **Calle Mayor** which holds the town's most notable landmark, the 16th c. **Parish Church of Santiago**, whose prominent tower beckons pilgrims inward to kneel at its baroque retablo and witness scenes from the martyrdom of Santiago and lives of other saints. On the left side of the church is a notable 14th c. barefoot Santiago Peregrino statue known locally as the Black Santiago (Santiago Beltza), who lost his dark skin in restoration. At the corner of the old town is the **San Pedro church**, with its three lively baroque-rococo retablos and a statue of the Virgen del Txori which, when it stood at a tower on the bridge, was said to have been washed daily by a small bird (*txori* in Basque).

🛏 Albergue Amalur 🇩 🇷 🇬 🇼 🇸 2/20, €11/-/-/-, Calle Cerco Viejo, tel 696 241 175

🛏 Albergue Padres Reparadores 🅞 🇩 🇰 🇼 🇸 12/100, €7/-/-/-, Plaza P. Guillermo Zicke, tel 663 615 795, space for tents

🛏 Santiago Apóstol (Camping El Real) 🇩 🇷 🇼 🇸 5/100, €12/-/-/-, Paraje El Real, **www.campingelreal.com**, tel 948 340 220, camping €8, +4–7 person bungalows, swimming pool. Located across river and above town

🛏 Albergue Estrella Guía 🅞 🇵 🇩 🇷 🇬 🇼 🇸 3/12 & 3/8, €15/-/40/55, Calle La Población 2, tel 622 262 431, hosts Natalia & José

🛏 Albergue Puente 🇵 🇩 🇷 🇬 🇰 🇧 🇼 🇸 5/30 & 4/8, €15/40/45/57, Paseo los Fueros 57, **http://alberguepuente.com**, tel 948 341 052

🛏 Jakue 🅞 🇵 🇩 🇷 🇬 🇰 🇼 🇸 4/43 & 28/56, €12/42/61/82, Calle Irunbidea 34, **www.jakue.com**, tel 948 341 017

Evening lights reflect off the surface of the Arga River in Puente la Reina (photo: Rod Hoekstra)

STAGE 5

Puente la Reina to Estella

Start	Puente la Reina, Plaza Mena
Finish	Estella, Plaza de los Fueros
Distance	21.6km
Total ascent	615m
Total descent	540m
Difficulty	Moderate
Duration	6¼hr
Percentage paved	30%
Albergues	Mañeru 4.8; Cirauqui 7.5; Lorca 13.1; Villatuerta 17.3; Estella 21.6

Wide open skies, wheat fields, vineyards and views over rolling hills make this a scenic and memorable stage. This is Camino walking at its loveliest, with moderate difficulty and ample rest stops. A short and picturesque detour off the track allows you to enjoy the heart of historic Estella, which is well worth extra time for touring and an overnight.

In **Puente la Reina**, continue left from the main square along Calle Mayor and cross the town's iconic bridge over the Arga. Turn left, cross a road to the left and descend on gravel past the waste treatment plant. Climb steeply through a pine forest until the path nestles alongside the A-12 'Avenida Camino de Santiago' highway. The domed tower of **Mañeru** beckons just 15min beyond.

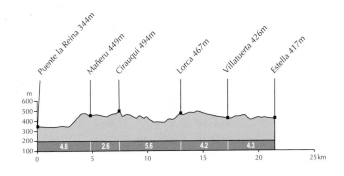

4.8KM MAÑERU (ELEV. 449M, POP. 419)  (686.7KM)

Mañeru includes many fine 16th–19th c. homes while its skyline is dominated by the 18th c. **Church of San Pedro** with its round tower offsetting the lantern cupola of its low, central dome. The church includes sculptures of a seated St Barbara, matron saint of the village, and a finely sculpted 16th c. crucifix.

⌂ Albergue El Cantero **P D R G K S** 3/26 & 4/8, €11/-/45/-, Calle La Esperanza 2, www.alberguelcantero.com, tel 948 342 142

The path remains on the south side of the A-12 and makes its way through grain fields and vineyards to picturesque **Cirauqui**.

2.6KM CIRAUQUI/ZIRAUKI (ELEV. 494M, POP. 476)  (684.1KM)

Although the town's name in Basque means 'nest of vipers,' Cirauqui is one of the most picturesque villages of the Camino. Photogenic from a distance, its winding streets exude their most medieval charm at dusk from the windows of the Maralotx albergue. The intricate Mudéjar portal of the 12th c. **Church of San Román** is a refined composition of geometric designs and sculpted characters. A medieval bridge on the outskirts of town plays a role in the *Codex Calixtinus* when two of the author's horses die after drinking water from the stream below.

⌂ Albergue Cirauqui Casa Maralotx **P D R G C W S** 3/26 & 2/4, €14/40/58/-, Calle Plaza Grande 4, www.alberguemaralotx.com, tel 678 635 208

Follow the path across the Roman bridge (**0.4km**), formerly part of the Roman Via Traiana, and continue as the route crosses the A-12 no fewer than four times in the

Rows of vines soak up sun below Cirauqui (photo: Rod Hoekstra)

next 6km. Watch for the pilgrim rest stop where volunteers are raising funds to build a permanent rest area and then pass under the unusual **modern aqueduct** (**4.1km**). After the last underpass you arrive on the Calle Mayor of tiny

5.6KM LORCA/LORKA (ELEV. 467M, POP. 135) 🛏 🄲 🅘 (678.5KM)

The village's name (the Arabic *alaurque* means 'battle') may refer to a 920 battle won by the Muslim king over King Sancho I of Navarre. The late 12th c. **Church of San Salvador** includes an 18th c. Santiago Peregrino.

🛏 Albergue de Lorca 🄿 🄳 🅁 🄺 🅆 🅂 🆉 3/12, €7/-/20/-, Calle Mayor 40, tel 948 541 190

🛏 La Bodega del Camino 🄿 🄳 🅁 🄶 🄺 🅆 🅂 2/13 & 6/11, €12/-/30/60, Calle Placeta 8, www.labodegadelcamino.com, tel 948 541 327

After Lorca, descend again to the valley floor where the trail picks up next to the quiet former highway, the NA-1110. The track shortcuts through fields, crosses the A-12 and arrives on the outskirts of **Villatuerta**, whose parish church, Our Lady of the Assumption, overlooks the valley.

4.2KM VILLATUERTA/BILATORTA (ELEV. 426M, POP. 1154) 🛉 ⊕ 🛏 🄲 🅘 (674.3KM)

The town sits on either side of the tiny Iranzu River, which is crossed by a two-arch Romanesque bridge. Gothic vaults grace the interior of the 14th c. **parish church**, where some say San Veremundo, Bishop of Irache and a Camino benefactor, was born. A plaque outside the church reads, 'Drink water, pilgrim; take rest, quench thirst and in the next stage know that a good wine will give you strength. Here was born San Veremundo who was abbot in Irache, who asked grace and marched showing his love of the Camino.'

🛏 Albergue Etxeurdina 🄿 🄳 🅁 🄺 🄱 🅆 🅂 2/18 & 2/4, €15/45/45/-, Río Iranzu 3, www.etxeurdina.com, tel 848 419 430

Continue downhill past the 11th-century **Ermita San Miguel**, visible for a great distance, to cross the NA-132 followed by the Ega River 400m later on the wooden treads of an iron bridge. Soon you are at the pilgrim office (**2.1km**) and the Curtidores albergue on the outskirts of **Estella**. Enjoy the lush, riverside park a few steps ahead, or head to the main part of Estella on the Puente de la Cárcel bridge just after the Santo Sepulcro church, whose doorway and imposing statuary are just left of the trail. The intricate, early 14th-century portal of this long-closed church includes scenes from the New Testament. Santiago Peregrino and the other apostles are depicted on the twin upper rows of statues. If you've crossed the Puente de la Cárcel bridge to enter town, turn left after the bridge and make your way down the picturesque main shopping street of the old city and turn right into the commodious main square, Plaza de los Fueros. Otherwise, there are ample pilgrim services on the south side of the river.

The warm afternoon keeps most walkers in the shade on Estella's Calle Mayor

4.3KM ESTELLA/LIZARRA (ELEV. 417M, POP. 13,668) ⏸ ⊕ ⬜ 🅒 ⓞ Ⓗ ⊕ 🅘 (670.0KM)

'Estella, where bread is good, wine excellent, meat and fish are abundant, and which overflows with all delights,' reads the *Codex Calixtinus* (Melzcher trans). After the town's founding in 1090 by King Sancho Ramirez at a bend of the Ega River it quickly grew to become a regional center and then one of the landmark cities of the Camino de Santiago. Medieval French immigrants clustered in their own quarter, as did Jews and native locals. The town's prosperity and diversity gave rise to an explosion of Romanesque architecture, surviving today in churches like the 12th–13th c. **San Pedro de la Rúa** on the south bank of the Ega, and the 12th c. **Church of San Miguel** whose north portal is a masterwork of Romanesque sculpture. San Miguel also includes a stunning 15th c. retablo behind its central altar. Although the **Church of San Juan Bautista** has Romanesque roots, its frequent remodeling dates to the early 20th c. Inside is an important 16th c. retablo with scenes from the Old Testament and the Holy Family. Located opposite the stairway to San Pedro de la Rúa is the 12th c. **Palace of the Kings of Navarre**, now a museum for the early 20th c. Basque painter, Gustavo de Maeztu. Pilgrimage to Santiago played an important role in the town's economic development, and by 1354 it contained six pilgrim hospitals. Estella's development reached an apogee in the 12th and 13th c., but in the 14th and 15th c. it began to decline due to wars with neighboring kingdoms and several outbreaks of the Plague. It was here in 1998 that a final peace with Basque separatists was signed. Estella holds festivals in honor of its patrons San Andrés and the Virgen del Puy on their feast days in August. Gastronomic delicacies include roast *gorrín* (suckling pig), trout, and *pochas* beans. A typical pilgrim activity is to relax in the **Plaza de los Fueros** and stroll along the shops of the adjacent **Calle Mayor**.

🔼 Albergue ANFAS Ⓓ Ⓡ Ⓖ Ⓚ Ⓦ Ⓢ 1/34, €8/-/-/-, Calle Cordeleros 7, www.albergueanfas.org, tel 639 011 688

🔼 Albergue Parroquial San Miguel Ⓓ Ⓑ Ⓦ Ⓢ 2/32, €Donation, Mercado Viejo 18, tel 948 550 431, mass daily at 7pm, run by volunteers, wifi at library

🔼 Hospital de Peregrinos Ⓓ Ⓚ Ⓦ Ⓢ 5/96, €6/-/-/-, Calle Rúa 50, tel 948 550 200

🔼 Ágora Hostel Ⓟ Ⓓ Ⓡ Ⓖ Ⓚ Ⓦ Ⓢ 2/20 & 3/11, €17/-/75/75, Callizo Pelaires 3, www.dormirenestella.com, tel 948 546 574

🔼 Albergue de Curtidores Ⓞ Ⓟ Ⓓ Ⓡ Ⓖ Ⓚ Ⓦ Ⓢ 9/42 & 2/4, €17/40/50/63, Calle Curtidores 43, www.lahosteriadelcamino.com, tel 663 613 642, renovated 17th c. tannery

🔼 Albergue de Rocamador Ⓓ Ⓡ Ⓖ Ⓚ Ⓦ Ⓢ 6/27 & 12/24, €13/20/32/-, Calle Rocamador 6, www.alberguescapuchinos.org/albergue, tel 948 550 549

🔼 Albergue Oncineda Ⓟ Ⓓ Ⓡ Ⓖ Ⓚ Ⓦ Ⓢ 28/155 & 2/4, €12/28/45/-, Calle Monasterio de Irache 11, www.albergueestella.com, tel 948 555 022, not open in 2022

🔼 Alda Estella Hostel Ⓟ Ⓓ Ⓡ Ⓖ Ⓚ Ⓢ 33/66, €14/44/53/-, Plaza de Santiago 41, www.aldahotels.es/alojamientos/alda-estella-hostel, tel 948 030 137

🔺 Camping Lizarra -/250, €12/-/-/-, Paraje de Ordoiz, www.campinglizarra.com, tel 948 551 733, swimming pool, bungalows and tent camping

STAGE 6
Estella to Los Arcos

Start	Estella, Puente de la Cárcel
Finish	Los Arcos, Plaza de Santa María
Distance	21.6km
Total ascent	520m
Total descent	490m
Difficulty	Moderate
Duration	6hr
Percentage paved	23%
Albergues	Ayegui 1.0; Irache Urbanización 4.2; Azqueta 7.5; Villamayor de Monjardín 9.3; Los Arcos 21.6

Under clear skies this stage is full of impressive scenery – mountains, valleys, grain fields and vineyards. Watch carefully for the option after the Irache wine fountain and turn right in the direction of Villamayor de Monjardín for the best views. The stretch between Villamayor and Los Arcos is one of the longest on the Camino without food or drink – unless you luck out with the presence of the food van 5km before Los Arcos. Still, it's best to plan ahead and pack some lunch and plenty of water.

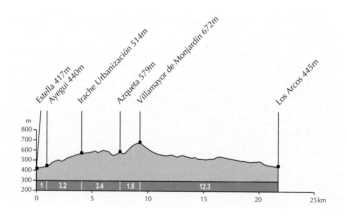

If starting from the center of **Estella**, return to the Camino by retracing your steps back across the bridge. Waymarks are scarce in the town's south neighborhood, but as the charming old quarter turns into the new automotive suburbs of **Ayegui** the signage improves.

1.0KM AYEGUI/AIEGI (ELEV. 440M, POP. 2241) 🏔 ⊕ ⬜ Ⓒ ⊚ ⊕ **(669.0KM)**

In 1060 King Sancho el de Pañalén gave Ayegui to the monastery at Irache, requiring it to supply the monastery with wine, wheat and volunteers.

🏠 Albergue Municipal San Cipriano Ⓞ Ⓓ Ⓡ Ⓚ Ⓦ Ⓢ 3/42, €10/-/-/-, Calle Polideportivo 3, www.facebook.com/pg/albergueayegui, tel 948 554 311

At the second roundabout the path turns up the hill onto a quiet backstreet behind apartment homes then returns to the main road which it crosses, aiming at the tall monastery building. Going straight at the roundabout leads to two supermarkets and a large sports store. In a few steps are first the blacksmith forges of Jesus Angel, who makes delightful Camino decorations, then the famous Irache free **wine fountain** (**1.8km**) and afterward the **Irache monastery**.

The first documentary evidence of the **Monastery of Irache** is from 958, although it is believed a monastic community existed here far earlier. Overlooking the Romanesque façade of the main building is an unusual,

Since 1991 Bodegas Irache has offered free wine to pilgrims

Byzantine-style domed tower with two adjacent cloisters. The interior is sparse, as is typical in Cistercian monastic style, but the central apse houses a 12th-century Romanesque image of the Virgin Mary. Saint Veremundo is the monastery's most famous abbot, remembered at his birthplace in Villatuerte. Across the drive, the modern **Bodegas Irache** has hosted a free wine fountain for thirsty pilgrims since 1991 (www.irache.com, fountain open daily 8am–8pm).

Continue up the hill where you are confronted with a choice (**0.6km**): straight ahead to Los Arcos via Luquin or a right turn to Los Arcos through Villamayor de Monjardín. The remote Luquin route crosses the A-12 and then climbs steeply to excellent views along the north slopes of wooded Montejurra. Beyond tiny Luquin it re-crosses the A-12 and rejoins the main route. The Villamayor option also boasts spectacular views, but its better services make it the preferred choice and it is therefore described as the main route here.

Alternative route via Luquin
To follow the quiet Luquin option, go straight at the fork crossing under the highway and climbing partway up Montejurra. Traverse the mountain on an undulating path of red dirt in a forest of holm oak, enjoying the shade and views. Coming to a wide gravel road views open to the cliffs across the wide valley. Continue climbing through forest before finally emptying out into rolling wheat fields and descending steeply on slippery rock into **Luquin** (bar, water, ⛰ Albergue Casa Tiago 🄿 🄳 🅁 🄺 🅆 🅂 🅉 2/14, €12/-/30/-, Calle San Martín 11, **www.alberguecasatiago.com**, tel 626 240 862)

Follow streets out of town steeply downhill. Watch signs as they point you across a quiet paved road and alongside the freeway before connecting to the main route across the freeway.

Main route via Villamayor
Soon pass a rest area with its fountain on the right and then pass

3.2KM IRACHE/IRATXE URBANIZACIÓN (ELEV. 514M, POP. 457) 🄷 🄲 ◉
(665.8KM)

▲ Camping Iratxe 26/52, €8/-/28/-, Avenida Prado de Irache 14, **www.campingiratxe.com**, tel 948 555 555, rooms and bungalows available

The dramatic cliffs of the Sierra de Lokiz in the Basaula Reserve of the Cantabrian Mountains appear to the north. A wide gravel path leads toward the soon-visible mountain behind Villamayor de Monjardín, but a summit on a mountain covered in holm oak intervenes, with a rest area (**1.6km**) on the far side. Afterward, ascend to the village of

Pilgrims walk among fields of lavender below the castle ruins atop Monjardín

3.4KM AZQUETA/AZKETA (ELEV. 579M, POP. 54) 🏠 ⬆ ◉ (662.5KM)

Although it is faced by a modern tower, inside the Church of San Pedro is all Gothic vaulted ceilings. The 16th c. baroque altarpiece is by Navarran artist Pedro Imberto.

🛌 La Perla Negra – Casa Peregrina 🅿 🆁 🅱 🅲 🆆 🆂 3/8, €-/-/45/-, Calle Carrera 18, www.facebook.com/PerlaNegraAlbergue, tel 627 114 797

Enormous views now open up to the left, right and behind, with the conical peak of 894m Mount Monjardín topped by its castle ruins ahead. Enter the town after passing the **Fuente de Moros** (Fountain of the Moors; **1.4km**) on the right and the modern winery on the left.

1.8KM VILLAMAYOR DE MONJARDÍN (ELEV. 672M, POP. 121) 🏠 ⊕ ⬆ ◉ (660.7KM)

The final Moorish stronghold in this region, Christian King Sancho Garcés captured the castle on Monjardín in 914. Atop the peak now are its ruins and alongside those, the tiny hermitage of San Esteban. In the town beneath, the portals of the Romanesque **Church of San Andrés** hold intricate carvings, while the interior is graced with a silver processional cross from about 1200. The church's tower, crowned with a tall cupola, dates from the 17th c. A large warehouse on the outskirts of town serves the Monjardín winery, known for its white wines.

🛌 Albergue Villamayor de Monjardín 🅿 🅳 🆁 🅶 🅺 🅱 🆆 🆂 🆉 3/20, €15/20/40/-, Calle Mayor 1, www.alberguevillamayordemonjardin.com, tel 948 537 139, host wrote a book about Villamayor

🛌 Oasis Trails Albergue 🅿 🅳 🆂 4/22 & 2/4, €11/35/40/-, Calle Plaza 4, www.oasistrails.org, tel 948 537 136, great homemade dinners

Looking beyond Villamayor on a clear day, the upcoming topography becomes visible – low, rolling hills covered in grain fields stretching into the far distance. The gravel path follows the general trajectory of the A-12 freeway but manages mostly to keep pilgrims among the fields and vineyards and away from the sounds of traffic. Except for the 200m jaunt to **Urbiola** (**1.2km**) across the highway, a sometimes-dry fountain (**1.0km**) and the iffy Flecha Amarilla food van (**3.9km**) there are no services on this 12.3km stretch. After the food van location, the outline of the San Gregorio Ostiense basilica near Sorlada can be seen far across the valley on a ridge to the right. **Los Arcos** appears first as a series of farm buildings, then suddenly low, closely spaced housing.

12.3KM LOS ARCOS (ELEV. 445M, POP. 1119) (648.4KM)

Known to the Romans as Curnonium, the narrow streets and stone homes of Los Arcos lend it the feel of a medieval town. Situated on the left bank of the Odrón River between Navarre, Aragon and Castile, the town found itself at the crossroads of regional conflicts in the 11th–19th c., making its sometimes a city of Castile, sometimes of Navarre. The **Santa María de la Asunción church** – built over the course of 600 years – is the town's primary architectural treasure and one of the most elaborate and ornate on the Camino Francés, featuring baroque decoration that covers the walls and ceilings. The main altar's stunning 17th c. walnut retablo depicts scenes from the Passion, the life of Mary, and the Apostles, including Santiago Peregrino. Seated in the middle is the 14th c. Gothic sculpture, Our Lady of Los Arcos. The building houses a prime 17th c. pipe organ and is crowned by an elegant 16th c. Renaissance bell tower. The **Felipe V arch** is all that is left of the town walls. The primary industry of Los Arcos is agriculture, especially grapes, olives, barley and wheat. Annual festivals include bullfighting and fighting with heifers, taking place on August 14–20.

Albergue Isaac Santiago D K W S 1/70, €6/-/-/-, Calle San Lázaro 6, tel 948 441 091

Albergue La Fuente Casa de Austria D R K W S 7/60, €10/-/-/-, Travesía del Estanco 5, **www.lafuentecasadeaustria.com**, tel 948 640 797

Albergue Casa de la Abuela P D R Cr W S 3/42 & 5/10, €15/35/45/-, Plaza de la Fruta 8, **www.casadelaabuela.com**, tel 948 640 250

Casa Alberdi O P D R Cr K W S 3/23 & 2/5, €15/-/46/-, Calle El Hortal 3, **www.alberguecasaalberdi.com**, tel 650 965 250, taxi service available

STAGE 7
Los Arcos to Logroño

Start	Los Arcos, Plaza de Santa María
Finish	Logroño, Plaza del Mercado
Distance	28.2km
Total ascent	580m
Total descent	645m
Difficulty	Moderately hard, due to length
Duration	8hr
Percentage paved	28%
Albergues	Sansol 6.9; Torres del Río 7.7; Viana 18.3; Logroño 28.2

The trail now crosses into the Spanish wine region of La Rioja, beginning fairly flat, but as it approaches Viana developing some steep ups and downs. The walk into Logroño may feel charmless and bleak. Even so, each successive town offers its rewards. Torres del Río for coffee, Viana for lunch, and Calle Laurel in Logroño for a delicious tapas dinner if you have budget and are in the mood to explore.

Leaving **Los Arcos**, a wide valley soon opens after the western gate of town and vineyards and vast fields of wheat appear. The road points its way across the valley to **Sansol**, whose church tower stands like a beacon to pilgrims across the plain.

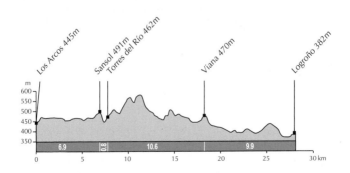

6.9KM SANSOL/SANTSOL (ELEV. 491M, POP. 103) 🚻 ⊕ 🛏 ◉ ⊕ (641.5KM)

Sansol, named after the fourth c. martyr San Zoilo, boasts several fine 16th–18th c. baroque palaces with festive coats of arms along the **Calle Mayor** and **Calle Real**. The 18th c. **Church of San Zoilo**, with its prominent tower visible for many miles, contains a dome painted in an Ascension theme.

🛏 Albergue Codés 🅳 🆁 🅶 🆆 🆂 2/24, €10/-/-/-, Calle Los Bodegones, www.facebook.com/alberguerestaurantecodes, tel 689 804 028

🛏 Albergue Karma 🅾 🅿 🅳 🆁 🆆 🆂 2/12, €6/-/-/-, Calle Taconera 11, tel 665 170 116

🛏 Albergue Sansol 🅳 🆁 🆆 🆂 1/26, €10/-/-/-, Calle Barrio Nuevo 4, www.facebook.com/alberguesansol.es, tel 609 203 206

🛏 Albergue Palacio de Sansol 🅿 🅳 🆁 🅺 🆆 🆂 5/32 & 5/15, €11/-/50/66, Plaza del Sindicato 1, **www.casaleuza.com/palaciodesansol**, tel 646 334 730 calls in English

Walk downhill steeply on flagstone pavers to the valley floor that separates Sansol from its sister town. Across a small river bridge is the lower section of charming and historic **Torres del Río**.

0.8KM TORRES DEL RÍO (ELEV. 462M, POP. 131) 🚻 ⊕ 🛏 ◉ ⊕ (640.7KM)

Like neighboring Sansol, Torres del Río hosts several fine baroque palaces festooned with coats of arms on their ornate façades. The town's treasure, though, is its 12th c. **Iglesia del Santo Sepulcro**, a carefully symmetrical building that evokes the Church of the Holy Sepulcher in Jerusalem, perhaps identifying it as a chapel of the crusading Knights Templar. Immediately the similarities with Santa María of Eunate outside Obanos are evident, sharing with that church its eight-sided form. On closer inspection the proportions make it stand out: the width of the dome is precisely equal to the height of the walls; the cylindrical stairway and the apse opposite are precisely equal in distance from the center of the central cylinder. The capitals atop the interior columns depict Christ's death and resurrection, again evoking its namesake church in Jerusalem. (Open daily 9am–1pm and 4.30–7pm, €1, *sello* available.)

🛏 Albergue Casa Mariela 🅿 🅳 🆁 🆆 🆂 5/44 & 4/8, €12/-/30/-, Plaza Padre Valeriano Ordóñez 6, **www. albergue-casa-mariela.negocio.site**, tel 603 359 218

🛏 Albergue La Pata de Oca 🅾 🅿 🅳 🆁 🅶 🆆 🆂 3/32 & 5/11, €10/-/50/75, Calle Mayor 5, https://alberguelapatadeoca.com, tel 948 378 457

The track continues past a stark and serene cemetery out of town and then begins a series of undulations, sometimes steep, as it crosses a number of valleys and ridges on its way to Viana, roughly following the NA-1110 highway. The approximate quarter-point of this stretch is reached at the **Virgen del Poyo chapel** (2.7km).

The Santo Sepulcro church in Torres del Río carries signs of a Crusader past

A monastery and pilgrim hospital long existed here, although the now-closed **chapel**, a last remnant, was built in the 19th c. 'Poyo' is from the Latin *podium*, meaning 'high place.'

Logroño and its region of La Rioja are now visible in the valley to the left, the Sierra de Codés mountains on the right, and the steeple of the main church of Viana – square with a tall cupola at its peak – on the ridge ahead.

Come alongside the NA-1110 (**3.8km**) for an efficient if unattractive entry to town. Once you are in the old city on the streets adjacent to the main church, **Viana**'s medieval character becomes more evident.

The skyline of Viana, last town in Navarre, comes into view

10.6KM VIANA (ELEV. 470M, POP. 4025) 🏨 ⊕ ⌂ 🅒 ⊚ ⊕ ⊕ (630.1KM)

Determined to create a frontier city that would function as a bulwark against Castile, in 1219 Navarran King Sancho VII (Sancho the Strong) consolidated several towns into one on the hilltop, naming it Viana. Over the intervening centuries it switched hands between Navarre and Castile repeatedly. Now Viana stands as the last Navarran town before entering La Rioja at Logroño, although the Basque language is spoken by only about 10% of its population. In 1507 one of Italy and Spain's most famous warriors, César Borja, son of Pope Alexander VI, was finally killed defending Viana on behalf of Carlos V. A bust of Borja is in the main plaza and his bones are interred in the **Church of Santa María**. This 13th–14th c. edifice features an elaborate 16th c. south portal, opening to a Gothic structure of three naves. Fine 18th c. neoclassical frescoes by Luis Paret in the Chapel of San Juan del Ramo depict the life of John the Baptist, while a 17th c. retablo of Santiago's life in the ambulatory may be a favorite of pilgrims. The nearby ruins of the 13th c. **Church of San Pedro** have a haunted feel. The town itself still holds a medieval flavor, with long, narrow east–west streets in the space between monumental stone buildings.

🛏 Albergue Parroquial de Viana 🅓 🅚 🅑 🅒 🅢 1/9, €Donation, Plaza de los Fueros, tel 948 645 037, pilgrim mass at 8pm

🛏 Albergería Andrés Muñoz 🅞 🅓 🅚 🅦 🅢 5/46, €8/-/-/-, Ruinas de San Pedro, www.viana.es/turismo/donde-dormir/albergues, tel 948 645 530, tri-level bunk beds

🛏 Albergue Izar 🅟 🅓 🅡 🅚 🅦 🅢 4/38 & 2/4, €10/-/30/-, Calle El Cristo 6, www.albergueizar.com, 948 090 002

The track now sadly leads down through modern streets with tall apartment towers into the workaday back alleys of suburban Viana. After crossing under an arterial the path arrives at a rest area adjacent to the **Virgen de Cuevas church** (**3.1km**, shade, tables, fountain), the last touch of comfort until the outskirts of Logroño. Continue through a pine forest bisected by the highway, which you cross on a tall **wooden highway bridge** (**1.6km**) to reach the first commercial estates of Logroño. Note the sign marking entry into La Rioja (**1.0km**).

> The least populous of Spain's 17 Comunidades Autónomas, **La Rioja** was created in 1833 to settle the long history of bloody disputes between its neighbors Castile and Navarre, with each wanting control of this rich agricultural region. Its name (from Río Oja) is first attested in the 11th century, and the region has since become famous as the center of the Spanish wine industry. Seven smaller rivers feed into the Ebro River in La Rioja, earning it the name 'Land of the Seven Valleys.'

The track follows a wide stretch of pink asphalt uphill then gradually narrows as it aims for the valley floor at Logroño itself, which stretches out directly ahead. Watch for the *sello* and snack stand of Felisa (**2.4km**), one of the Camino's true saints, who seems to feel the pain of weary pilgrims. The lush park along the Ebro makes up for the otherwise forlorn industrial entry to town. Steps lead up to a pilgrim info center at the foot of **Logroño**'s signature landmark, the Puente de Piedra bridge (**1.1km**). Either follow the official track along Calle Ruavieja to walk among the suited politicians of the nearby Riojan government offices (and miss the old center of town), or continue a few blocks south toward Calle Portales to experience the center of vibrant and sophisticated Logroño and its majestic concathedral.

9.9KM LOGROÑO (ELEV. 382M, POP. 150,876) ▥ ⊕ 🛏 Ⓒ ⊚ ⊚ Ⓗ ⊕ ⊕ 𝒊 (620.2KM)

The capital of Spain's wine-growing region, Logroño may also be the gastronomic capital of the Camino de Santiago. Within the narrow confines of a few cozy blocks, **Calle Laurel** hosts over 50 *taperías*, tiny restaurants that offer *pinchos* (like tapas) to accompany Rioja's bold *tinto* (red) Tempranillo wines. Look also for delightful Riojan *blanco* and *rosado* blends. The tapas bars open around 7.30 but become busy with diners after 9pm. Third largest among Camino Francés cities, Logroño has a rich history with roots among Celts and Romans. The town was retaken from Muslim control in 755 and in 1095 Alfonso VI granted it a charter (*fuero*) that for the first time in Spanish history freed peasants from serfdom. Given its central location, the city changed hands after attacks by neighboring kingdoms in 1073, 1134, 1160, 1176, 1369, 1375, 1460 and 1521, not to mention being taken by Napoléon's troops in the 19th c. and suffering in the Carlist Wars of the 1830s. The incessant conflicts left modern Logroño with only a few historic architectural treasures. The **Puerta del Revellín**, also named the 'Camino Gate' for passage of Santiago pilgrims, is a treasured remnant of the 16th c. city walls. The co-cathedral (meaning it shares a bishop with other cathedrals) of **Santa María de la Redonda** houses 10 Hispano-Flemish works by Melgar and Gallego and a Hispano-Flemish retablo on the left side of the main church with an Adoration of the Magi theme that includes a black magus. The church's most beloved feature is a crucifixion painting in the ambulatory behind the main altar, attributed to **Michelangelo** but perhaps it is a copy made by his students since several similar paintings exist in other European cities. The Romanesque/Gothic **San Bartolomé church** (13th c.) features an intricate 15th c. portal with scenes from the Crucifixion of Christ as well as the life and martyrdom of San Bartolomé. The portal of the **Church of Santiago el Real** is topped by an enormous sculpture of Santiago, and a 16th c. Santiago is in its retablo. The city is not without monuments to a bloody past. The Logroño City Library is built on the site of the Casa de la Inquisición, site of heretic and witch trials, and just 18km southwest of town is Clavijo, site of the 844 battle where legends say Santiago returned to lead Christians to victory against a Muslim army led by 'Abd ar-Rahman II.

🛏 Albergue de Peregrinos 🄳 🄺 🅆 🅂 3/62, €10/-/-/-, Calle Ruavieja 32, **www.asantiago.org/albergues**, tel 941 248 686

🛏 Albergue Parroquial Santiago El Real 🄾 🄳 🄺 🄱 🄲 1/30, €Donation, Calle Barriocepo 8, **http://santiagoelreal.org/peregrinos**, tel 941 209 501

🛏 Albergue Albas 🄾 🄿 🄳 🅁 🅆 🅂 1/26 & 1/2, €14/-/40/-, Plaza Martínez Flamarique 4, **www.alberguealbas.es**, tel 941 700 832, 688 766 475

🛏 Albergue Para Peregrinos Logroño 🄾 🄿 🄳 🅁 🄶 🄺 🄱 🄲 🅆 🅂 8/38 & 8/16, €15/36/49/69, Calle Capitán Gallarza 10, **www.facebook.com/pg/alberguelogrono**, tel 941 254 226, Pensión La Bilbaina in the same building

🛏 Hostel Entresueños 🄾 🄿 🄳 🅁 🄶 🄺 🅆 🅂 14/110 & 5/17, €10/-/40/-, Calle Portales 12, **www.hostellogrono.com**, tel 941 271 334

🛏 Santiago Apóstol Logroño 🄿 🄳 🅁 🄺 🅆 🅂 5/66 & 6/17, €10/-/40/60, Calle Ruavieja 42, tel 635 371 036

The Concathedral of Santa María de la Redonda towers over central Logroño (photo: Rod Hoekstra)

⛺ Winederful Hostel and Café P D R G K S 2/18 & 5/10, €16/-/50/-, Calle Herrerías 2–14, **www.facebook.com/winederfulhostel**, tel 941 139 618

▲ Camping La Playa Avenida de la Playa 6, **www.campinglaplaya.com**, tel 941 252 253, bungalows, private rooms and tent camping

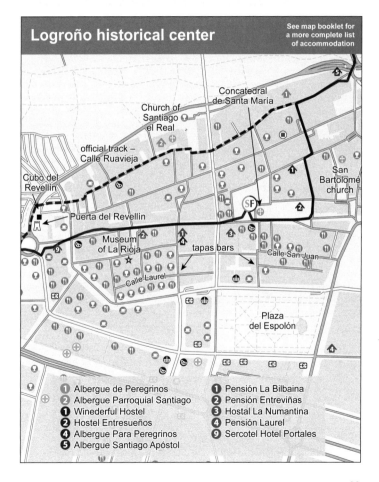

Logroño historical center

See map booklet for a more complete list of accommodation

Concatedral de Santa María

Church of Santiago el Real

official track – Calle Ruavieja

Cubo del Revellín

San Bartolomé church

Puerta del Revellín

Museum of La Rioja

tapas bars

Calle San Juan

Calle Laurel

Plaza del Espolón

1 Albergue de Peregrinos
2 Albergue Parroquial Santiago
1 Winederful Hostel
2 Hostel Entresueños
4 Albergue Para Peregrinos
5 Albergue Santiago Apóstol

1 Pensión La Bilbaina
2 Pensión Entreviñas
3 Hostal La Numantina
4 Pensión Laurel
9 Sercotel Hotel Portales

STAGE 8
Logroño to Nájera

Start	Logroño, Plaza del Mercado
Finish	Nájera, bridge over Najerilla River
Distance	28.5km
Total ascent	490m
Total descent	385m
Difficulty	Moderately hard, due to length
Duration	7¾hr
Percentage paved	26%
Albergues	Navarrete 12.5; Sotés (turn-off) 16.5; Ventosa (turn-off) 18.1; Nájera 28.5

Despite this being a long stage, an overnight at Nájera makes sense due to its size, importance, and quantity of pilgrim services. The first part of the walk is very pleasant as it follows a pedestrian walkway to a quiet lake. Some road-walking before and after Navarrete takes away some of the charm, but the extravagant retablo of the parish church at Navarrete is an unforgettable spectacle. Venture into Nájera's old quarter for an intriguing exploration into Spanish history. A 700m option to Ventosa gives the possibility of refreshment on the long and dry stretch before Nájera.

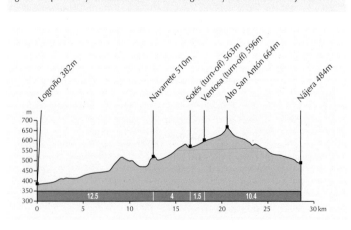

Leave central **Logroño** on Calle Murrieta, following it until the Camino arrows place you among strolling locals on a lovely pedestrian trail leading through Parque San Miguel (**2.3km**) and ending at the park surrounding **Pantano de La Grajera** (**3.4km**). The Río Iregua was dammed in 1883 to create the small lake and neighboring marshes that have become a rich riparian zone and welcome refuge of greenery. Despite its slightly sulfurous smell, the lake attracts sport fishermen and wildlife and also includes a snack bar (**0.5km**).

The track passes a pilgrim rest area (**1.3km**, fountain) and soon begins to climb on gravel through olive groves and vineyards toward a gravel path above the LO-20 highway, which it follows toward the ridge and monumental **Toro sign** (**2.5km**).

The 14m **'Osborne Bulls'** (Spanish: Toros de Osborne) are billboards originally designed by Thomas Osborne Mann and constructed in the 1950s to advertise Brandy de Jerez. EU law now forbids billboard advertising of alcoholic beverages, but these images were judged so inherently Spanish that 91 of the signs were allowed to remain throughout Spain, although the advertiser's name was intentionally blacked out.

Follow the N-120 arterial downward toward Navarrete, which you can now see partly ringing a hill across the valley ahead. Pass ruins of the medieval pilgrim hospital of **San Juan of Acre** (**1.4km**). After finally crossing the valley a short climb takes you into

12.5KM NAVARRETE (ELEV. 510M, POP. 2919) ⃞ ⊕ △ ⃞ ⃝ ⊕ ⊕ (**607.7KM**)

Navarrete's streets cluster in a semi-circle around mount **Cerro Tedeón**, capped for centuries by a strong, protective fortress. Storehouses (*bodegas* in Spanish) for mushrooms and wine are burrowed into caves under the mountain. Long used by pilgrims, the Calle Mayor is also known as 'Calle Santiago.' At its exact center is the **Iglesia de la Asunción**, a must-see treasure of Riojan medieval architecture. The centerpiece of the 17th–18th c. High Gothic building of three naves is its 17th c. retablo by Fernando de la Peña, a work of stunning complexity and lavish ornamentation in an almost overwhelmingly intricate composition. The **sacristy museum** houses a fine collection of liturgical garments, metalwork and paintings. (Church open 9.30am–8.30pm, mass Mon–Sat 8pm, Sun 10am and 1pm. Donation of €1 req. A pilgrim blessing is held after each mass.)

⌂ Albergue de Navarrete D K W S 3/34, €10/-/-/-, Calle San Juan, www.asantiago.org/albergues, tel 941 440 722

⌂ La Casa del Peregrino Ángel D R K C W S 1/18, €12/-/-/-, Calle Las Huertas 3, www.alberguenavarrete.wordpress.com, tel 630 982 928, exclusively for pilgrims

⌂ A la Sombra del Laurel P D R G C W S 1/6 & 7/14, €15/30/45/60, Carretera de Burgos 52, www.alasombradellaurel.com, tel 639 861 110

⌂ Albergue Buen Camino P D R W S 1/6 & 2/3, €12/25/35/-, Calle La Cruz 2, www.alberguebuencamino.es, tel 941 440 318

Navarrete's Iglesia de la Asunción has one of the most lavish of all Camino retablos

⌂ Albergue Hostel Pilgrim 🅿 🄳 🅁 🅆 🅂 5/32 & 12/24, €10/30/35/-, Calle Abadía 1, www.facebook.com/hostelpilgrims, tel 691 699 725

⌂ Albergue Turístico El Cántaro 🅿 🄳 🅁 🄶 🄺 🅆 🅂 2/17 & 5/11, €12/25/35/50, Calle Herrerías 16, www.albergueelcantaro.com, tel 941 441 180

⌂ El Camino de las Estrellas 🅿 🄳 🅁 🄳 🄲 🅆 🅂 3/38 & 4/8, €10/-/40/-, Carretera de Burgos 9, www.facebook.com/elcaminodlasestrellas, tel 618 051 392

Leave town on the street named for pilgrim saint San Roque and rejoin the N-120, which you walk along until just after the town's cemetery. Here rests the historic and intricate **Romanesque portal** (**1.2km**) of the pilgrim hospital of San Juan of Acre, passed on the entry to Navarrete. The track then veers off the highway and onto a wide gravel farm road which blessedly takes you back among the vineyards and olive groves. Just after a winery, an option to turn left toward the services of Sotés (**2.8km**) now appears.

4.0KM TURN-OFF TO SOTÉS (AT 2KM OFF TRACK) (ELEV. 563M, POP. 297)
🄸 🔼 ◉ (603.7KM)

While it requires a steep and otherwise unnecessary detour, if you find yourself in Sotés take a moment to visit the 17th c. Church of San Martín with its four altarpieces, 13th c. Romanesque Virgin and 18th c. image of Santiago Peregrino. From Sotés follow the LR-341 west to Ventosa which returns to the main route.

⌂ Albergue San Martín 🄳 🅁 🄺 🅆 🅂 2/8, €10/-/-/-, Calle San Miguel 67, tel 650 962 625

Very soon another option appears – to turn left toward Ventosa. This recommended detour adds only 700m to the day and offers the only services, save the occasional food truck, in the desolate but beautiful stretch before Nájera.

1.5KM TURN-OFF TO VENTOSA (ADDITIONAL 0.7KM) (ELEV. 596M, POP. 166) 🄸 🔼 ◉ (602.2KM)

The tower of the town's **Church of San Saturnino** can be seen for many miles. Known to have existed since at least the 11th c., Ventosa is the site of the 1367 Battle of Nájera between King Pedro I of Castile and his stepbrother Don Enrique de Trastámara who aspired to his throne. King Pedro's 10,000 Castilian, British, Gascon, Moorish and Mallorcan troops overwhelmed the 4500 Castilian, French and Aragonese troops of Don Enrique.

⌂ San Saturnino 🅿 🄳 🅁 🄶 🄺 🅆 🅂 🅉 6/42, €13/-/35/-, Calle Mayor 33, tel 941 441 899

The Ventosa option returns to the main track and both climb the ridge to the 664m **Alto San Antón** (**2.4km**), a pleasant viewpoint that separates the valleys of Navarrete and Nájera.

Ruins of a monastery and pilgrim hospital are still visible to the right of the trail. From these heights, **views** on a clear day include the peak of San Lorenzo (2271m) to the southwest and the towns of Tricio, Nájera and Huércanos from left to right ahead. Nájera can be identified from the distance by red cliffs that stand between it and its western environs.

The wide gravel track continues down the valley, aiming at an enormous white grain elevator (**6.0km**) on the east side of the town. Continue past the sports center (**1.0km**) straight through town to find **Nájera**'s pleasant center at the

A model of the Virgin statue said to have been found in a Nájera cave in 1044 by King García II

bottom of the hill, along the river. Continue to the bridge over the Najerilla River to find the charming riverfront walk and historic heart.

10.4KM NÁJERA (ELEV. 484M, POP. 8144) ▥ ⊕ ⬓ Ⓒ ◉ ⊕ ⊕ (591.8KM)

The undistinguished entry to Nájera belies its outsized role in Spanish history. The town, whose name in Arabic means 'between the cliffs,' sits astride the Najerilla River against a tall wall of red bluffs. According to legend, in 1044 García III, King of Navarre, was hunting along the Najerilla when his hawk followed a dove into a cave in the cliff. Entering the grotto's deep recesses, the king saw a brilliant glow, and when he approached he realized the light was emanating from a statue of the Virgin Mary. He commanded a church to be built at the cave opening and then a monastery – **Santa María la Real** – which sits today up against the mountainous wall, sheltering the cave opening and the king's Virgin statue which is now ensconced in the church's lavish retablo. García III, who would die later at the Battle of Atapuerca (also on the Camino trail), was buried at the cave opening. Later, his tomb and those of over two dozen of his successors would be crowded around this holy place. Undistinguished from the exterior, the monastery complex – now a museum – includes fine Gothic cloisters and other treasures. The monastery (for a time a cathedral) would become a spoil of war, fought over by bishops and kings through much of its history. Many of its treasures were lost to the French when the town was occupied and ransacked by Napoléon's troops, but its story and architecture still inspire (www.santamarialareal.net, open mornings and afternoons Tues–Sun, €4). Also significant is the nearby 17th c. **Real Capilla and Parroquia de la Santa Cruz**, with its soaring half-dome and 13th c. Gothic crucifix. Nájera is best enjoyed with outdoor refreshments along the west riverbank, south of the bridge.

🔺 Albergue de Peregrinos de Nájera 🅞🅓🅚🅦🅢 1/90, €Donation, Plaza de Santiago, tel 941 440 776, volunteer *hospitaleros*

🔺 Albergue Las Peñas 🅞🅟🅓🅡🅖🅦🅢🅩 2/6, €10/-/35/-, Calle Costanilla 56, **www.facebook.com/AlbergueLasPenyas**, tel 621 209 432

🔺 Albergue de peregrinos Sancho III - La Judería 🅟🅓🅡🅖🅦🅢 -/18 & 4/8, Calle Constantino Garrán 13, **www.lajuderiasanchoiii.com/albergue**, tel 941 361 138

🔺 Albergue Nido de Cigüeña 🅟🅓🅡🅚🅦🅢 2/12 & 2/5, €15/15/30/50, Calleja Cuarta San Miguel 4, **https://alberguenajera.es**, tel 611 095 191

🔺 Pensión Calle Mayor 🅟🅓🅡🅢 1/8 & 4/8, €15/-/30/-, Calle Dicaran 5, tel 941 360 407

🔺 Puerta de Nájera 🅟🅓🅡🅖🅚🅦🅢 9/39 & 4/8, €15/-/40/-, Calle Ribera del Najerilla 1, **https://alberguedenajera.com**, tel 941 362 317

STAGE 9

Nájera to Santo Domingo de la Calzada

Start	Nájera, bridge over Najerilla River
Finish	Santo Domingo de la Calzada, Plaza del Santo (cathedral square)
Distance	22.1km (including Cirueña café extension)
Total ascent	460m
Total descent	305m
Difficulty	Easy
Duration	6hr
Percentage paved	36%
Albergues	Azofra 6.2; Cirueña 15.7; Santo Domingo de la Calzada 22.1

A relaxing stage that gently undulates among shallow valleys and low ridges, filled at first with vineyards then with wheat fields. At stage end is Santo Domingo de la Calzada, one of the Camino's iconic towns with a long history of pilgrim service. A little patience and an extra 500m each way into central Cirueña afford a pleasant place for a mid-stage break.

Before heading out of **Nájera** the trail passes the Monasterio de Santa María la Real (**0.4km**). It then continues first on sidewalk then on asphalt and finally on a wide gravel road through a pine forest. Just after a gap in the natural ridge of reddish-purple stone a

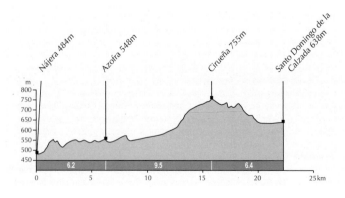

sweeping view of vineyards and farms opens up to the west. Crossing the valley, look back for a vista from this side of the ridge behind Nájera and notice the silhouette of the Cross of Nájera on the peak behind. **Azofra**, with its squarish church tower, is just ahead, and you enter on its Calle Mayor.

6.2KM AZOFRA (ELEV. 548M, POP. 200) 🍴 ⊕ 🛏 🅲 ⑩ ⊕ (585.5KM)

From the Arabic for 'the tribute,' this sleepy town has long served pilgrims, although its 12th c. pilgrim hospital is long gone. The **Nuestra Señora de los Ángeles church** harkens from the 17th c. and contains paintings of pilgrim saints Santiago and San Roque. The town is perhaps most notable as the jumping-off point for pilgrims who want to see a treasure of Spanish history – the nearby **Monastery of San Millán de la Cogolla**, a UNESCO World Heritage Site. Located 14km south of Azofra off the LR-206/7 highways, this monastery complex is considered the birthplace of the Spanish Castilian language. The monastery (actually two monasteries – the 'lower' 11th c. Monasterio de Yuso and the 'upper' 6th c. Monasterio de Suso) can be reached on foot or by taxi from Azofra (http://monasteriodesanmillan.com). A journey on the LR-206 to San Millán has the added benefit of passing the Santa María de Cañas monastery, with its beautiful windows, altarpiece and cloisters (www.monasteriodecañas.es).

🛏 Azofra Municipal Albergue Ⓞ Ⓓ Ⓚ Ⓦ Ⓢ 30/60, €10/-/-/-, Calle Las Parras 7, www.azofra.org/Albergue-Municipal, tel 941 379 325

Pass the municipal albergue a block on the right, then head down and out of town, first on sidewalks and then off to the left on a gravel farm road that heads toward the A-12 motorway (**2.3km**). Along the way, pass a medieval *rollo*: a tall, stone column that functioned as a judicial and administrative marker and where executions were held. Walk near the highway for a brief time, then head back across wheat fields and scattered vineyards toward a low ridge. Atop the rise is a **rest area** (**5.0km**, shade and fountain) and beyond lies the Rioja Alta **golf course clubhouse** (**0.9km**, www.golfrioja.com) and a development of golf resort homes at the edge of **Cirueña**. Instead of following the arrows to the right after town, walk left about 500m to find refreshment at Bar Jacobeo just after the parish church.

9.5KM CIRUEÑA (ELEV. 755M, POP. 131) 🍴 🛏 ⑩ (576.1KM)

Known today for its Rioja Alta golf course, most of the now-forgettable village's medieval architecture has disappeared due to frequent plundering by neighboring towns.

🛏 Virgen de Guadalupe Ⓟ Ⓡ Ⓒ Ⓦ Ⓢ 6/11, €-/15/30/-, Calle Barrio Alto 1, https://albergue-virgendeguadalupe.webnode.es, tel 638 924 069

Retrace your steps along the road to find the arrows and then the roundabout that houses a pilgrim sculpture (**0.5km**) of thick sheet metal. Turn left to cross two valleys

The last hints of snow fade from mountains visible after Cirueña (photo: Rod Hoekstra)

toward Santo Domingo. The second valley, with its broad view across fields, is one of the most photographed places on this portion of the Camino Francés. Atop the opposite ridge see Santo Domingo and its cathedral tower, just 45min ahead. Pass the **municipal football field** (**4.6km**) then stay straight as the main road of the new town becomes the Calle Mayor of the old. Continue to the cathedral, its adjacent tower and the Parador hotel, each holding down its own side of **Santo Domingo**'s central square.

6.4KM SANTO DOMINGO DE LA CALZADA (ELEV. 638M, POP. 6369)
▮ ⊕ ▲ Ⓒ ◉ ⊕ ⊕ 𝒊 (569.7KM)

In the 11th c. young Domingo García of Viloria fared poorly in his studies in nearby monasteries, so he became a hermit along the pilgrim road, clearing the then-forested trails around the Oja River. Here, Saint Gregorio Ostiense, who admired his road-improvement work, befriended and encouraged him. Domingo was soon building bridges and hospitals for pilgrims. King García III granted him the ruins of an old fortress which Domingo rebuilt, creating the small town that ultimately would bear his name. Crown jewel of the current town is its **cathedral**, begun in 1098 with many additions through the 18th c., including a beautiful baroque bell tower across the street that can be climbed for a view of the surrounding territory. The cathedral includes intricate Gothic decoration with a 16th c. choir screen (*trascoro*) that narrates the life of Santo Domingo. Around the apse is a series of chapels, some built as early as the 13th c., each with its own artistic treasures, most notable being the recently discovered Hispano-Flemish paintings in the Capilla de Santa Teresa. The cathedral cloister houses an **ecclesiastical museum**. Across from the cathedral's south entrance is the **Ermita de Nuestra Señora de la Plaza**, a 16th c. Gothic-style building that holds a statue of the Virgin Mary. Also in town are the 17th c. **Monasterio de las Bernardas** and the 16th c. **Monasterio de San Francisco**. The **Parador hotel** was originally built by Santo Domingo himself as a pilgrim hospital. By the 20th c. it was in ruins, but now is preserved as a luxury hotel with a prime view of the town's central square. Portions of the 13th–14th c. **city walls** can still be seen in the northwest part of the old town. According to the *Codex Calixtinus* and other sources, a German pilgrim family of two parents and a son were eating in a local inn on their way to Santiago when the daughter of the establishment propositioned the young man. Being devoted to his pilgrimage he declined the advance, upon which the maid concealed some of the church's silver in his bags and reported him to the authorities. After being tried, he was hung in the town square and his remains left to decay there while his heartbroken parents continued to Santiago. On their way home they visited the gallows and discovered their son – alive. His weight, he said, had been held by Santiago the entire time, and would they please take him down? They brought notice of the miracle to the local magistrate who at that moment was roasting two chickens for dinner. On hearing the news he scoffed, saying, 'He's as alive as these chickens I'm roasting.' At that moment the chickens jumped off the spit and ran down the street. To this day, chickens, rumored to be descendants of the original two, are kept in the cathedral along with a piece of the gallows on which the young man was hanged.

🛏 Casa de la Cofradía del Santo Ⓞ Ⓓ Ⓡ Ⓚ Ⓢ 11/70, €11/-/-/-, Calle Mayor 38, www.alberguecofradiadelsanto.com, tel 941 343 390, laundromat in front of albergue

🛏 Abadía Cicterciense Ⓟ Ⓓ Ⓚ Ⓦ Ⓢ 6/32 & 78/156, €9/38/50/80, Calle Mayor 29, www.cister-lacalzada.com/albergue, tel 941 340 700, private rooms at Calle Pinar 2

Worth the splurge due to location on the main square:
🛏 Parador de Santo Domingo de la Calzada Ⓞ Ⓟ Ⓡ Ⓖ Ⓢ 61/122, €-/-/77/103, Plaza del Santo 3, www.parador.es/en, tel 941 340 300

Flying buttresses support the tall walls of the cathedral at Santo Domingo de la Calzada (photo: Rod Hoekstra)

109

STAGE 10
Santo Domingo de la Calzada to Belorado

Start	Santo Domingo, Plaza del Santo
Finish	Belorado, Plaza Mayor
Distance	22.5km
Total ascent	425m
Total descent	295m
Difficulty	Easy
Duration	6¼hr
Percentage paved	28%
Albergues	Grañón 6.5; Redecilla del Camino 10.6; Castildelgado 12.2; Viloria de Rioja 14.1; Villamayor del Río 17.5; Belorado 22.5

In spite of following alongside the N-120 highway, this stage has many advantages – beautiful views of rolling hills and frequent stops at tiny villages. The albergue at Grañón is renowned for its friendly communal dinners and nights in the church attic. The other towns are more convenient than memorable, until sweet Belorado, a charming if decrepit riverside town with many pilgrim services.

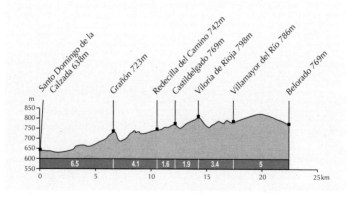

Pilgrim boots rest on a windowsill at a Grañón albergue (photo: Rod Hoekstra)

From the plaza in **Santo Domingo**, continue past the cathedral and cross the Oja River (**0.6km**) on a **bridge** originally built by Santo Domingo. The center of the original span, built in the mid 11th c., was replaced in the 18th c. with a similar design. Veer onto a wide gravel path that will take you back and forth between fields and the N-120. Toward the top of the upcoming ridge are a metal **cross** and benches (**2.8km**) that memorialize the otherwise-forgotten history of disharmony between neighboring Grañón and Santo Domingo. Soon the dome-roofed octagonal tower of Grañón's parish church appears.

6.5KM GRAÑÓN (ELEV. 723M, POP. 275) 🏨 ⛪ 🏧 🅿 ⭘ (563.2KM)

Atop a ridge separating parts of a key east–west road, Grañón has been occupied since pre-Roman times. Its compact layout follows the perimeter of its now-vanished medieval walls. At one time the town hosted two monasteries as well as a pilgrim hospital that was located on the plaza across from the **Church of San Juan Bautista**. This otherwise unremarkable church hosts a Renaissance retablo inspired by the main altarpiece at the cathedral in Santo Domingo. The building's albergue is known in pilgrim lore as one of the friendliest, most atmospheric Camino overnights.

🛏 Casa de Las Sonrisas 🅞 🅓 🅑 🅒 🅦 🅢 7/24, €Donation, Calle Mayor 16, https://alberguelacasadelassonrisas.com, tel 687 877 891

🛏 Hospital de Peregrinos San Juan Bautista 🅞 🅓 🅚 🅑 🅒 🅢 2/40, €Donation, Calle Mayor 1, www.facebook.com/alberguegranon.larioja, tel 633 915 800, much beloved for its setting inside the church and warm hospitality

🛏 Nuestra Señora de Carrasquedo 🅞 🅟 🅓 🅡 🅦 🅢 2/14 & 6/12, €8/24/32/48, Camino de la Ermita 45, tel 627 341 907

Follow the trail down into the broad valley of wheat and sunflowers until you're walking uphill toward the next town. Signs welcome you to the Burgos Province of Castile and León (**2.1km**, Spanish: Castilla y León).

Geographically the largest of Spain's Autonomous Communities, **Castilla y León** is divided into nine provinces, of which the Camino Francés crosses three – Burgos, Palencia and León. Castilla y León encompasses the northern Meseta, drained by the Río Duero and its many tributaries. In the ninth c. the Kingdom of León consisted of all the non-Muslim regions of the north-west Iberian Peninsula. In the 11th c. Castile and Galicia were separated out, and in the 12th c. Portugal. It was not until 1983 that Old Castilla and the Province of León were joined as a single Autonomous Community. Some of Spain's great cities – Segovia, Salamanca, Ávila, Palencia, Zamora, and of course Burgos and León – lie in the region as well as by some counts about 60% of the architectural, artistic, historical and cultural treasures of Spain.

Continue among fields and cross the N-120 to find a pilgrim information office (**1.7km**) at the outskirts of

4.1KM REDECILLA DEL CAMINO (ELEV. 742M, POP. 127) 🔢 ⊕ 🔳 ◉ ❶ (559.1KM)

The medieval pilgrim hospital to San Lazaro is now an albergue. The town's church hosts a unique baptismal font in the Byzantine or Mozarabic style, thought to be from the 10th or 11th c. Note the coiled serpent at the base of the font's eight pillars, signifying the triumph of baptism over evil.

🏠 Albergue Essentia 🅳 🆁 🆆 🆂 2/10, €12/-/-/-, Calle Mayor 34, www.facebook.com/alberguessentia, tel 606 046 298

🏠 San Lázaro Redecilla del Camino 🅾 🅳 🅺 🅲 🆆 🆂 5/50, €5/-/-/-, Calle Mayor 24, tel 947 585 221

Carefully cross the highway and pick up the trail alongside it opposite the town. The sound of cars and trucks is oddly abrasive after days in the countryside. The path aims at **Castildelgado** with its square church tower near the tall radio beacons.

1.6KM CASTILDELGADO (ELEV. 769M, POP. 40) 🔢 🔳 ◉ (557.4KM)

Established at least as early as 926, Castildelgado takes its name from a 16th c. bishop of Burgos, Jeronimo Delgado, a prominent clergyman and the town's favorite son. Delgado is buried in the 16th c. **Church of San Pedro**.

🏠 Albergue Bideluze 🅿 🅳 🆁 🅲 🆆 🆂 🆉 3/16, €12/-/35/-, Calle Mayor 8, www.alberguebideluze.com, tel 947 585 271

Pass by the church and plaza with its fountain and the nearby 1746 hermitage of Santa María del Campo. Walk downhill on a steep but well-groomed gravel path to take up a position once again alongside the highway. Soon the path diverts away from the N-120 and toward **Viloria de Rioja** with its albergues, bar, and picturesque brick-and-stucco church.

1.9KM VILORIA DE RIOJA (ELEV. 798M, POP. 62) 🏠 ◉ (555.6KM)

It was here that in 1019 Santo Domingo de la Calzada was born. The town's parish church still houses the font where he was baptized.

⌂ Albergue Parada Viloria **D R B C W S** 3/16, €8/-/-/-, Calle Bajera 37, www.facebook.com/pg/bajera37, tel 610 625 065, no other food services available nearby

⌂ Refugio Acacio y Orietta **D R B C W S** 1/10, €25/-/-/-, Calle Nueva 6, www.acacioyorietta.com/hospedagem, tel 947 585 220, Paulo Coelho connection

Now the path returns north to resume its partnership with the highway before arriving at **Villamayor**, which you enter one block off the highway (the fountain is sadly non-potable).

3.4KM VILLAMAYOR DEL RÍO (ELEV. 786M, POP. 253) 🍴 🏠 ◉ (552.2KM)

Sometimes called 'The Town of Three Lies' because it is not a *villa* (city) nor *mayor* (big) and its *arroyo* (stream) hardly qualifies as a river.

⌂ San Luis de Francia **D R C W S** 6/24, €5/-/-/-, Carretera de Quintanilla, www.facebook.com/alberguesanluisdefrancia, tel 947 580 566

The path again follows the highway and makes a long, gentle climb toward the distant ridge. Carefully cross the highway (**3.9km**) to a shaded rest area and then follow a quiet gravel road into **Belorado**. The track winds around the center of town, one block off the Plaza Mayor with its banks, restaurants, tourist information center and shops, giving you three potential left turns to get to the circular square at the heart of this little town.

5.0KM BELORADO (ELEV. 769M, POP. 1852) 🍴 ⊕ 🏠 🄲 ◉ ⊕ ⊕ (547.2KM)

Belorado sits astride the Tirón River in a narrow pass at the foot of the northern slopes of the Montes de Ayago, a strategic location that explains its long history as a fortified stronghold. By the 13th c. it had eight churches as well as French, Castilian, Jewish and Muslim quarters. The 20th c. was hard on the town's longstanding leather industry, and many older buildings stand abandoned. The 15th c. **Church of Santa María** is a pilgrim favorite, with a stone retablo featuring sculptures of both Santiago Peregrino and Santiago Matamoros as well as a Romanesque Virgin Mary. Caves behind the church were once homes to hermits. Above are the sparse ruins of the **Castillo de Belorado**, a fortification begun as early as the 9th c. but abandoned by the 17th. Just off the Plaza Mayor is the 17th c. **Church of San Pedro** whose rococo altarpiece is topped part of the year by a statue of a beheaded San Vitores.

🔺 Albergue El Corro **O P D R K C W S Z** 4/45, €8/15/30/36, Calle Mayor 68, **www.facebook.com/pg/alberguelcorro**, tel 947 581 419

🔺 Albergue Parroquial de Belorado **D B W S** 1/20, €Donation, Plaza San Francisco 71, tel 947 580 085, next to Santa María Church, breakfast with donation

🔺 Cuatro Cantones **D R G K C W S** 5/65, €12/-/-/-, Calle Hipólito López Bernal 10, **www.cuatrocantones.com**, tel 947 580 591, swimming pool

🔺 Albergue A Santiago **P D R K W S** 8/98 & 22/44, €10/32/42/-, Camino de los Paules, **www.a-santiago.es**, tel 677 811 847, swimming pool

🔺 Albergue El Caminante **P D R G C W S** 1/22 & 8/17, €6/25/35/45, Calle Mayor 36, **www.alberguecaminobelorado.es**, tel 656 873 927

🔺 Albergue El Salto **P D R G W S** 2/24 & 2/4, €15/-/-/-, Camino de los Cauces, **www.elsalto.eu**, tel 669 415 636

A quiet street in central Belorado

STAGE 11
Belorado to San Juan de Ortega

Start	Belorado, Plaza Mayor
Finish	San Juan de Ortega, monastery
Distance	24.0km
Total ascent	570m
Total descent	335m
Difficulty	Moderate
Duration	6¾hr
Percentage paved	9%
Albergues	Tosantos 4.8; Villambistia 6.7; Espinosa del Camino 8.3; Villafranca Montes de Oca 11.9; San Juan de Ortega 24.0

Today's stage begins along the route of the N-120 highway surrounded by flat fields of grain until Villafranca Montes de Oca where it climbs through forests over the Montes de Oca to San Juan de Ortega. The first section is fairly flat with frequent bars and pilgrim services, while the latter is a moderate ascent with no services except a food van near the top. San Juan de Ortega sports an historic monastery, but only one albergue, one bar and one restaurant. For more choices continue on the few additional kilometers to Agés or Atapuerca.

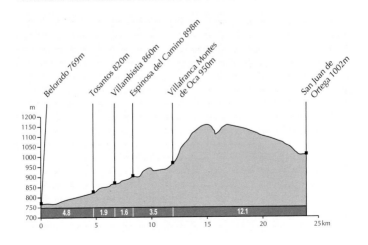

The Ermita de la Virgen de la Peña sits above Tosantos

In **Belorado**'s Plaza Mayor, find your way to the alley left of the San Pedro church and then turn right onto the Camino track, following it through town, past the Our Lady of Bretonera (Clarisas) convent (**0.6km**) and out to the highway. After crossing the highway, cross also the four-arched **Tirón River bridge** (**0.4km**), noticing the rest area adjacent. The path passes a **gas station** (**0.4km**) and a shady rest area (**2.5km**, fountain) before arriving on the back street of **Tosantos**.

4.8KM TOSANTOS (ELEV. 820M, POP. 56) 🍴 ⚑ ◉ (542.4KM)

Legend holds that in 712 a sacred image of the Virgin Mary was hidden in a cave above town under a bell to protect it from Muslims. The cave, visible above on the cliffs across the highway, now holds a chapel, the **Ermita de la Virgen de la Peña**, where the statue (actually from the 12th c.) spends part of the year. When not in the cave chapel, it is housed in the town's 17th c. **Church of San Esteban**. Pilgrims will find services on the opposite side of town across the highway, although the town's two bars are closed on Mondays.

🏠 **Albergue Los Arancones** Ⓞ Ⓓ Ⓡ Ⓦ 1/16, €12/-/-/-, Calle de la Iglesia, tel 693 299 063, will not open in 2022

🏠 **San Francisco de Asís Tosantos** Ⓓ Ⓑ Ⓒ Ⓢ 3/30, €Donation, Calle Santa Marina 2, tel 947 580 371, breakfast and dinner with donation

Leave town by walking uphill on a wide gravel drive. The sound of cars and long-haul trucks fades into the distance as you edge away from the road toward **Villambistia** with its white stucco tower that can be seen for several miles.

1.9KM VILLAMBISTIA (ELEV. 860M, POP. 44) 🏨 ♻ ◉ (540.5KM)

The **parish church** hosts a 16th c. retablo.

⛺ Albergue Municipal San Roque ◉ Ⓓ Ⓡ Ⓑ Ⓒ Ⓦ Ⓢ 1/12, €10/-/-/-, Plaza Mayor 1, tel 687 669 734

Partway to Espinosa del Camino, pass a shaded rest area (**1.1km**) near the highway. Carefully cross the road and enter the town a block behind its highway frontage.

1.6KM ESPINOSA DEL CAMINO (ELEV. 898M, POP. 43) 🏨 ♻ ◉ (538.9KM)

A 12th c. image of San Indalecio, disciple of Santiago in the evangelization of the Iberian Peninsula, can be seen in the **Parish Church of La Asunción**.

⛺ La Campana de Pepe ◉ Ⓓ Ⓡ Ⓑ Ⓒ 2/10, €17/-/-/-, Calle Villafranca, **https://lacampanadepepe.blogspot.com**, tel 678 479 361, half board included

A wide gravel path leads out of town toward a narrow valley filled with wheat fields and framed by mountains on three sides with wind turbines to the right. Come to a stone ruin after the ridge and see all that remains of the sixth–eighth c. San Felices hermitage (**1.8km**). You can now see to the left the profile of Villafranca Montes de Oca. Before arriving in town, the track forces you onto a narrow path alongside the highway, where the nearby whooshing of trucks requires a hand on your hat to keep it from blowing away. A small footbridge crosses over the tiny **Oca River** (**1.4km**), and then the path spits you out beside the busy roadway and its narrow channel through

3.5KM VILLAFRANCA MONTES DE OCA (ELEV. 950M, POP. 125) 🏨 ♻ ◉ (535.3KM)

Ruins of the Roman city of Auca north of town document the long pedigree of this village whose bishop, San Indalecio, was said to have been appointed by Santiago himself. The 19th c. **Church of Santiago Apóstol** holds a statue of Santiago Peregrino. Of the town's three medieval pilgrim hospitals, the one remaining is the 14th c. **San Antón Abad**, now a hotel/albergue. The name 'Villafranca' likely refers to immigration of French peoples to the town, encouraged by rulers to fill in lands left empty in the Reconquista. The **Montes de Oca** are a ridge of high, rolling hills that separate the Ebro River drainage into the Mediterranean from the Duero drainage into the Atlantic. The forests of this range once were inhabited by wolves and thieves that preyed on hapless pilgrims.

🛏 Albergue de Peregrinos de Villafranca Montes de Oca **D R K W S** 4/60, €5/-/-/-, Calle Mayor 17, tel 691 801 211

🛏 San Antón Abad **P D R G S** 4/30 & 3/6, €15/-/50/-, Calle Hospital 4, www.hotelsanantonabad.com, tel 947 582 150, additional private rooms in adjacent hotel with breakfast included at €-/63/75/-

Turn uphill before the parish church and begin the day's long climb, first on a narrow rubble-strewn path and then on a wide gravel drive. The N-120 highway blessedly fades into the distance as the path is submerged for many miles into forests of oak and pine. Partway uphill is a rest area (**1.3km**, picnic tables, fountain) with a viewpoint over the mountains to the south. At the first summit are a few sun-bathed picnic tables and a **concrete monument** (**2.3km**, 1149m elev.).

Burgos was the capital of the Nationalist forces during the **Spanish Civil War** of the 1930s, and opposing leaders were often taken in the middle of the night and their bodies found the next day. The monument remembers the lives of men who were assassinated in 1936; their bodies were dumped at this site.

Exterior of the monastery at San Juan de Ortega

Here also the N-120 highway reasserts itself to the left. In 1.2km the track meets and follows a super-highway-sized swath of clearing that continues for the next 1½hr. 'El Oasis' food truck (**1.9km**) can usually be found on this stretch. After a time the track leaves the wide clearing (**3.6km**), turning left onto a narrow path in a forest of oak and pine. The forest ends in a wide meadow and the white, Spanish baroque façade of **San Juan de Ortega** appears. Pass a steel sculpture and an interpretive center before arriving at the monastery with its albergue, bar and restaurant.

12.1KM SAN JUAN DE ORTEGA (ELEV. 1002M, POP. 20) 🏨 🛗 (523.2KM)

When Juan Velázquez of Quintanaortuño was shipwrecked on his 1109 pilgrimage to Jerusalem, he promised he would dedicate his life in service to pilgrims if he survived. When he returned home, he became a co-worker of Santo Domingo, helping to build bridgeworks for safer pilgrim travel. He soon focused his efforts on the stretch of Camino running through the wolf- and thief-infested forests of the Montes de Oca and dedicated his outpost church to San Nicolás de Bari. Before long he attracted the attention of leaders in Burgos, who after his death helped the subsequent monastery fulfill its mission of pilgrim safety and care. Juan Velázquez himself is said to have built the three 12th c. apses of the **Church of San Juan de Ortega** that bears his name. Inside the church, note the elaborate columnar capitals, including the large capital that narrates the Annunciation, Visitation and Nativity. The 15th c. alabaster tomb of San Juan by Gil de Siloé narrates his miracles. A Gothic baldacchino covers the sepulcher while the tomb itself lies below in the crypt. Twice a year at equinox a single shaft of light precisely illuminates the Virgin statue at sunset.

🛏 Albergue Monasterio San Juan de Ortega **D C W S** 3/60, €10/-/-/-, Calle de la Iglesia 9, **www.alberguesanjuandeortega.es/albergue**, tel 947 569 913, pilgrim mass and blessing at 6pm

🛏 El Descanso de San Juan **O D R C W S** 1/7, €15/-/-/-, San Juan de Ortega, tel 690 398 024

STAGE 12
San Juan de Ortega to Burgos

Start	San Juan de Ortega, monastery
Finish	Burgos, Plaza Santa María (cathedral main entrance)
Distance	26.8km
Total ascent	275m
Total descent	420m
Difficulty	Moderate
Duration	7hr
Percentage paved	51%
Albergues	Agés 3.6; Atapuerca 6.2; Cardeñuela Riopico 12.6; Orbaneja Riopico 14.7; Castañares 19.3; Burgos 26.8

After the climb of 150m to Cruz de Atapuerca the day is a gradual downhill walk, with scenic and cosmopolitan Burgos at stage end. A poorly marked option at the Burgos airport allows pilgrims to choose between an industrial entry to the city via the official route, or a more relaxed entry along a riverfront park.

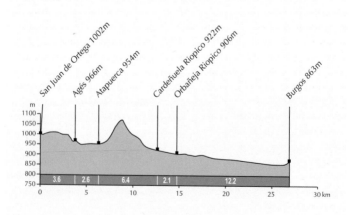

From **San Juan de Ortega**, after the monastery, continue along the drive and soon veer left to pick up the wide dirt path under trees that will take you most of the way to Agés. As the forest ends you realize you are on the long spur of a ridge pointing out into a spacious valley with wide vistas over many miles. Atapuerca is on the right, and before long **Agés** appears below on the left.

3.6KM AGÉS (ELEV. 966M, POP. 62) 🖼 ⊕ 🛏 (519.5KM)

The Battle of Atapuerca took place just outside town in 1054 between the armies of two brothers – García Sánchez II of Navarre and King Ferdinand I of Castile. Lovers of Paulo Coelho's mystic tomes will want to stop at El Alquimista (The Alchemist) bar. The **Iglesia de Santa Eulalia** is a quiet and serene space, worth a visit for reflection.

🛖 Albergue El Pajar de Agés ⓄⓅⒹⓇ🅖🅒ⓌⓈ🅩 3/24, €12/-/40/-, Calle Ochabro 12, www.elpajardeages.es, tel 686 273 322

🛖 Albergue Fagus Ⓓ🅖ⓌⓈ 5/22, €13/-/-/-, Calle Adobera 14–16, www.alberguefagus.com, tel 947 561 329

🛖 Albergue Municipal La Taberna ⓄⒹⓇ🅖ⓌⓈ 1/36, €9/-/-/-, Calle del Medio 21, www.alberguedeages.com, tel 947 400 697

Pass the fountain and continue on the quiet asphalt road, coming to the turn-off for Atapuerca's CAREX archeological museum (**1.8km**).

2.6KM ATAPUERCA (ELEV. 954M, POP. 187) 🖼 🛏 ⊕ (517.0KM)

In 1976 archeologists discovered Europe's most ancient hominid remains in nearby limestone caves. The oldest cave yielded remains of humanoid ancestors from up to 1.2 million years ago. The **CAREX Experimental Archeology Center and Archeological Park** (1km north of the track, closed Mon, www.atapuerca.org, tel 947 421 000) offers tours focused on the study of archeology, while the remains themselves rest at the Museo de la Evolución Humana in Burgos.

🛖 Albergue La Hutte ⓄⒹ🅚Ⓦ 1/16, €10/-/-/-, Calle En Medio 36, www.burgosturismorural.com, tel 947 430 320, basic kitchen

🛖 La Plazuela Verde ⓄⒹⓇ🅖🅚ⓌⓈ 1/10, €14/-/-/-, Calle San Polo 41, https://laplazuelaverde.es/, tel 654 301 152

🛖 Albergue El Peregrino Ⓟ Ⓓ🅖🅚ⓌⓈ 6/30 & 6/12, €11/-/40/-, Calle Camino de Santiago 25, www.alberguatapuerca.com, tel 661 580 882

Continue through the village and turn left at the signs, heading uphill past a picnic area on a rough path of sometimes jagged stones beneath scattered stands of holm oak, to arrive at **Cruz de Atapuerca** (**2.3km**, elev. 1071m). Just beyond this tall cross is a spectacular vista toward Burgos and the vast Meseta beyond. Continue downhill and pick up a dirt road below the quarry, entering the rolling hills and grainfields of the Pico River drainage. After ½hr pass the entry to the town of **Villalval** (**2.5km**, no services) and continue gradually downhill on the quiet paved road.

6.4KM CARDEÑUELA RIOPICO (ELEV. 922M, POP. 111) 🏠 ⬛ (510.6KM)

🏠 Albergue Municipal La Parada **O D R W S** 2/12, €7/-/-/-, Calle Real 28, tel 646 249 597, next to La Parada bar

🏠 Albergue Santa Fe **P D R G C W S** 2/15 & 6/10, €8/30/40/-, Calle Los Huertos 2, www.baralberguesantafe.com, tel 626 352 269

🏠 Albergue Vía Minera **P D R G C W S** 6/58 & 7/24, €8/10/40/-, Calle La Iglesia 1, http://albergueviaminera.blogspot.com, tel 652 941 647, swimming pool

Continue down the road, now called 'Calle Real,' through scattered houses to reach Cardeñuela's larger neighbor, where the road narrows abruptly.

2.1KM ORBAÑEJA RIOPICO (ELEV. 906M, POP. 177) 🏠 ⬛ (508.5KM)

🏠 Cantina El Peregrino **D R G W S** 3/18, €7/-/-/-, Calle Principal 1, www.facebook.com/albergueelperegrino, tel 947 430 980

After town the paved road continues to descend before rising to an overpass for the AP-1 freeway (**0.7km**) and then descending to arrive at an important choice.

In spite of the lack of signage to advise you, here (**1.0km**) you face the decision of whether you will turn left to enter the city south of the airport through the Castañares-Burgos riverfront park and trail system, or go straight and walk on sidewalks alongside a wide and noisy industrial boulevard north of the airport.

Alternative route around south of airport
For a quieter and gentler entry (just 100m longer), turn left before the red-roofed apartment homes and descend to a wide gravel path that first draws closer to the freeway and then heads along the fence line of the airport's southern perimeter. Follow the path along the south border of the airport, arriving in 3.7km at the town of **Castañares**.

3.7KM CASTAÑARES (ELEV. 884M, POP. 283) 🏠 ⬛ ◉ (503.9KM)

🏠 Hotel HM Versus Burgos **O P R G K S** 14/28, €-/55/55/70, Calle Mayor 26, www.hotelversus.es, tel 947 474 977

The Arco de Santa Maria once served both as the main gate of Burgos and its town hall

Continue on, entering a lovely park system, ultimately passing a riverfront beach (2.9km) and then crossing into central Burgos on a rust-colored pedestrian bridge (2.2km). Turn left on Calle de Fernán Gonzalez to come to Burgos Cathedral.

Main route around north of airport

After circling around the NE tip of the airport runways, come to the N-1, a wide, industrial highway sprinkled with factories, warehouses, trucker motels and shady clubs. At Santa Maria la Real y Antigua church (7.0km, 14th c.) the landscape changes to modern, suburban apartment blocks, continuing to follow the N-1, which is blessedly surrounded by busy shops and cafés. At a small park on the right (1.1km) the route diverges onto Calle San Roque before turning two blocks to the right at the N-627 and continuing on Avenida de la Paz to the old city walls at Arco San Juan (2.2km). Continue west along Calle Fernán Gonzalez to the cathedral in **Burgos**.

12.2KM BURGOS (ELEV. 863M, POP. 176,608) 🏨 ⊕ 🛏 🄲 ◉ ◉ Ⓗ ⊕ ⊕ ❶ (496.4KM)

This city of El Cid 'Campeador' (born Rodrigo Díaz de Vivar) has many claims to fame. It was site of a visit by Christopher Columbus to King Ferdinand and Queen Isabella, was besieged by Napoléon during the Peninsular War, and was the base of Francisco Franco's rebel Nationalist government. Modern-day Burgos retains much of its charming medieval architecture in its pedestrianized center with its crown jewel being the dazzling **Cathedral of Santa María**, a UNESCO World Heritage Site. Here at the cathedral exit on the south side receive a *sello* stamp. Admission to the vast building is €4.50. Rent a €3 audio guide, and head upstairs for a look at some of the most elaborate and beautiful ecclesiastical architecture in all of Spain (http://catedral-deburgos.info). Walk clockwise around the interior to enjoy the main building and its 18 chapels, highlighted by the **fly-catcher clock**, the spectacular **St Anne Chapel** and the **Golden Stairs** designed by a student of Michelangelo. See if you can identify the male/female characteristics of the **Chapel of the High Constable**. Back outside and adjacent to the cathedral is the **Church of San Nicolás** and the 465 figures of its remarkable 16th c. altarpiece. Downhill toward the river stands the picturesque **Arco de Santa María**, main entrance to the old city and once the town hall. The nearby **Plaza Mayor** is an excellent place for lunch, tapas or dinner. Along the river is the **Paseo del Espolón**, a lovely pedestrian stroll under carefully pruned plane trees with shops and outdoor cafés. The **statue of El Cid** stands just beyond the end of the Paseo. This military leader of the Reconquista is still Burgos' favorite son, and statues of his friends and family members adorn the nearby **San Pablo bridge**. If you have time and a scientific inclination, cross the bridge to the **Museo de la Evolución Humana**, resting place of many of the Atapuerca archaeological finds. Just outside town are two key Burgos attractions – the **Monasterio de las Huelgas** with its Royal Pantheon of Castilian monarchs; and the **Cartuja de Miraflores**, a 15th c. Carthusian monastery and architectural gem. An evening walk or tourist train ride to the **Castle of Burgos** allows a sunset view over the cathedral and the vast Meseta beyond.

🛖 Albergue de Peregrinos Emaús 🅳 🅱 🅲 🆂 4/20, €8/-/-/-, Calle San Pedro de Cardeña 31a, **www.facebook.com/albergueemaus**, no tel, breakfast with donation

🛖 Albergue Santiago y Santa Catalina 🅳 🆆 1/16, €6/-/-/-, Calle Lain Calvo 10, tel 947 207 952

🛖 Casa de Cubos 🅾 🅳 🆆 🆂 6/150, €10/-/-/-, Calle Fernán González 28, **www.caminosantiagoburgos.com/albergues/#11**, tel 947 460 922

🛖 Hostel Catedral Burgos 🅿 🅳 🆁 🅶 🆆 🆂 23/116 & 14/28, €19/-/46/66, Plaza Huerto del Rey 5, **www.hostelburgos.com**, tel 623 115 887

🔺 Camping Fuentes Blancas 🅳 🆁 🆆 🆂 -/-, €See website, Carretera Fuentes Blancas km3, **www.campingburgos.com**, tel 947 486 016, albergue, bungalows and spaces for tents available

Worth the splurge due to location overlooking the cathedral.
🛖 Crisol Mesón del Cid 🅾 🅿 🆁 🅶 🆂 49/94, €-/-/68/91, Plaza Santa María 8, **www.mesondelcid.es**, tel 947 208 715, views overlooking cathedral for €10 extra

The statue of El Cid holds down one end of the Paseo del Espolón in central Burgos

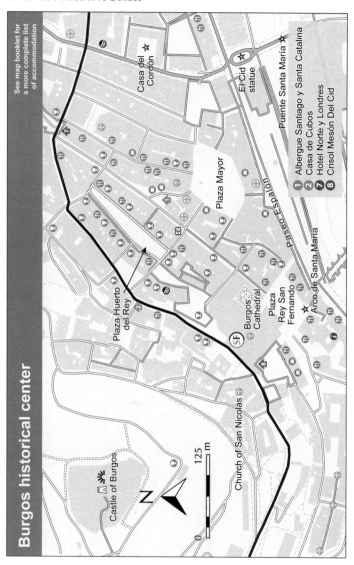

Burgos historical center

See map booklet for a more complete list of accommodation

Casa del Cordón

El Cid statue

Puente Santa María

① Albergue Santiago y Santa Catalina
② Casa de Cubos
⑦ Hotel Norte y Londres
⑧ Crisol Mesón Del Cid

Plaza Mayor

Paseo Espolón

Arco de Santa María

Plaza Huerto del Rey

Burgos Cathedral

Plaza Rey San Fernando

Church of San Nicolás

Castle of Burgos

125 m

N

Stones placed on a trailside monument after El Burgo
Ranero mark pilgrim prayers and memories

SECTION 3:
BURGOS TO LEÓN

SECTION 3: BURGOS TO LEÓN

In pilgrim lore, the flat, dry central section of the Camino Francés – the Meseta – is its most difficult. Grainfields stretch across changeless, shadeless scenery composed of miles of... well, nothing. Anxious about boredom or heat, some pilgrims skip this portion of the walk, but those who take on the challenge often end up remembering the Meseta as their favorite part.

Drained by the Duero River, which flows west toward Portugal and the Atlantic, the northern 'high' Meseta is surprisingly cold in winter due to its average 800m altitude. Weather patterns bring fewer clouds and less rain, which make it most always sunny and warm in summer. Pilgrims first meet the Meseta a few kilometers east of Burgos and then finally bid it *adieu* past

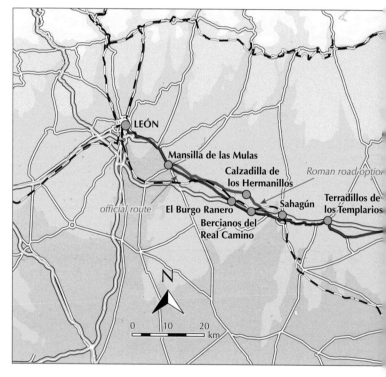

León. In spring it is a seemingly infinite blend of the color green, with fields of wheat, rye and other grains dancing in its winds. Summer sees these same fields wave their gold and amber colors in the warm breezes. In late summer, autumn and winter, the vastness is covered by a crazy quilt of chestnut-brown and red furrowed soil, awaiting the spring rains and plantings which start the cycle over. Spring through fall, red poppies joyfully dot the landscape. Except for noise from an occasional car or tractor, the trademark sounds of the Meseta are silence, birdsong and the whistling of wind over the vast and empty fields.

The cosmopolitan cities of Burgos and León serve as its margins, and the region in-between them is sprinkled with charming but empty-feeling villages. As with other rural residents around the world, local Spaniards have abandoned quiet agrarian regions for livelier cities, and their absence is felt. Cafés and parks find the remaining elderly Spanish farmers playing cards or casting the *bocce* ball. Left behind by previous generations is a smattering of

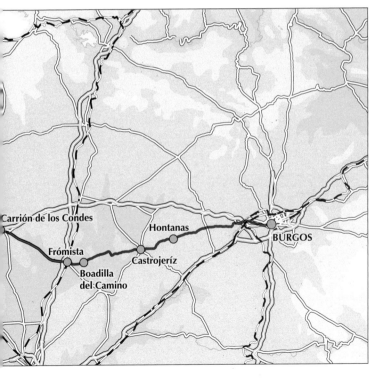

architecture and art that offers a window into past centuries when the towns were full of youth and steeped in Christian devotion.

In the later stages of the Meseta, ask for river crayfish or quail, specialties of the Province of Palencia. Leonese delicacies include the *cocido maragato* chickpea stew and *botillo* stuffed meat.

And there are other surprises – the nostalgic grandeur of Santa María la Blanca, the quiet cloister of San Zoilo, the narrow streets at the center of Carrión de los Condes. Pilgrims can choose to walk a day-long stretch of ancient Roman road, complete with its original paving. With a little imagination, a night's stay in a monastery-turned-hotel will bring out the inner monk or nun. After a day's walk, a brief nap, some pilgrim laundry scrubbing, a cool drink and some deep conversation with other walkers, the best end of the day is watching the sun slowly set in flaming colors over the flat and distant horizon.

PLANNING

The road branches to two fairly equidistant alternatives after Sahagún, either following the better-serviced and shadier Stages 17A and 18A through Bercianos del Real Camino or the more solitary option on Roman roads of Stages 17B and 18B. The two routes are sometimes only a few hundred meters apart and both converge at Mansilla de las Mulas.

WHAT NOT TO MISS

Find extra time to visit the most charming and largest towns of the Meseta – Carrión de los Condes and Sahagún (Stage 17) – and experience their architectural treasures. Medieval churches at Villalcázar de Sirga and Frómista (both Stage 15) are must-sees. The most memorable overnight lodging on this stretch is outside Carrión at the San Zoilo monastery, where monks' quarters adjacent to a Renaissance cloister have been transformed into hotel rooms. Arrival at León brings the opportunity to enjoy its elegant cathedral and fascinating Basílica de San Isidoro. On Friday and Saturday nights throngs of thirsty college students fill the restaurants and pubs of León's Húmedo quarter, with an occasional sandal- and shorts-clad pilgrim among the otherwise well-dressed crowd.

STAGE 13

Burgos to Hontanas

Start	Burgos, Cathedral of Santa María
Finish	Hontanas, municipal albergue
Distance	31.7km
Total ascent	420m
Total descent	415m
Difficulty	Moderately hard, due to length and elevation changes
Duration	8½hr
Percentage paved	25%
Albergues	Tardajos 10.7; Rabé de las Calzadas 13.0; Hornillos del Camino 20.9; Arroyo San Bol 26.7; Hontanas 31.7

Burgos quickly fades into the background and the vast scale of the Meseta now becomes clear. Towns are fewer and smaller, but their connection to the medieval Camino becomes more evident. Today's topography includes one of the Meseta's few memorable hills, and the walk is quite free of shade.

In **Burgos**, continue along the street behind the cathedral as it travels through the old city walls at Arco San Martín, and follow the yellow arrows along sidewalks across the pedestrian bridge over the Arlanzón toward the **University of Burgos** (1.5km). Note the 'Statue in Homage to the Pilgrim' that marks the site of a medieval pilgrim hospital, now converted to the university's law school. The track quickly leads to parkland and

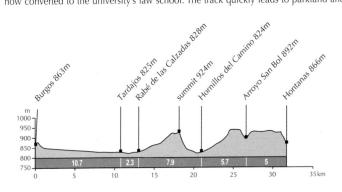

The first steps into the vast Meseta are among low, rolling hills covered in fields of grain

then farmland, passing a rest area (**3.6km**, fountain) before it weaves through a tangle of highway interchanges. After finally crossing the A-231 highway (**6.6km**), cross the familiar N-120 once again and then the Arlanzón a final time before heading into

10.7KM TARDAJOS (ELEV. 825M, POP. 950) 🔟 🏠 🆑 ◎ ⊕ ⊕ (485.6KM)

Situated at the crossroads of two major Roman thoroughfares, the ancient town of Tardajos served as an important bulwark against the Muslim south. One of its now-vanished churches, La Magdalena, was host to St Francis of Assisi during his pilgrimage to Santiago.

🛏 Albergue Municipal de Tardajos 🅓 3/18, €Donation, Calle Asunción, tel 947 451 189

🛏 Albergue La Fábrica 🅟 🅓 🅡 🅖 🅦 🅢 4/14 & 6/12, €13/40/50/56, Camino de La Fábrica 27, www.alberguelafabrica.com, tel 620 111 939

🛏 La Casa de Beli 🅟 🅓 🅡 🅖 🅦 🅢 5/34 & 7/15, €10/40/50/75, Avenida General Yagüe 16, https://lacasadebeli.com, tel 947 451 234

Walking north out of town on a paved road amongst the fields, arrive at

2.3KM RABÉ DE LAS CALZADAS (ELEV. 828M, POP. 227) 🔟 🏠 (483.3KM)

The town's treasure is the Romanesque relief of the Crucifixion in the **Santa Marina church** (13th c.).

🛏 Albergue Libéranos Domine 🅞 🅓 🅡 🅒 🅦 🅢 4/24, €12/-/-/-, Plaza Francisco Riberas 10, www.liberanosdomine.com, tel 695 116 901, Clementina is your host

Pass the unremarkable Ermita de la Virgen (**0.3km**) on the left, a gateway into fields of the local cash crop of turnips. Now at the Meseta proper, everything seems small before the vastness of this high plain. Pass a rest area (**2.3km**, no water) and continue on a path of sharp stones, first uphill in fields to a summit (**3.0km**) and then downhill steeply with a sweeping view ahead and into

7.9KM HORNILLOS DEL CAMINO (ELEV. 824M, POP. 57) ▯ ⊕ ▱ (475.4KM)

Although the name 'Hornillos' likely refers to ovens or smelters located here in the Middle Ages, the town's establishment dates from ancient times. The plain **San Román church** was originally the site of a pre-Roman *castro* (fortress). Since the Middle Ages the town's main street has been the Camino Francés main route, and at the height of the Camino, Hornillos was home to several pilgrim hospitals. Look for the cross of Santiago and a chalice carved onto a house on the right after the town's first crossroads, which marks the original site of the pilgrim hospital of Sancti Spiritus.

🛖 Albergue de Hornillos del Camino ⦿ 🄳 🅁 🄺 🄲 🅆 🅂 3/15, €10/-/-/-, Calle San Román 3, http://hornillosalbergue.es/en/home/, tel 689 784 681

🛖 Albergue El Afar 🄳 🅁 🄺 🄲 🅆 🅂 3/20, €12/-/-/-, Calle Cantarranas 8, http://elalfardehornillos.es, tel 654 263 857

🛖 Hornillos Meeting Point 🄿 🄳 🅁 🄶 🄺 🅆 🅂 3/32 & 5/10, €9/38/42/-, Calle Cantarranas 3, www.hornillosmeetingpoint.com, tel 608 113 599

🛖 La Casa del Abuelo ⦿ 🄿 🄳 🅁 🄺 🄱 🅆 🅂 5/10 & 11/22, €20/45/55/-, Calle Real 44, https://lacasadelabuelohornillos.webnode.es, tel 661 869 618

The cross of the Order of Santiago looks out over wind turbines after Hornillos (photo: Rod Hoekstra)

Continue on the main street through town back into farmlands, climbing to a plateau ending at a **cross of Santiago viewpoint** (5.1km). Look for signs directing you to the left for one of the Camino's favorite albergues – one of only a few scattered buildings in this otherwise empty valley.

5.7KM ARROYO SAN BOL (ELEV. 892M, POP. 0) ⬛ (469.7KM)

Set in a small gully or *arroyo* watered by a spring, this albergue offers a serene if secluded overnight. With no nearby village, those who love a quiet setting and a communal paella meal will find a memorable sojourn here. Nearby are sparse remains of the 11th c. Monastery of San Baudillo.

🔼 Albergue San Bol **D R K C W S** 1/10, €10/-/-/-, Arroyo de San Bol, www.alberguesanbol.com, tel 606 893 407

Continue straight on through farmland going gradually uphill on rough, reddish-brown gravel stones, again among grainfields and stands of wind turbines. Pass on your right 🔼 Albergue Fuente Sidres **D R G W S** 2/12, €15/-/-/-, Camino de Santiago, www.alberguefuentesidres.es, tel 686 908 486, ecological hostel opened 2021. Since it sits low in its own *arroyo*, the only signs of the next charming but isolated village are utility lines and a cell phone tower.

5.0KM HONTANAS (ELEV. 866M, POP. 73) 🍴 ⬛ ◉ (464.7KM)

Tucked into a hidden valley, the tower of Hontanas' 14th c. **Church of the Immaculate Conception** is the first sign of village life. As pilgrimage ebbed after the 18th c. the village took on a ghost-town-like character, but with the revival of the Camino in the late 20th c. much of its vibrancy has returned, as evidenced by the renewal of the former San Juan pilgrim hospital, now a thriving albergue.

🔼 Albergue Santa Brígida **P D R G K C W S Z** 3/16, €10/-/55/70, Calle Real 15, www.alberguesantabrigida.com, tel 628 927 317

🔼 Albergue Juan de Yepes **P D R G K C W S** 5/34 & 4/9, €10/-/55/70, Calle Real 1, www.alberguejuandeyepes.com, tel 638 938 546

🔼 El Puntido **P D R G K W S** 7/40 & 8/18, €8/-/32/45, Calle Iglesia 6, www.puntido.com, tel 947 378 597

STAGE 14
Hontanas to Boadilla del Camino

Start	Hontanas, municipal albergue
Finish	Boadilla del Camino, Church of Santa María
Distance	28.8km
Total ascent	375m
Total descent	460m
Difficulty	Moderately hard, due to its length as well as the steep climb and descent after Castrojeríz
Duration	7¾hr
Percentage paved	31%
Albergues	Monasterio de San Antón 5.7; Castrojeríz 9.4; Ermita de San Nicolás 18.5; Itero de la Vega 20.5; Boadilla del Camino 28.8

The wide horizons of this stage plus the topography fill it with unforgettable images, particularly of views going up and down the steep Alto de Mostelares just after Castrojeríz. Other than a few very scattered and tiny towns, this region is empty of most everything except fields and wind farms. Bring plenty of water for the 10km stretch after Castrojeríz, which is devoid of fountains and services.

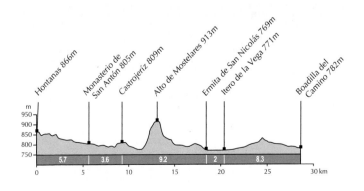

In **Hontanas**, after passing the municipal swimming pool (**0.4km**) the pavement turns to a dirt and gravel track (**0.4km**). A narrow, sometimes muddy trail traverses the hillside above the lovely **Garbanzuelo stream**, gradually leading downhill to turn right on an asphalt road (**3.3km**) under trees.

5.7KM MONASTERIO DE SAN ANTÓN (ELEV. 805M, POP. 0) 🔼 (459.0KM)

The Order of San Antón, begun in 1093 in France, was dedicated to treatment of people suffering from ergotism, sometimes called 'St Anthony's Fire,' caused by ingestion of contaminated flour. At its height the Order sponsored hundreds of hospitals throughout Europe to treat the disease, which could be cured with good food as well as ample wine to dilate the blood vessels. The symbol of the Order was a blue tau (T-shaped) cross. Here, the San Antón monastery and hospital, whose ruins date mostly from the 14th c., served as headquarters for the Order in Castile and Portugal. Pilgrims arriving late would shelter under the roof that connected the arches sprawling over the Camino road, and the Order's monks would feed them through niches in the walls. The remains of what must have been an impressive building include a carved portal and the church's rose window, highlighting the tau symbol. The Order of San Antón disbanded finally in 1787.

🔺 Hospital de Peregrinos de San Antón 🇩 🇧 🇨 🇸 1/12, €Donation, Convento de San Antón, **http://fundacionsananton.org**, breakfast and dinner with donation, no electricity or phone

Continue on the paved road under trees to the Colegiata de Santa María del Manzano church (**2.4km**) on the northern flank of town, with the imposing castle ruins visible above.

3.6KM CASTROJERÍZ (ELEV. 809M, POP. 819) 🔲 ⊕ 🔼 🇨 ◉ ⊕ (455.4KM)

Known in Roman times as Castrum Sigerici, the tall mesa with its castle above has long stood guard over the territory. The town of Castrojeríz is wrapped in a crescent shape around the **castle mountain** and the pilgrim road functions as its historic main artery. Tradition holds that Santiago saw a vision of the Virgin Mary in an apple tree and was so excited he leaped heavily onto his horse, causing a hoof print in a solid rock, which can now be viewed outside the south door of the **Santa María del Manzano** (trans: 'Saint Mary of the Apple Tree') church. The building houses a 13th c. painted statue of the Virgen del Manzano and 18th c. rococo paintings by the master Antonio Raphael Mengs. The **Church of Santo Domingo**, now a museum, hosts important tapestries while the **Church of San Juan de los Caballeros** houses a 16th c. Flemish altarpiece and painted roof beams in the cloister.

🔺 Albergue de Peregrinos Casa Nostra 🇩 🇰 🇼 🇸 3/26, €8/-/-/-, Calle Real de Oriente 52, tel 947 377 493

🔺 Albergue de San Esteban 🇴 🇩 🇷 🇧 🇸 1/30, €7/-/-/-, Calle Castillo 4B, tel 947 377 001

For centuries the castle above Castrojeríz has looked down to the Santa María del Manzano church

CASTROJERIZ

🛏 Albergue El Camino Verge de Montserrat **O D R K C W S** 3/10, €10/-/-/-, Calle Real de Oriente 79, **www.albergueelcaminovm.com**, tel 633 538 993

🛏 Albergue Rosalía **D R G K C W S** 3/30, €12/-/-/-, Calle Cordón 2, **www.alberguerosalia.com**, tel 637 765 779

🛏 Albergue A Cien Leguas **O P D R G W S** 2/24 & 5/11, €12/40/60/75, Calle Real de Oriente 78, **www.acienleguas.es**, tel 947 562 305

🛏 Albergue Orión **P D R G K W S** 3/22 & 3/7, €12/40/50/60, Avenida de la Colegiata 28, **www.facebook.com/orionalbergue**, tel 649 481 609

🛏 Albergue Ultreia **P D R C W S** 3/27 & 3/6, €12/38/50/68, Calle Real de Oriente 77, **http://albergueultreiacastrojeriz.com**, tel 947 378 640, Olga and José are your hosts, tents welcome

🏕 Camping Camino de Santiago **D R W S** 1/30, €check website, Avenida Virgen del Manzano, **www.campingcamino.com**, tel 947 377 255, also has Casa Rural

While the tiny town seems to go on forever, it is only 2–3 blocks wide as it curls around the foot of the mountain behind it. Continue across the valley floor, crossing the **Odra River** (**2.1km**) and climbing the steep and imposing **Alto de Mostelares** (elev. 913m) – another reminder that the flat Meseta is not so flat after all. Atop the long, gravel road leading to its summit sits a small, dry, shaded rest area (**1.5km**) with views back to Castrojeríz that somewhat soften the 12% incline.

The albergue at Ermita de San Nicolás is overseen by volunteers from the Italian pilgrim confraternity

Continue to the other side of the plateau for an extraordinary view that stretches beyond grainfields to the far horizon. The 18% downhill grade is blessedly on concrete. Enter the desolate and beautiful valley that offers vast views in all directions. After a rise, come to a modest fountain and rest area (**4.1km**). Don't miss the dirt footpath (**0.9km**) to Puente Fitero that comes before an asphalt intersection.

9.2KM ERMITA DE SAN NICOLÁS (ELEV. 769M, POP. 0) 🖼 (446.2KM)

Originally an outpost of the Order of the Hospitallers of St John of Jerusalem, the building dates to the 12th–13th c. In 1995 it was restored to its original use and is now run as an albergue by the Italian Confraternity of San Jacopo.

⌂ Hospital de San Nicolás de Puente Fitero 🅳 🅲 🆂 1/12, €Donation, Ermita de San Nicolás, **www.confraternitadisanjacopo.it**, pilgrim foot-washing ceremony, breakfast with donation

In 300m cross **Puente Fitero**, the massive 11th-century stone bridge (remodeled in the 17th century) over the Pisuerga River, which is also the border between the provinces of Burgos and Palencia. Turn right along the river, joining a well-maintained gravel road and soon arriving at

2.0KM ITERO DE LA VEGA (ELEV. 771M, POP. 171) 🏨 ⊕ 🏪 **(444.2KM)**

Tracing its roots to as early as 950, Itero de la Vega grew as part of repopulation efforts after expulsion of the Muslims from northern Spain. At the entrance to town, the 13th c. **Ermita de la Piedad** contains an image of Santiago.

🔺 Albergue Hogar del Peregrino 🅞 🄳 🅚 🅒 🅦 🅢 4/8, €12/-/-/-, Calle Santa María 17, tel 979 151 866

🔺 Albergue La Mochila 🅞 🄳 🅁 🅚 🅦 🅢 5/28, €6/-/-/-, Calle Santa Ana 3, tel 979 151 781

🔺 Municipal Albergue 🅞 🄳 🅚 1/13, €5/-/-/-, Plaza de la Iglesia 3, tel 605 034 347

🔺 Albergue Puente Fitero 🅞 🄿 🄳 🅁 🅦 🅢 2/22 & 7/14, €8/30/40/48, Calle Santa María 3, https://clickturismo.es/hostalpuentefitero, tel 979 151 822

A rest area with a fountain marks the exit from town. The long, sometimes gradual climb ahead is marked by four oddly terraced but unplowable hilltops, **Los Oteros** (**4.1km**, 832m elev., literally 'The Knolls'). After crossing their ridge, follow the rough, reddish-brown two-track trail as it makes its mostly shadeless way to the tiny town of

8.3KM BOADILLA DEL CAMINO (ELEV. 782M, POP. 123) 🏨 🏪 **(436.0KM)**

Boadilla's circular plan indicates protective walls once surrounded it. In its heyday the village supported four churches, a monastery and two pilgrim hospitals, although the 16th c. **Santa María de la Asunción** is the only modern survivor. Note the plateresque altarpiece, the pulpit in a mixture of styles and the Romanesque baptismal font. The ornate 15th c. *rollo* (gibbet column) just east of the church celebrates the town's independence from overlords in larger nearby towns, allowing them to hang their criminals locally. Doves are raised in dovecotes among the neighboring fields to provide natural insecticide and fertilizer, and they can be seen gathering in the evenings in large flocks.

🔺 Juntos Albergue de Peregrinos 🄿 🄳 🅁 🅖 🅒 🅦 🅢 🅩 2/12, €12/-/35/-, Calle Mayor 7, https://juntos-albergue.com, tel 682 181 175

🔺 En El Camino 🄿 🄳 🅁 🅦 🅢 4/70 & 16/32, €9/35/45/55, Plaza El Rollo, www.boadilladelcamino.com, tel 979 810 284, 979 810 999

STAGE 15

Boadilla del Camino to Carrión de los Condes

Start	Boadilla del Camino, Church of Santa María
Finish	Carrión de los Condes, Plaza Santa María
Distance	25.3km
Total ascent	245m
Total descent	195m
Difficulty	Easy
Duration	6½hr
Percentage paved	17%
Albergues	Frómista 6.0; Población de Campos 9.7; Revenga de Campos 13.3; Villarmentero de Campos 15.3; Villalcázar de Sirga 19.5; Carrión de los Condes 25.3

After a pleasant few kilometers along a shady canal, the day consists mostly of gravel trails alongside the quiet P-980 highway. Ample services at regular intervals allow plenty of options for food and drink, while the architectural gems in Frómista, Villalcázar and Carrión de los Condes delight the devout, the historian and the artist.

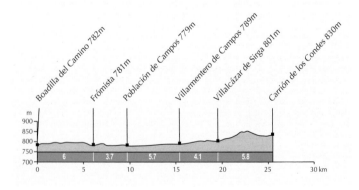

Follow the concrete Calle Mayor out of **Boadilla**. With the last buildings you are once again on a gravel road, this time framed with scattered tall trees. Turn left and soon rise to the top of a levee along the pleasant, lazy **Canal de Castilla** (**1.9km**) that will accompany you as far as the **canal locks** (**3.3km**) on the outskirts of **Frómista**.

6.0KM FRÓMISTA (ELEV. 781M, POP. 804) 🍴 ⊕ ◪ 🅒 ◉ ◉ ⊕ ⊕ 𝒊 (430.0KM)

The name of this farming capital may come from the Latin word for grain, *frumentum*. Although the vibrant agricultural town was founded by the Celts and continued by the Romans and Visigoths, after its destruction by the Muslims it lay deserted. In the 10th c. the countess of Castilla encouraged its repopulation. Frómista was a refuge for Jews who had been expelled from neighboring towns, but the mass expulsion of Jews in 1492 led to the town's slow demise again until construction of the Canal de Castilla in 1773 returned it to its former role as an agricultural center of the high Meseta. Because stone is scarce in this region, many of its architectural treasures from previous centuries have been repurposed, including its two former pilgrim hospitals. The 11th c. **Church of San Martín** is a notable exception. This jewel of Romanesque architecture was designed to be a diminutive replica of Aragon's Cathedral of Jaca and is well worth a careful visit. Note the sculpted corbels and metopes supporting the roof. Look on the interior for the exquisite narrative columnar capitals and enjoy the simplicity of the Romanesque design. A 16th c. Santiago statue reaches out to pilgrims for a moment of contemplation. In addition, the 16th c. Gothic **Church of San Pedro** holds a lovely 15th c. retablo with stunning images in the Hispano-Flemish style.

A series of locks once allowed boats to navigate deep into the Meseta along the Canal de Castilla at Frómista (photo: Rod Hoekstra)

🔺 Albergue Betania **D** **R** **K** **S** 2/9, €Donation, Avenida del Ejército Español 26, tel 638 846 043, open October to May

🔺 Albergue de Frómista **D** **R** **W** **S** 6/46, €12/-/-/-, Plaza San Martín, tel 979 811 089

🔺 Albergue Estrella del Camino **D** **R** **C** **W** **S** 3/32, €12/-/-/-, Avenida del Ejército Español, tel 979 810 399

🔺 Albergue Luz de Frómista **P** **D** **R** **K** **W** **S** **Z** 4/26, €10/-/25/-, Avenida del Ejército Español 10, www.albergueluzdefromista.com, tel 979 810 757, Anita and Gabriel are pilgrims

🔺 Albergue Vicus **O** **D** **R** **K** **W** **S** 2/6, €10/-/-/-, Avenida Ingeniero Rivera 25, tel 617 483 264

Leave town on a sidewalk of pink and white pavers, passing along two round-abouts before greeting what soon will become the all-too-familiar site of a roadside gravel track between evenly spaced concrete pylons along the P-980 roadway. Pass the **Ermita de San Miguel** (**3.2km**) just before entering

3.7KM POBLACIÓN DE CAMPOS (ELEV. 779M, POP. 137) 🍴 🛏 ⊚ (426.3KM)

Once home to two pilgrim hospitals. The tiny Romanesque 13th c. **Ermita de San Miguel** at the entrance to town was a chapel of the Knights of Malta.

🔺 Albergue de Población de Campos **O** **D** **R** **K** **W** **S** 1/18, €5/-/-/-, Calle Fuente Nueva 5, tel 979 811 099, adjacent to the hostal

🔺 Albergue La Finca **O** **D** **R** **G** **W** **S** 2/20, €10/-/-/-, Carretera de Carrión Km 16, www.facebook.com/AlbergueFinca, tel 620 785 999

After the fountain and bar at the town square, return to the P-980, cross a multi-arched stone bridge over the Ucieza River and take your place again on the gravel trail alongside the road, coming to a rest area and fountain (**3.2km**). Continue through **Revenga de Campos** (**0.4km**, café), a tiny and quiet town of low brick-and-stucco build-ings, noting the 12th–15th-century church followed by a shaded rest area (**0.2km**).

5.7KM VILLARMENTERO DE CAMPOS (ELEV. 789M, POP. 20) 🛏 (420.6KM)

🔺 Albergue Amanecer **D** **R** **K** **C** **S** 2/20, €7/-/-/-, Calle José Antonio, tel 629 178 543, breakfast with donation

Continue along the roadside trail, this time aiming at the village with an outsized white-and-brick-faced church, the Iglesia de Santa María la Blanca.

4.1KM VILLALCÁZAR DE SIRGA (ELEV. 801M, POP. 172) 🏨 ⊕ 🏧 ◉ (416.5KM)

Originally called Villasirga ('town of the road'), after construction of the massive, fortress-like **Church of Santa María la Blanca** the Arabic word *alcázar* (castle) was added to its name. Although emigration has slowly reduced the size of this once considerable town, what is left of the grand church after the Lisbon earthquake of 1755 and the despoiling by Napoléon in 1808 still radiates the medieval prominence of the village. Villalcázar's fame came from the miracles of the church's namesake – the White Virgin – who bestowed blessings on passing pilgrims. The 13th c. statue of the White Virgin is the centerpiece of the 13th–16th c. retablo behind the main altar of this church which is very much worth a visit. To the left is a 16th c. altarpiece honoring San Antonio, and to the right the Chapel of Santiago has another 16th c. retablo recounting the life of Santiago himself. Look also under the rose window for three tombs, masterworks of 13th–14th c. sculpture. (Open daily except during mass; €1 with *credencial* with €1 coin-operated lights.)

🔺 Albergue Villalcázar de Sirga 🄳 🄺 🅆 🅂 2/20, €Donation, Plaza del Peregrino, tel 979 888 041

🔺 Albergue Tasca Don Camino 🄿 🄳 🅁 🄲ⁿ 🅆 🅂 3/26 & 7/14, €12/25/40/-, Calle Real 23, tel 979 888 163

Continuing along the P-980, head now toward the white grain towers and domed church steeple of **Carrión**.

5.8KM CARRIÓN DE LOS CONDES (ELEV. 830M, POP. 2150)
🏨 ⊕ 🏧 🄲 ◉ ⊕ ⊕ 🛈 (410.7KM)

Sadly, Carrión carries the name of its infamous counts (*condes* in Spanish) – who scandalously mistreated the daughters of El Cid. Perhaps better suited as namesake would be the town's favorite son, the 15th c. Marquis de Santillana, one of the greatest of Spanish poets. In medieval times this once-flourishing agricultural city hosted 13 parishes and 14 pilgrim hospitals. Some of its splendor can still be seen in its remaining churches. The Christ above the 12th c. portal of the 19th c. **Church of Santiago** set the style for similar artistic pieces throughout Castilla. Look in the interior for images of the 24 Old Men of the Apocalypse on the bands of molding beneath the main arches as well as the capitals celebrating good deeds. The precious 12th c. **Church of Santa María del Camino** celebrates the defeat of the Moors at this location by Vermudo I. Its Romanesque portal is oldest in town and its statue of the Virgin dates also from the Romanesque period. A site of historic significance located at the exit to town, across the river, is the **Monastery of San Zoilo**, once headquarters to a network of monasteries and pilgrim hospitals and for centuries site of the tombs of Carrión's infamous counts. The wondrous ceilings of the splendid cloister date from the Renaissance, and the plateresque façade which faces the pilgrim trail is from the 17th c. The monastery is now converted to a hotel, offering pilgrims a memorable modern taste of medieval cloister life.

143

The 12th-century portal of the Church of Santiago in Carrión de los Condes set the style for similar portals throughout the region

⏶ Albergue de Santa María del Camino **D K W S** 3/58, €5/-/-/-, Calle Clérigo Pastor 2, **www.viastellarum-comunidadelaconversion.blogspot.com.es**, tel 979 880 768, pilgrim mass at 8pm with the famous singing nuns at 6:30pm

⏶ Albergue Espíritu Santo **O D W S** 7/96, €10/-/-/-, Plaza de San Juan 4, tel 979 880 052, seasonal prayer service 4:30pm

⏶ Monasterio de Santa Clara **P D R K W S** 4/30 & 9/18, €8/25/50/-, Calle Santa Clara 1, **https://clarisascarrion.blogspot.com/**, tel 979 880 837

⏴ Camping El Eden **D W** Calle Tenerías 11, **https://ciudaddecarrion.wixsite.com/campingeleden**, tel 979 880 714, tent area and restaurant available

Worth the splurge for a monks'-eye view:
⏶ Hotel Real Monasterio San Zoilo **P R C S** 49/94, €-/64/84/104, Calle San Zoilo 23, **https://sanzoilo.com**, tel 979 880 050, some rooms in former monk quarters

STAGE 16

Carrión de los Condes to Terradillos de los Templarios

Start	Carrión de los Condes, Plaza Santa María
Finish	Terradillos de los Templarios, parish church
Distance	26.4km
Total ascent	195m
Total descent	145m
Difficulty	Easy
Duration	6¾hr
Percentage paved	28%
Albergues	San Zoilo 0.8; Calzadilla de la Cueza 17.3; Ledigos 23.4; Terradillos de los Templarios 26.4

The vast wilderness of grainfields between Carrión de los Condes and Calzadilla de la Cueza marks one of the longest stretches of Camino without formal services (although there is an informal bar partway). Afterward the tiny villages dotting the path offer sparse options. Plan in advance for plenty of food, water and cash for a three-day stretch with very few services.

After enjoying the many shops and monuments along the Calle Santa María in **Carrión de los Condes**, continue downhill and cross the Carrión River (**0.5km**, tables and fountain) to reach **San Zoilo** and its lovely monastery/hotel (**0.3km**). Walk past the

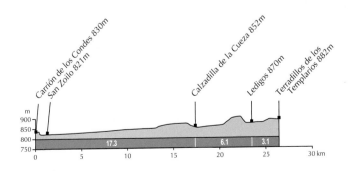

The vast stretch before Calzadilla de la Cueza that follows the ancient Roman road is one of the longest on the Camino without reliable services

roundabout where the original Camino trail, once the Roman Via Aquitana, is now the paved PP-2411 roadway. It begins as an oddly narrow asphalt driveway, then soon becomes a two-lane road, still very quiet as it passes ruins of the 12th-century **Abbey of Benevívere (5.0km)**. After a time it comes to an intersection with another asphalt road (**0.7km**), and the Camino trail itself continues on white gravel. Note a picnic area on the right (**1.8km**), a welcome sight on this isolated but beautiful stretch. Come to the seasonal **Bar Oasis (2.4km)** and, if it is open, enjoy the only services until Calzadilla. A shaded rest area (**2.9km**) marks the approximate three-quarter point between Carrión and **Calzadilla**, which is hidden in the wooded valley at long last ahead.

17.3KM CALZADILLA DE LA CUEZA (ELEV. 852M, POP. 52) 🍴 🛏 ◉ (393.4KM)

Calzadilla (lit. 'little road') of the Cueza River, this town embodies the humble style of this sub-region of the Meseta, known as the Tierra del Campo, where construction is still occasionally of the adobe style. The Church of San Martín houses a 16th c. retablo by Juan de Juni.

🏠 Albergue Camino Real Ⓞ Ⓓ Ⓡ Ⓦ Ⓢ 2/24, €8/-/-/-, Trasera Mayor 8, tel 616 483 517, swimming pool

🏠 Albergue Municipal de Calzadilla de la Cueza Ⓟ Ⓓ Ⓡ Ⓚ Ⓦ Ⓢ Ⓩ 2/36, €5/-/-/-, Calle Mayor 36, tel 979 180 921

Pick up a trail alongside the familiar N-120 highway, at this point a rather quiet road. Climb the ridge ahead and partway down the opposite side arrive at the town of

6.1KM LEDIGOS (ELEV. 870M, POP. 66) 🍴 ⛪ ◉ (387.3KM)

Some say the tiny and humble town's 17th c. parish church is the only place on all of the Camino Francés where all three images of Santiago can be seen – Santiago the Pilgrim, Santiago the Apostle and Santiago Matamoros.

⛺ Albergue El Palomar 🄿 🄳 🅁 🅆 🅂 2/47 & 5/10, €6/-/20/-, Calle Ronda de Abajo 23, www.albergueelpalomar.com, tel 979 883 605

⛺ Albergue La Morena 🄾 🄿 🄳 🅁 🄶 🄺 🄲 🅆 🅂 1/18 & 9/18, €15/-/40/-, Calle Carretera 3, www.alberguelamorena.com, tel 979 064 052

In the right season, the smell of scotch broom fills the air on the roadside path to nearby

3.1KM TERRADILLOS DE LOS TEMPLARIOS (ELEV. 882M, POP. 78)
🍴 ⛪ ◉ (384.2KM)

Originally only 'Terradillos,' the medieval relationship to the Knights Templar was added to the town's name only in the 20th c. The brick **Church of San Pedro** includes a 17th c. altarpiece and 14th c. crucifix.

⛺ Jacques de Molay 🄿 🄳 🅁 🅆 🅂 🆉 8/50, €10/-/25/-, Calle la Iglesia 10, tel 979 883 679

⛺ Albergue Los Templarios 🄿 🄳 🅁 🄶 🅆 🅂 7/28 & 12/24, €10/30/42/55, Camino de Santiago & N-120, www.alberguelostemplarios.com, tel 667 252 279

STAGE 17A

Terradillos de los Templarios to Bercianos del Real Camino

Start	Terradillos de los Templarios, parish church
Finish	Bercianos del Real Camino, Plaza Comunión
Distance	24.5km
Total ascent	255m
Total descent	285m
Difficulty	Easy
Duration	6½hr
Percentage paved	16%
Albergues	Moratinos 3.4; San Nicolás del Real Camino 6.2; Sahagún 14.5; Bercianos del Real Camino 24.5

On this stage, at Calzada del Coto, pilgrims are faced with the choice of a shaded, better-serviced and manicured walk under plane trees (Stages 17A and 18A) or the desolate-but-beautiful Roman road option (Stages 17B and 18B). Before the choice, the mid-sized town of Sahagún offers important services to help prepare for the spare, tiny villages ahead that infrequently dot the vast landscape. The track gradually rises and then descends across gently undulating farmland planted mostly with grain and sunflowers.

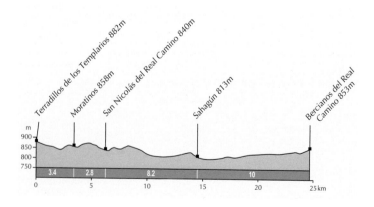

Underground hobbit-like bodegas store food and wine for local residents in the western Meseta

From **Terradillos**, follow the white gravel track downhill and out of town at first toward the bottom of the valley. Pass a rest area and hand-pump well (**2.2km**) and then afterward ascend to the familiar rolling hills of grain and to **Moratinos**.

3.4KM MORATINOS (ELEV. 858M, POP. 61) 🏠 🛏 ◉ (380.8KM)

A hill in the center of town is laced with Hobbiton-like underground wine-storage cellars (*bodegas*).

🔺 Albergue Hospital San Bruno P D R G W S 3/30 & 2/4, €12/-/45/-, Calle Ontanón 9, tel 672 629 658

🔺 Albergue Moratinos O P D R G W S 3/20 & 8/16, €10/40/50/60, Calle Real 12, www.hostalmoratinos.es, tel 628 257 160, jacuzzi available

Soon you are greeted with a sweeping view of the oncoming territory, including first San Nicolás and then the far distant white grain elevators of Sahagún. **San Nicolás** appears as a collection of brick homes with some humble barns made of adobe.

2.8KM SAN NICOLÁS DEL REAL CAMINO (ELEV. 840M, POP. 46)
🛏 🔷 ◉ (378.0KM)

Named for San Nicolás de Bari and the Royal (*real* in Spanish) Way.

🛏 Albergue Laganares San Nicolás 🅳 🅡 🅒 🅦 🆂 4/20, €10/-/-/-, Plaza Mayor 1, www.facebook.com/AlbergueSanNicolasdelRealCaminoLaganares, tel 979 188 142, vegetarian food available

After town the trail heads to the N-120 highway to use its bridge for crossing the **Sequillo River** then returns to a brown gravel track that crosses quiet farms south of the N-120, crossing again to come to the charming **Ermita de la Virgen de Puente** (5.2km, no fountain), a chapel across a small bridge.

A 12th c. construction in the Mudéjar (Muslim-Iberian) style, the **hermitage** may have once served as a pilgrim hospital. It and the neighboring medieval bridge mark the first buildings in the Province of León.

Cross under the highway bridge to enter **Sahagún** and carefully follow the somewhat confusing yellow arrows that direct you west along Calle Antonio Nicolás.

8.2KM SAHAGÚN (ELEV. 813M, POP. 2837) 🛏 ⊕ 🔷 🅒 ◉ ◉ ⊕ ⊕ 🛈 (369.8KM)

Sahagún is the largest town between Burgos and León. In the early fourth c. the missionary brothers, Saints Facundo and Primitivo, were martyred on the banks of the Cea River and a Visigothic church was built over the site of their deaths. Sahagún is a contraction of the name San Facundo and refers to the prominent monastery, named for one of the brothers, around which the town grew. Soon a city followed, much contested between Muslim and Christian factions in the 9th and 10th c. By the 11th c. Sahagún was second only to León in prominence in the kingdom and at its height hosted nine parishes of diverse ethnic groups. Ruins of the **Royal Monastery of San Benito**, a 15th c. renaming of the powerful Monastery of San Facundo, stand adjacent to the **Arch of San Benito**, one-time façade of its church, now the iconic monument of the town. The monastery's 19th c. clock tower still stands, as does part of the Chapel of San Mancio that dates from the 12th c. The stone-and-brick **Church of San Tirso** is a Mudéjar masterpiece, prototypical for the town's other Romanesque-Mudéjar churches, including the completely brick 13th c. **Church of San Lorenzo** with its Jesus Chapel and Cofradía building housing the town's processional image. The 16th c. **Church of the Holy Trinity** was resurrected from ruins in 1993 and now serves as the municipal albergue, home of the **tourist information center** (which offers a halfway-point certificate to qualifying pilgrims) and the municipal auditorium. Look also for the **Madres Benedictinas museum** with its goldsmith displays and baroque chapel.

🛏 Albergue de Peregrinos Cluny 🅞 🅓 🅚 🅦 🆂 1/64, €5/-/-/-, Travesía del Arco 87, www.turismosahagun.com/locales/albergue-municipal-cluny/, tel 987 781 015, 13th–16th c. building

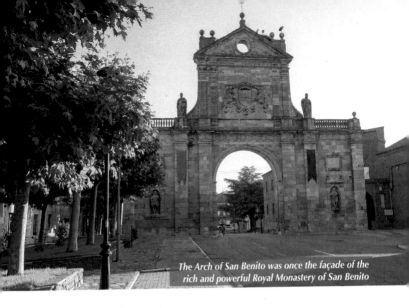

The Arch of San Benito was once the façade of the rich and powerful Royal Monastery of San Benito

⌂ Albergue Santa Cruz 🄿 🄳 🅁 🄺 🄲 🅆 🅂 10/40 & 9/18, €6/10/20/-, Calle Antonio Nicolás 40, www.alberguesensahagun.es, tel 650 696 023, breakfast available with donation

⌂ Albergue Viatoris 🄿 🄳 🅁 🄺 🅆 🅂 6/50 & 12/24, €5/18/25/36, Travesía El Arco 25, tel 987 780 975

▲ Camping Pedro Ponce www.turismosahagun.com/camping-municipal, tel 987 780 415

Pass the landmark Arch of San Benito and the charming stone bridge that crosses the **Cea River**. Soon you are introduced to a unique feature of the next many miles – a white gravel path alongside the road under uniformly spaced plane trees. Here the trees are large and offer glorious shade. As this road approaches the N-120 highway to the right, signs begin to appear for Calzada del Coto, aiming cars across the freeway, where you come to an important choice.

4.2KM JUNCTION TO CALZADA DEL COTO (ELEV. 819M, OP. 0) NO SERVICES (365.6KM)

Although it is very poorly marked on the ground, this is the fork that separates Stages 17/18A and 17/18B, so your choice here will dictate your itinerary for the next day and a half. Go straight to remain on Stage 17A through Bercianos (described here) or turn right for Stage 17B to Calzadilla (see below).

151

Going straight along toward Bercianos, find yourself on a brown gravel track with a series of signboards depicting the choice you already made at the important junction. Cross under railroad tracks (**3.0km**, picnic tables) and then come to the simple and rough **Virgen de Perales hermitage** and former pilgrim hospital of Cebreiro monks (**1.4km**, tables, no fountain). The town of **Bercianos** soon greets you first with its barns and then its welcome cafés and bars.

5.8KM BERCIANOS DEL REAL CAMINO (ELEV. 853M, POP. 202) 🍴 ⊕ 🛏 ◉ (359.8KM)

The name Bercianos most likely derives from residents of the Bierzo region, brought here to repopulate the area after the Reconquista, perhaps explaining why Cebreiro monks hosted the Perales pilgrim hospital.

🛖 Albergue de Peregrinos **D K B C W S** 5/44, €Donation, Calle Santa Rita 11, tel 987 784 008, community breakfast

🛖 Bercianos 1900 **D R G W S** 2/20, €15/-/-/-, Calle Mayor 49, www.bercianos1900.com, tel 669 282 824

🛖 Albergue La Perala **P D R G W S** 6/24 & 17/34, €12/30/40/50, Camino Francés, www.facebook.com/pg/LaPeralaAlbergue, tel 685 817 699

🛖 Albergue Santa Clara **O P D R G K W S** 1/8 & 6/12, €15/25/30/-, Travesía Comunión 2, www.facebook.com/Albergue-Santa-Clara, tel 605 839 993

STAGE 17B

Terradillos de los Templarios to Calzadilla de los Hermanillos

Start	Terradillos de los Templarios, parish church
Finish	Calzadilla de los Hermanillos, municipal albergue
Distance	27.7km
Total ascent	290m
Total descent	285m
Difficulty	Moderate, due to road surface
Duration	7½hr
Percentage paved	40%
Albergues	Moratinos 3.4; San Nicolás del Real Camino 6.2; Sahagún 14.5; Calzada del Coto 19.3; Calzadilla de los Hermanillos 27.7

You have chosen the desolate-but-beautiful Roman road, probably the loneliest option of the Camino. Walked by few pilgrims, the track follows the Via Traiana – with no shade of plane trees and no facilities save Calzadilla de los Hermanillos until Mansilla de las Mulas (although connecting roads to Reliegos and Burgo Ranero allow access over a few extra km to services). The rounded rock surface of the Roman road can be uncomfortable under thin-soled shoes.

From **Terradillos** follow the directions for Stage 17A, above, as far as the option (**4.2km**) located just before Calzada del Coto. Here turn right and cross the A-231 highway bridge into the village.

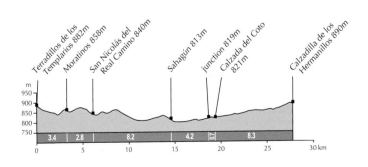

4.9KM (FROM SAHAGÚN) CALZADA DEL COTO (ELEV. 821M, POP. 260)
⏸ 🛏 ◉ (364.9KM)

Calzada was a possession of Sahagún's Monastery of San Facundo from the 10th–19th c. and houses the **Church of San Esteban** as well as the 15th c. **Hermitage of San Roque**, pilgrim saint.

⬆ Albergue de Peregrinos San Roque ◉ D W S 2/36, €Donation, Calle La Era 14, tel 674 587 001

Go ahead through the village on Calle Real and continue onto a gravel road. Follow this through a scrubby environment of bushes and long grass then cross a railway bridge (**2.1km**), ascending gently through wheat fields and small eucalyptus groves to reach

8.3KM CALZADILLA DE LOS HERMANILLOS (ELEV. 890M, POP. 144)
⏸ ⊕ 🛏 ◉ (356.6KM)

The *hermanillos* of the town's name are the 'little brothers,' monks of the Sahagún monastery, who were responsible for some of the town's early settlement.

⬆ Albergue San Bartolomé D W 6/24, €Donation, Calle Mayor 28, tel 987 330 023

⬆ Albergue Vía Trajana P D R G W S 3/10 & 5/10, €15/-/35/-, Calle Mayor 55, www.albergueviatrajana.com, tel 987 337 610

STAGE 18A

Bercianos del Real Camino to Mansilla de las Mulas

Start	Bercianos del Real Camino, Plaza Comunión
Finish	Mansilla de Las Mulas, Plaza del Pozo
Distance	26.8km
Total ascent	140m
Total descent	195m
Difficulty	Easy
Duration	7hr
Percentage paved	18%
Albergues	El Burgo Ranero 7.7; Reliegos 20.7; Mansilla de las Mulas 26.8

A uniform stage of unremarkable farmlands that tests the ability of pilgrims either to pass the time in conversation with friends or make peace with solitude. Mansilla de las Mulas is the largest of the villages and offers full pilgrim services.

From **Bercianos** the arrows point you again onto the familiar roadside path under trees, this time along the LE-6701, a quiet lane adjacent to the A-231 freeway. The vast spaces are dotted by occasional barns or stands of trees, but in the remote reaches of the walk the trees along the path are slender and offer little shade. The crossings under the freeway (**5.9km**) then the high-speed rail line (**0.3km**) are among the few highlights of this stretch. Continue into

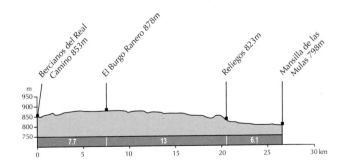

7.7KM EL BURGO RANERO (ELEV. 878M, POP. 751) 🏛 ⊕ 🔼 ◉ ⊕ ◉ (352.1KM)

The town's name either means 'Town of the Frogs' (ranas) for its frog pond or comes from a collapsed form of 'Town of the Granary' (granero). In pre-modern times thousands of sheep would be herded through here as they traveled between northern mountain pastures in the summer and warm summer fields further south. A train station on the Venta de Baños–León line is located a few hundred meters northeast of town.

🔼 **Albergue Domenico Laffi** 🄾 🄳 🄺 🅦 🅂 4/32, €Donation, Calle Fray Pedro del Burgo 11, tel 987 330 023, tents accepted on the lawn

🔼 **Albergue La Laguna** 🄿 🄳 🄡 🄺 🅦 🅂 2/20 & 5/10, €12/-/40/-, Calle La Laguna 12, tel 637 958 180

🔼 **Hospedería Jacobea El Nogal** 🄿 🄳 🄡 🄺 🅦 🅂 2/13 & 4/10, €8/20/20/30, Calle Fray Pedro del Burgo 42, tel 667 207 454

Continue through town and assume your position again on the roadside path. The faint outline of the Picos de Europa mountains appear in the far distance to the right, a hint of the Montes de León you will cross in a few days' time. Pass the end of the runway of a tiny **airport** (**6.8km**) and then a rest area (**1.1km**) at the entrance to the town of Villamarco, visible to the left just 1km off the trail. Turn under a second set of **railroad tracks** (**2.6km**), pass through a low arroyo (seasonal stream bed) and enter

13.0KM RELIEGOS (ELEV. 823M, POP. 231) 🏛 🔼 ◉ (339.1KM)

Known as Palantia in Roman times, three Roman military roads converged here. The largest modern meteorite to fall in Spain fell on the Calle Real in 1947, sinking to a depth of 35cm. Portions of the 17.3kg meteorite are kept at the National Museum of Natural Sciences in Madrid.

🔼 **Albergue Las Hadas** 🄿 🄳 🄡 🄶 🅦 🅂 🅉 2/16, €13/40/45/-, Calle Real 42, **https://alberguelashadas.com**, tel 987 317 915

🔼 **Albergue Municipal Don Gaiferos** 🄾 🄳 🄺 🅂 4/44, €5/-/-/-, Calle La Escuela 24, tel 987 317 801

🔼 **Albergue Gil** 🄿 🄳 🄡 🄶 🅦 🅂 2/14 & 4/9, €12/-/40/50, Calle Cantas 28, tel 987 317 804

🔼 **Albergue La Parada** 🄿 🄳 🄡 🄺 🅦 🅂 6/36 & 2/4, €10/-/40/-, Calle La Escuela 7, tel 987 317 880

🔼 **Albergue Vive tu Camino** 🄿 🄳 🄡 🄶 🄒 🅦 🅂 1/6 & 3/6, €13/-/45/-, Calle Real 56, **www.facebook.com/alberguevivetucamino**, tel 670 885 959

🔼 **La Cantina de Teddy** 🄿 🄳 🄡 🄶 🅂 2/10 & 2/4, €9/40/50/70, Camino Real, tel 987 190 627

Many of the medieval walls of Mansilla de las Mulas still stand (photo: Mike Wells)

It's back to the roadside path again, which just before Mansilla points you to an **overpass** above the N-601 highway (**5.1km**), although it is just as easy to cross (with care) the highway itself here. **Mansilla**'s pointed church towers lead the way, and after passing through its medieval walls the town square is just ahead on quiet, pedestrian Calle Santa María.

6.1KM MANSILLA DE LAS MULAS (ELEV. 798M, POP. 1913) 🍴 ⊕ △ ⊂ ◉ ⊕ ⊕ (332.9KM)

From the Latin *mansilla* (for 'small estate') and once a market town of horses, mules and donkeys (hence *las mulas*), the town has long served as a perimeter defense for neighboring León. About three-quarters of its **medieval walls** remain. Look for the 14m-high wall remnants on the town's west side. The 18th c. **Church of Santa María** is built on 12th c. foundations and contains a baroque altarpiece.

🛏 Albergue Amigos del Peregrino 🄳 🅆 🅂 8/74, €5/-/-/-, Calle del Puente 6, tel 661 977 305

🛏 Albergue El Jardín del Camino 🄾 🄳 🅁 🄶 🅆 🅂 2/36, €12/-/-/-, Camino de Santiago 1, www.alberguedeeljardindelcamino.com, tel 600 471 597

🛏 Albergue Gaia 🄾 🄳 🅁 🄺 🅆 🅂 2/18, €10/-/-/-, Avenida Constitución 28, https://alberguedegaia.wordpress.com, tel 987 310 308, breakfast with donation

STAGE 18B

Calzadilla de los Hermanillos to Mansilla de las Mulas

Start	Calzadilla de los Hermanillos, municipal albergue
Finish	Mansilla de Las Mulas, Plaza Del Pozo
Distance	23.9km
Total ascent	80m
Total descent	170m
Difficulty	Moderate, due to road surface
Duration	6hr
Percentage paved	20%
Albergues	Mansilla de las Mulas 23.9

Flat as flat can be, with only the occasional passing train as entertainment in the vast fields of grain as you make your way along an ancient Roman roadway.

From **Calzadilla**, pass through grain fields on a quiet asphalt road and cross the **Payuelos Canal** twice (**0.9km**, then **2.1km** later) to reach a T-junction (**0.2km**) to El Burgo Ranero. The asphalt ends here. The Alto de Payuelos Canal is part of a major scheme that brings water from the upper reaches of the Esla River to irrigate the previously arid lands between Sahagún and León. Go ahead onto a lonely gravel track and descend gently through fields with the Cantabrian Mountains visible on the northern horizon and a railway line beyond the fields to the left.

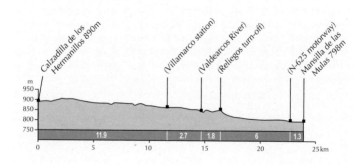

A small portion of the Roman road is kept in place behind a low wooden fence (photo: Mike Wells)

The track gradually becomes closer to the railway until it passes alongside a level crossing at the now-closed **Villamarco station** (**8.7km**). Continue parallel with the railway on a rougher track, eventually descending to cross a new bridge over the **Valdearcos River** (**2.7km**) that has recently replaced a fording point. Soon after the bridge, the track route has been skewed to the left to preserve a long section of original Roman road behind a wooden rail fence.

The Roman road is part of the **Via Traiana** that originally connected Bordeaux in France with the Roman gold mining town of Astorga. Emperors and legions passed this way, as did the armies of the Moors and Charlemagne.

Continue over the canal again and reach the Reliegos turn-off (**1.8km**). Turn right, now on a gravel road, descending into the Esla River valley with Mansilla de las Mulas visible ahead. The pink building complex across fields to the right is a high-security prison. Come to the N-625 road (**6.0km**) and enter **Mansilla** through the Arco de Santa María gate, following Calle La Concepción to reach Plaza del Pozo.

23.9KM MANSILLA DE LAS MULAS (ELEV. 798M, POP. 1913)
⬛ ⊕ 🛏 Ⓒ ▣ ⊕ ⊕ (332.8KM)

For more details see end of Stage 18A.

STAGE 19
Mansilla de las Mulas to León

Start	Mansilla de las Mulas, Plaza del Pozo
Finish	León, Cathedral of Santa María
Distance	19.1km
Total ascent	230m
Total descent	190m
Difficulty	Moderate, with a few hills
Duration	5hr
Percentage paved	45%
Albergues	Puente Villarente 6.1; Arcahueja 10.7; León 19.1

An ambivalent stage as the tranquil farms and fields are left behind for the hectic but vibrant and engaging provincial capital of León. While Friday and Saturday nights bring youthful partygoers to its historic heart, delicious tapas can be found any evening in the Romántico and Húmedo quarters of this energetic mid-sized city.

Leave **Mansilla** on the medieval, now automobile, bridge over the Elsa River (**0.4km**) and take up a wide path under trees alongside the busy N-601 arterial. Continue through **Villamoros de Mansilla** (**4.3km**, bakery). The sound of automobiles becomes

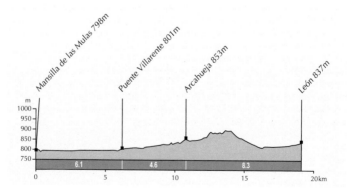

monotonous until a brief and sudden interval of green at the crossing of the Porma River (**1.1km**, rest area) alongside the historic stone bridge at

6.1KM PUENTE VILLARENTE (ELEV. 801M, POP. 238) ⊞ ⊕ △ Ⓒ ◉ ⊕ (326.8KM)

This tiny village, known mostly for its **17-arch bridge** over the Porma, was host to two pilgrim hospitals in the Middle Ages. The two-story building with the large archway to the left after the bridge was one.

🔺 Albergue El Delfin Verde 🅿 🅓 🆁 🅖 🆂 3/20 & 15/30, €5/25/40/55, Calle Carretera General 15, http://complejoeldelfinverde.es/albergue-delfin-verde-leon, tel 987 312 065, swimming pool, 2022 private rooms only

🔺 Albergue San Pelayo 🅿 🅓 🆁 🅖 🆆 🆂 2/10 & 10/20, €12/38/45/65, Calle El Romero 9, http://alberguesanpelayo.com, tel 987 312 677

Continue on harsh sidewalks among scattered auto-oriented establishments until a gravel path (**1.3km**) branches off on the right and heads for a quiet valley between roadways accompanied by a more welcome soundtrack of birdsong. Cross the road that heads toward Sanfelismo (**1.9km**) and then cross under the freeway, go through fields and steeply up into the town of

4.6KM ARCAHUEJA (ELEV. 853M, POP. 203) ⊞ △ Ⓒ ◉ (322.3KM)

Although the town traces its roots to the 12th c., its close proximity to León has caused much of its traditional adobe-and-brick architecture to be replaced by a hodge-podge of modern buildings.

🔺 Albergue La Torre 🅞 🅟 🅓 🆁 🅖 🆆 🆂 2/20 & 7/27, €10/25/35/50, Calle Juan Carlos I 19D, www.alberguetorre.es, tel 987 205 896

The track turns left on asphalt toward a collection of commercial dealerships on a frontage road for the nearby freeway, and then immediately heads steeply on a gravel trail to a hill above the road. Ahead you see a **blue pedestrian bridge** (**3.1km**) which allows you to cross the busy N-601 freeway. Soon cross above the LE-30 highway (**0.8km**) and join Avenida de Madrid into town. Veer left onto Calle Martinez (**1.2km**), cross the ancient Puente Castro (**0.4km**) and then carefully follow the yellow arrows and brass scallop shells mounted in the sidewalk as you finally enter the city walls at Puerta Moneda (**1.9km**). Watch carefully for brass scallop shell medallions on the pavement as they guide you through a shopping district of the old city before turning you right on Calle Ancha and bringing you in a few blocks to the grand, glorious, Gothic Cathedral of Santa María de León.

The Cathedral of León is a treasure of High Gothic architecture (photo: Rod Hoekstra)

8.3KM LEÓN (ELEV. 837M, POP. 126,192) 🏨⊕🔼🅲◉Ⓜ🅗⊕✚ ℹ️ (313.9KM)

Established in AD70 as headquarters for the Roman Seventh Legion (hence the city's name). the delightful center city of León maintains its Roman layout, with north–south streets encompassed by solid walls with four city gates. For three centuries it was capital of the Kingdom of León, building on its economic base in the gold trade and as wool capital of the vast pasturelands of the high Meseta. In 1063, King Fernando I brought the bones of San Isidoro, Archbishop of Seville, to León and housed them in a Romanesque complex for their adoration. The **Basilica of San Isidoro**,

Stained glass at the Cathedral of León shares colorful stories from ancient and medieval times (photo: Rod Hoekstra)

its adjacent **Museo de San Isidoro** and the **Pantheon of Kings** are now premiere sites of Spanish art history (open daily year-round, €5 guided tours only, www.museosanisidorodeleon.com). During this same period León was home to a vibrant Jewish community and here its favorite son, Moses de León, compiled the *Zohar*, foundational books of Jewish kabbala mysticism. Prosperity brought a desire for grand monuments, and the 13th c. **Cathedral of León**, built in less than 100 years, stands out as a uniquely unified and graceful monument of High Gothic architecture that was saved from collapse by a 19th c. structural intervention. Its many chapels contain important works of art, but the building is best remembered for its brilliant stained glass (open daily except during special events, no tours during mass when entry is free, €6 cathedral, €5 museum supports non-stop renovations, www.catedraldeleon.org, audio guide recommended). León was an important stop on the Camino Francés and hosted several pilgrim hospitals, including one at the 16th c. **Monastery of San Marcos**, now repurposed as the luxurious **Parador de León** hotel. Famed Catalan architect Antoni Gaudí used local materials to construct the **Casa Botines**, and his statue sits on a nearby bench admiring his work. Adjacent **Calle Ancha** is the ideal venue for pilgrim watching and outdoor dining. The **Húmedo quarter**, south of the cathedral in the old city, comes alive on Friday and Saturday nights with youthful revelers from the many colleges of the 12,000-student University of León.

🛏 Albergue Benedictinas Carbajalas **O D W S** 4/135, €7/-/-/-, Plaza Santa María del Camino 3, www.alberguesleon.com, tel 680 649 289, breakfast with donation

🏠 Check in León **O D R G K W S** 2/40, €10/-/-/-, Avenida Alcalde Miguel Castaño 88, www.checkinleon.es, tel 686 956 896

🏠 Globetrotter Hostel **D R G K** 5/46, €15/-/-/-, Calle Paloma 8, www.globetrotterhostel.es, tel 987 103 267

🏠 Hostel Covent Garden **P D R G K S Z** 5/20, €20/45/45/-, Calle Ancha 25, www.facebook.com/HostelCoventGarden, tel 601 082 002

🛏 Albergue León Hostel **O P D R G K W S** 3/20 & 3/6, €18/-/45/-, Calle Ancha 8, http://leonhostel.es, tel 987 079 907

🛏 Albergue Muralla Leonesa **P D R G K W S** 13/64 & 7/17, €13/-/34/45, Calle Tarifa 5, https://alberguemurallaleonesa.com, tel 987 177 873

🛏 Albergue San Francisco de Asís **O P D R G K W S** 12/24 & 11/26, €13/18/36/45, Avenida Alcalde Miguel Castaño 4, www.alberguescapuchinos.org/albergue, tel 987 215 060

🛏 Albergue Santo Tomás de Canterbury **P D R G K W S** 3/28 & 6/17, €12/-/60/45, Avenida de La Lastra 53, https://alberguesantotomas.com, tel 987 392 626

🏠 Hostel Quartier León Jabalquinto **P D R G** 4/54 & 4/22, €15/-/-/45, Calle Juan de Are 2, https://quartierleon.com, tel 987 539 750

Worth the splurge to stay in a famous former pilgrim hospital:
🛏 Parador de León **O P R G S** 234/388, €consult website, Plaza San Marcos, 7, www.parador.es, tel 987 237 30

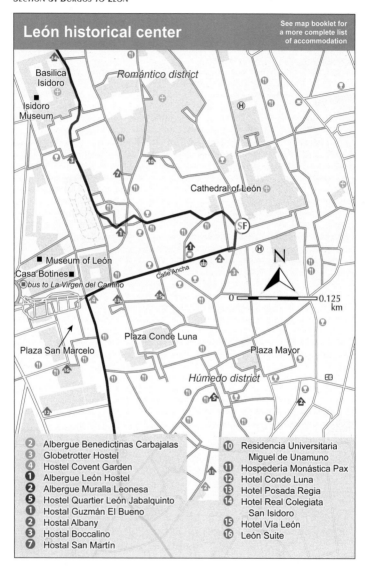

León historical center

See map booklet for a more complete list of accommodation

Romántico district

Basilica Isidoro

Isidoro Museum

Cathedral of León

Museum of León

Casa Botines

bus to La Virgen del Camino

Calle Ancha

0   0.125 km

Plaza San Marcelo

Plaza Conde Luna

Plaza Mayor

Húmedo district

N

❷ Albergue Benedictinas Carbajalas
❸ Globetrotter Hostel
❹ Hostel Covent Garden
❶ Albergue León Hostel
❷ Albergue Muralla Leonesa
❺ Hostel Quartier León Jabalquinto
❶ Hostal Guzmán El Bueno
❷ Hostal Albany
❸ Hostal Boccalino
❼ Hostal San Martín

❿ Residencia Universitaria
   Miguel de Unamuno
⓫ Hospedería Monástica Pax
⓬ Hotel Conde Luna
⓭ Hotel Posada Regia
⓮ Hotel Real Colegiata
   San Isidoro
⓯ Hotel Vía León
⓰ León Suite

SECTION 4:
LEÓN TO SARRIA

A thirsty pilgrim drinks from a gourd at San Justo de la Vega

SECTION 4: LEÓN TO SARRIA

Two days' walk after León the flat fields of the Meseta are replaced by mountainside forests of tall trees and then, at the highest elevations, a low carpet of purple heather and Spanish lavender. Near the summit of the Camino's highest point stands Cruz de Ferro, an iron cross atop a mound of stones and pilgrim memorabilia that safeguards years of pilgrim tears and prayers.

The following downhill paths pit knees against gravity and boots against slippery gravel until crossing a bridge into the cool, riverside confines of Molinaseca. Starting here, the charming and historic Bierzo valley welcomes pilgrims with castles, ancient churches, verdant vineyards, and tasty wines. Afterward, at the summit of a day-long climb, pilgrims can join tourists to explore the picturesque mountaintop village of O Cebreiro to gaze into the region's Celtic roots.

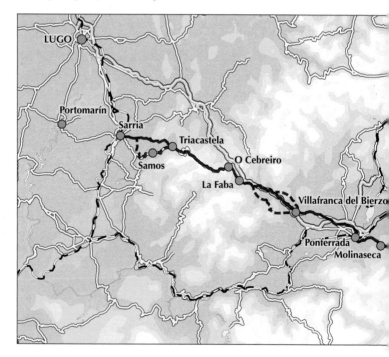

O Cebreiro is also the gateway into Galicia, an area long sequestered from the rest of Spain by the tall Cantabrian Mountains. Before modern highways connected Spanish regions, it was far easier to cross the coastal valleys from Galicia into Portugal than it was to climb over the mountain passes into Spain, making modern Galicia sound and feel more like Lisbon than Madrid.

The differences run deep. Observant pilgrims will notice that Galician villages lack the central plazas seen in most Spanish towns. In fact, Galicia does not really have *pueblos* or villages, but simply *lugares* (from the Latin *locus*

– 'place'). These 'places' are houses and barns clustered at an intersection of roads that, when followed, dribble off toward more pastures and fields. They bustle with the farming and storing of crops and the herding, milking and feeding of dairy cattle as the region does its share to bring fresh dairy products to the kitchens and tables of Spain.

PLANNING

1 Just after León is an important option – either walk along the N-120 roadway through Villadangos del Páramo or take the recommended

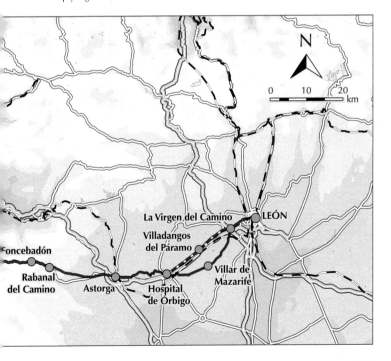

2km longer option along quiet farm roads and fields through Villar de Mazarife.

2 Because the first 7km after central León is often judged to be the most unpleasant portion of the Camino, pilgrims sometimes bus through León's western suburbs to La Virgen del Camino and pick up the walk there. The staging in this guide assumes that option, while without the bus option the stages León to Mazarife to Astorga to Foncebadón work out just as well.

3 The steep descent into Molinaseca will wear on most anyone's knees, so tough-soled footwear tread is important for that half-day.

4 At Triacastela the main route takes a quick but hilly path to Sarria while a longer and lovelier variant travels through Samos, home to Spain's oldest monastery and one of the most frequently chosen of the optional delights on the Camino Francés.

WHAT NOT TO MISS

Allow extra time to wander the cathedral and pilgrims' museums in Astorga and be certain to bring a small stone or small memento to leave at the foot of Cruz de Ferro, just after Foncebadón. Spend the few euros necessary to tour the Templar castle at Ponferrada and enjoy a glass of world-famous Bierzo wine in Cacabelos (Stage 24) or Villafranca del Bierzo. The unforgettable *cebreiro* cheese at O Cebreiro (Stage 26) is made from raw milk and drizzled with local honey. The variant to the Samos monastery on Stage 27, although a few kilometers longer, offers a final tranquil break before the days fill with pilgrims at Sarria.

Leaving the Astorga cathedral (photo: Rod Hoekstra)

STAGE 20
León to Hospital de Órbigo

Start	León, Cathedral of Santa María
Finish	Hospital de Órbigo, Iglesia de San Juan Bautista
Distance	35.7km (31.4km on Villadangos variant); subtract 7.4km with bus option to La Virgen
Total ascent	325m (225m on variant)
Total descent	345m (245m on variant)
Difficulty	Easy (or moderately hard due to distance without bus option)
Duration	9¼hr (7hr walking following bus transfer; 8hr on variant)
Percentage paved	67% (41% via Villadangos variant due to roadside gravel paths)
Albergues	Trobajo del Camino 3.9; La Virgen del Camino 7.4; Oncina de la Valdoncina 11.2; Villar de Mazarife 21.2; Villavante 31.1; Hospital de Órbigo 35.7. (Variant: Valverde de la Virgen 11.2; Villadangos del Páramo 20.3; San Martín del Camino 24.5)

A long stage that is broken up either by taking a bus to La Virgen del Camino or by spending an overnight partway at quiet Villar de Mazarife. Although the official track follows the N-120 on a roadside path through Villadangos del Páramo, the Villar de Mazarife option is the more tranquil choice and is treated here as the primary route.

Instead of walking the first 7–8km through grim suburbs, a bus from central León to La Virgen del Camino shortens the otherwise soulless first hours. (Begin at BBVA Bank at Plaza Santo Domingo, blue Alsa City bus M1A, €1.35, weekdays every 30min from 6.15am–10.15pm, Sat hourly, Sun bi-hourly).

If you've chosen to walk from **León** to La Virgen, follow the yellow arrows from the cathedral square past San Isidoro (**0.4km**), then through the medieval walls and off toward the river and the sumptuous Parador hotel (**1.1km**), formerly home of the San Martín pilgrim hospital. Cross the **Bernesga River** where the modern, less charming suburbs of León begin. Cross a green metal **pedestrian bridge** over train tracks (**1.6km**) and enter the suburb of

3.9KM TROBAJO DEL CAMINO (ELEV. 836M, POP. 20,951) ⊞ ⊕ ⊡ ⓒ ◉ ⊕ ⊕ (310.0KM)

This modern suburb traces its roots to a small Roman town at this location.

⌂ Hostal El Abuelo ⊡ ⓡ ⓖ 26/52, €-/38/50/70, Calle los Mesones 6, www.hostalelabuelo.es, tel 987 801 044

⌂ Hotel Alfageme ⓞ ⊡ ⓡ ⓖ ⓢ 30/78, €-/42/51/60, Calle Alfageme 55, www.hotelalfageme.es, tel 987 840 490

Gradually the apartments are replaced by commercial warehouses as the arrows aim us alongside the familiar N-120 highway (**2.9km**) as it bisects the suburban settlement of

3.5KM LA VIRGEN DEL CAMINO (ELEV. 906M, POP. 5079) ⊞ ⊕ ⊡ ⓒ ◉ ⊕ (306.5KM)

Named after an apparition of Mary in 1505, this dormitory town for León has a large Dominican convent and a stunning modern church, the **Basílica de la Virgen**, the most notable modern architecture on the Camino Francés. Dominican friar Francisco Coello designed the marble-clad building, which consists of a brutalist nave with a separate slender concrete spire. The front is decorated with modern, 6m-tall Josep Subirachs statues of Mary and the 12 apostles, including Santiago who points toward the Camino. An early 16th c. statue of the Virgin graces the baroque main altarpiece inside.

⌂ Albergue Don Antonino y Doña Cinia ⓓ ⓚ ⓦ ⓢ 2/40, €7/-/-/-, Avenida Padre Eustoquio 16, www.lavirgendelcamino.info/wordpress/albergue-de-peregrinos, tel 615 217 335

Cross the N-120 highway and follow an asphalt road downhill left and quickly into the open fields south of La Virgen. Soon comes the **option for the Villadangos variant** (described under 'Villadangos del Páramo variant,' below).

For the quieter Mazarife option, turn left to cross a bridge over the Astorga–León highway (**1.5km**) and then follow an echoey underpass (**0.3km**) beneath the Ruta de la Plata highway before arriving at **Fresno del Camino** (**0.2km**, food, bus, 18th c. Church of San Andrés). Come now to terrain unlike what we've seen previously on the Meseta. In place of wide fields of grain are savanna-like fields of scrub grass and scattered oak trees over rolling hills. Cross railroad tracks (**1.4km**) and an *arroyo* (stream bed) before entering

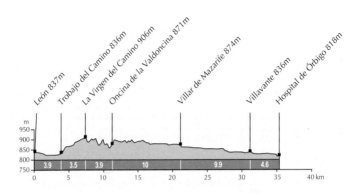

3.9KM ONCINA DE LA VALDONCINA (ELEV. 871M, POP. 38) 🏨 🛒 ◉ (302.7KM)

Most likely from the Latin *uncina*, meaning 'curve,' the Valdoncina is a region of low moors. The town includes a 1926 **Church of San Bartolomé**, formerly a hermitage, which incorporates an earlier *espadaña* (bell tower/wall).

🛖 Albergue El Pajar de Oncina ⓄⒻⒹⓇⓀⒷⒸⓌⓈⓏ 1/8, €10/-/30/-, Calle Arriba 2, www.facebook.com/elpajardeoncina, tel 677 567 309

Pilgrims rest in the shade at Oncina de la Valdoncina

The track leads up and out of town on a red dirt road, starting a 10km stretch interrupted by just one small town. Now the terrain is even more savanna-like, with a wide, flat, farmless grassland punctuated by occasional trees. After a time, scattered grain fields begin to appear as arrows lead toward the landmark cantilevered water tower of **Chozas de Abajo** (5.6km, fountain; the town's café is past the water tower, two blocks off the track). Leave town on a narrow asphalt road winding toward Villar de Mazarife and its tulip-shaped water tower, which you reach after a rest area and fountain (**3.8km**).

10.0KM VILLAR DE MAZARIFE (ELEV. 874M, POP. 360) 🍴 ⊕ 🗘 ◉ (292.7KM)

Mazarif, head of a prominent family from Córdoba, led the repopulation of this area in the ninth c. The 16th c. **Santiago Church** is made of mud walls and mortar, with art from the 18th to early 20th c. The town also holds a small **museum** at the former home of the artist known as Monseñor (Luis López Casado) and another **museum** to the telegraph and telephone.

🏠 Albergue El Refugio de Jesús Ⓞ Ⓓ Ⓡ Ⓚ Ⓦ Ⓢ 12/50, €7/-/-/-, Calle Corujo 13, www.facebook.com/AlbergueDeJesus, tel 987 390 697

🏠 Albergue San Antonio de Pádua Ⓞ Ⓟ Ⓓ Ⓡ Ⓒ Ⓦ Ⓢ 3/50 & 8/16, €10/-/30/-, Camino León 33, www.facebook.com/pg/alberguesanantoniodepadua, tel 987 390 192

🏠 Albergue Tío Pepe Ⓟ Ⓓ Ⓡ Ⓒ Ⓦ Ⓢ 5/20 & 6/12, €12/50/60/-, Calle Teso 2, www.alberguetiopepe.es, tel 987 390 517, breakfast included for pilgrims staying in the private rooms

Catch a two-lane asphalt road out of town and into spacious, irrigated fields of corn, wheat and rye. This straight-as-an-arrow road narrowly bypasses **La Milla del Páramo** (6.3km), visible to the right, and after intersecting another road it turns to gravel in the long and equally straight approach to

9.9KM VILLAVANTE (ELEV. 836M, POP. 232) 🍴 🗘 ◉ ◉ (282.8KM)

The town hosts a railway stop on the León–Astorga line and the 17th c. **Church of Santa María de las Candelas**.

🏠 Albergue Santa Lucía Ⓟ Ⓓ Ⓡ Ⓒ Ⓒ Ⓦ Ⓢ 1/23 & 2/4, €10/-/28/-, Calle Doctor Vélez 17, www.alberguesantalucia.es, tel 987 389 105

After some gardens and barns the track follows along the railway line (**0.8km**) then makes a straight shot toward the highway beyond. Crossing the AP-71 highway bridge (**2.0km**), the track continues along the road (disregard the many arrows pointing left), crosses the N-120 (**0.7km**) and heads toward a large brick water tower. Turn left through the tiny suburb of **Puente de Órbigo** (**0.7km**) where the pavement turns to cobblestones before crossing the famous bridge into

4.6KM HOSPITAL DE ÓRBIGO (ELEV. 818M, POP. 976) 🏨 ⊕ 🛏 Ⓒ ◉ ⊕ (278.2KM)

Hospital de Órbigo is located where the Via Traiana Roman road crossed the Órbigo River. This now-quiet river carried a much greater flow before the Barrios de Luna dam upstream was completed in 1951. The town's strategic location led it to be site of battles in 452 between the Suevi and Visigoths and in 878 between Alfonso I and the Moors. The name derives from the town's famous Camino de Santiago pilgrim hospital. The ruins of the pilgrim hospital founded by the order of San Juan of Jerusalem stand close to the 13th c. **Paso Honroso bridge**, one of Spain's oldest Gothic spans. Today only four of its 19 arches are original. Spurned by his lover in 1434, Suero de Quiñones, a Leonese knight, determined to prove himself the foremost knight of Europe, issued a challenge to all comers. That year for one summer month on the field south of the bridge Suero broke over 300 lances of his opponents while other knights and Holy Year pilgrims looked on. Finally content with his show of courage – though it didn't change his lover's mind – he made a pilgrimage to Santiago where he donated a bejeweled necklace to the cathedral. The necklace rests now on the bust of Santiago El Menor in Santiago Cathedral's Chapel of the Relics.

🏠 Albergue Karl Leisner Ⓓ Ⓡ Ⓚ Ⓦ Ⓢ 10/92, €8/-/-/-, Calle Álvarez Vega 32, tel 987 388 444

🏠 Albergue Verde Ⓟ Ⓓ Ⓡ Ⓑ Ⓒ Ⓦ Ⓢ Ⓩ 2/28, €11/25/30/-, Avenida Fueros de León 76, www.facebook.com/albergueverde, tel 607 671 670, breakfast and dinner with donation

🏠 Albergue Casa de los Hidalgos Ⓟ Ⓓ Ⓡ Ⓖ Ⓦ Ⓢ 2/18 & 3/6, €14/35/40/-, Calle Álvarez Vega 36, http://casadeloshidalgos.com, tel 699 198 755

🏠 Albergue La Encina Ⓞ Ⓟ Ⓓ Ⓡ Ⓖ Ⓦ Ⓢ 4/16 & 3/6, €12/-/44/-, Avenida Suero de Quiñones, www.complejolaribera.com, tel 987 361 087, swimming pool

🏠 Albergue San Miguel Ⓟ Ⓓ Ⓡ Ⓖ Ⓚ Ⓦ Ⓢ 1/18 & 3/6, €10/30/35/-, Calle Álvarez Vega 35, http://alberguesanmiguel.com, tel 988 388 285

▲ Camping Don Suero de Quiñones €consult website, Calle Álvarez Vega, www.hospitaldeorbigo.com/index.php/municipio/camping, tel 987 388 206

Villadangos del Páramo variant

South of La Virgen del Camino turn right at the **option** marker (**0.4km**) and continue parallel with the main road, eventually through scrubland to pass under the A-66 motorway (**1.5km**). Turn right after the tunnel to return to the N-120 and continue on the roadside pathway to reach

3.8KM VALVERDE DE LA VIRGEN (ELEV. 891M, POP. 7358) 🏨 🛏 ◉ (298.7KM)

The bell tower at beginning of the village has five huge storks' nests.

🏠 Albergue La Casa del Camino Ⓓ Ⓡ Ⓖ Ⓦ Ⓢ 1/32, €8/-/-/-, Camino El Jano 2, http://alberguelacasadelcamino.com, tel 987 303 455

Storks build their nests in the espadaña of the Valverde de la Virgen church (photo: Mike Wells)

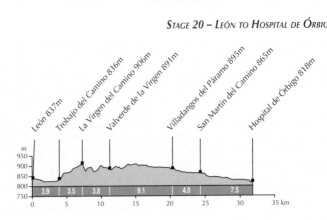

Walk uphill through the village then continue uneventfully on the roadside path-way to **San Miguel del Camino** (**1.4km**, restaurant, grocery store, fountain).

Again, join the road through the village, regaining the roadside pathway after the end of the built-up area. Soon reach a low summit (922m) then come to a confluence of modern industrial estates and housing developments.

7.2KM URBANIZACIÓN CAMINO SANTIAGO (ELEV. 898M, POP. 233)
🍴 🚲 🛏 ◉ (291.6KM)

⛰ Hotel Avenida III 🅾 🅿 🆁 🅶 🆂 65/130, €-/49/61/82, Carretera León-Astorga Km 17, https://hotelavenidaiii.com, tel 630 250 882

Follow the asphalt service road, crossing the N-120 toward the old part of

1.9KM VILLADANGOS DEL PÁRAMO (ELEV. 895M, POP. 1096)
🍴 🚲 🛏 🅲 ◉ ✚ (289.7KM)

Although the town has Roman roots, it stood abandoned during the Muslim period until repopulation beginning in the ninth c. Here in September 1111 Leonese and Galician forces were defeated in battle by Alfonso I El Batallador of Aragón. The town's modern **church**, which preserves its 18th c. bell tower, includes statues of Santiago Matamoros and Santiago Peregrino. Previously a livestock and subsistence farming town, a 1967 project introduced a network of canals for irrigation of potatoes, corn and sugar beets.

⛰ Albergue de Villadangos del Páramo 🅾 🅳 🆁 🅺 🆆 🆂 7/80, €7/-/-/-, Carretera de León-Astorga, tel 627 010 490

🔺 Camping Camino de Santiago 🆁 🅶 🆆 🆂 €consult website, Carretera N-120 Km 324, www.campingcaminodesantiago.com, tel 987 680 253, swimming pool

Cross the bridge over the Páramo Canal (**0.3km**) and follow the gravel track ahead through trees first, then cross the N-120 (**0.4km**) to follow the path off the left shoulder of the road and into

4.0KM SAN MARTÍN DEL CAMINO (ELEV. 865M, POP. 519) 🍴 🛏 ◉ (285.7KM)

Archeology from the area indicates Asturian settlements here in prehistory, although the town is first mentioned in 12th c. documents.

🏠 Albergue La Casa Verde **P D R K B W S Z** 1/8, €10/-/27/-, Travesía de la Estación 8, **www.facebook.com/alberguelacasaverde**, tel 646 879 437

🏠 Albergue Municipal San Martín del Camino **D R K B C W S** 2/46, €6/-/-/-, Carretera de León-Astorga 56, tel 676 020 388, breakfast and dinner with donation

🏠 Albergue Santa Ana **P D R C W S** 2/40 & 12/24, €8/-/25/-, Avenida El Peregrino 12, **https://albergue-peregrinos-santa-ana.business.site**, tel 654 111 509

🏠 Albergue Vieira **O P D R C W S** 6/36 & 2/4, €10/-/35/-, Avenida Peregrinos, **www.facebook.com/AlbergueVieira**, tel 987 378 565, swimming pool

At the end of the village, cross the canal (**0.6km**) and immediately turn left onto the roadside pathway, continuing as it returns to the main road, which you follow until just before **Puente de Órbigo**. Here the track finally departs the N-120 (**5.6km**) and joins the Mazarife route (**0.5km**) to continue onwards into **Hospital de Órbigo**.

The golden field beside the bridge at Hospital de Órbigo was the scene of a famous series of jousting contests in 1434 (photo: Rod Hoekstra)

STAGE 21
Hospital de Órbigo to Astorga

Start	Hospital de Órbigo, Iglesia de San Juan Bautista
Finish	Astorga Cathedral
Distance	17.4km
Total ascent	310m
Total descent	255m
Difficulty	Moderate, due to elevation changes
Duration	4¾hr
Percentage paved	51%
Albergues	Villares de Órbigo 2.6; Santibáñez de Valdeiglesias 5.3; San Justo de la Vega 13.3; Astorga 17.4

From Hospital de Órbigo, the Meseta's vastness is replaced with rolling hills, scrublands, and only the occasional field of grain. The climb to Astorga is the official end of the Meseta, and the town serves as gateway to the Montes de León just behind.

Make your way out of **Hospital de Órbigo**, turning left to enter grainfields again, soon arriving at the red tile roofs of

2.6KM VILLARES DE ÓRBIGO (ELEV. 826M, POP. 672) 🏚 ⊕ 🛆 ⊕ (275.6KM)

Sometimes a scent of garlic fills the air in this farming village whose main crops are garlic, onion, leeks and peppers, all irrigated by the Órbigo River. Santiago Matamoros is proudly displayed at the altar of the Santiago parish church.

🔺 Albergue El Encanto 🅿 🅳 🆁 🅶 🅺 🆆 🆂 1/10 & 6/14, €14/40/55/-, Camino Santiago 23, https://albergueelencanto.es, tel 682 860 210

🔺 Albergue Villares de Órbigo 🅿 🅳 🆁 🅶 🅺 🆆 🆂 3/19 & 3/7, €12/30/40/50, Calle El Arnal 21, http://alberguevillaresdeorbigo.com, tel 722 833 373

Make your way on a new and very wide gravel road (**0.6km**, rest area) at first gradually up the ridge ahead. A narrower gravel track shortcut picks up to the right and then the signs direct pilgrims onto the LE-6451 roadway, heading further uphill to

2.7KM SANTIBÁÑEZ DE VALDEIGLESIAS (ELEV. 846M, POP. 155) 🏠 🅿 (272.9KM)

A loudspeaker on the bell tower of the village church loudly announces Sunday mass, although otherwise the tiny modern church with its images of Santiago Matamoros is usually locked.

🏠 Albergue Camino Francés 🅿 🅳 🅁 🅖 🅒 🅦 🅢 🆉 3/16, €10/-/42/-, Calle Real 56, www.onlypilgrims.com/en/camino-frances-128/, tel 626 165 266

🏠 Albergue Parroquial de Santibáñez 🅳 🅁 🅒 🅢 4/20, €6/-/-/-, Travesía Carromonte Bajo 3, tel 987 377 698, half board, bed, breakfast and community dinner €16

🏠 L'Abilleiru – Albergue Rural 🅿 🅳 🅁 🅖 🅒 🅦 🅢 2/6 & 3/6, €25/-/50/-, Calle Real 44, www.labilleirualberguerural.com, tel 615 269 057

Until San Justo de la Vega there is just one pilgrim kiosk for food and refreshment. Check your provisions and stock up here. Continue past the municipal albergue up and out of town, at first between the cattle shed and barn of a farm, and then in a wilderness of scrub trees covering the ridge. After four small summits, come to the **House of the Gods kiosk** (**5.0km**), a favorite pilgrim stop. Beginning in 2009, pilgrim friend David Vidal offered warm hospitality in this off-the-grid rest area. Soon come to the **Santo Toribio cross** (**1.6km**, rest area, no fountain), a viewpoint from which you can see Astorga across the Tuerto River valley. Walk downhill to join a sidewalk on the N-120a (**0.6km**) into

8.0KM SAN JUSTO DE LA VEGA (ELEV. 850M, POP. 1908) 🏠 ⊕ 🅿 ⊚ ⊕ (264.9KM)

Although it feels like a suburb of Astorga, which looms above, San Justo has a long pedigree, likely having its start in the sixth–eighth c. The parish church includes a 16th c. tower, a 16th c. image of patron saint Gregorio Español, and a modern altarpiece by the artist Sendo. In the Middle Ages the town hosted a pilgrim hospital.

🏠 Hostal Juli 🅿 🅁 🅖 🅦 🅢 12/24, €-/25/45/60, Calle Real 56, tel 987 617 632

Continue along the N-120a toward Astorga and its cathedral, quite visible on the hill above. Views of the two-towered temple distract from the slow entry into the city. Cross the **Tuerto River** (**0.6km**) and later some narrow railroad tracks (**1.9km**) on an intricate bridge of ramps and switchbacks. Across the N-120a and atop the hill inside town, a Roman mosaic is under a shed cover immediately to the right, followed by the Roman museum (**0.9km**). Walking farther through town over pedestrian streets, pass through the Plaza España with its charming clock tower and shops and continue following the arrows to the Bishop's Palace and cathedral, a few blocks ahead.

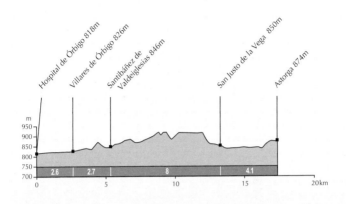

Hospital de Órbigo 818m
Villares de Órbigo 826m
Santibáñez de Valdeiglesias 846m
San Justo de la Vega 850m
Astorga 874m

m
950
900
850
800
750
700

2.6 | 2.7 | 8 | 4.1

0 | 5 | 10 | 15 | 20km

The Bishop's Palace in Astorga, designed by Antoni Gaudí, now houses a pilgrim museum (photo: Rod Hoekstra)

4.1KM ASTORGA (ELEV. 874M, POP. 11,264) 🔲 ⊕ ◻ ◖ ◉ ◉ ⊕ ⊕ ❶ (260.8KM)

A capital of the Astur tribe in ancient times, the Romans named this regional capital Asturicas Augustus, using it as an outpost on the Via Traiana to guard the mountain mines to the west. Because of its prominence, both St Paul and Santiago were said to have visited here and its third c. bishopric is one of Spain's oldest. Nearly 2km of the **Roman walls**, rebuilt many times, can be seen on the town's northwest flank. The tall walls didn't save the city from being sacked first by the Visigoths in 456 then by Muslim invaders in 714. In about 850 Astorga was recaptured in the Reconquista and through the 17th c. prospered as a major pilgrim supply center on the Camino Francés and Via de la Plata, which converge here. At its Camino zenith it boasted 21 pilgrim hospitals, and none less than St Francis of Assisi stayed at the Hospice of San Roque here in 1214. Pilgrims enter town at the **Plaza de San Francisco**, passing the **Monasterio de San Francisco** and Roman ruins that include the 50m **Ergástula tunnel**. Continuing to the **Plaza España**, the 17th c. *ayuntamiento* (town hall) is topped by a mechanical clock from 1748 with figures wearing costumes of the local Maragato mountain people. After pausing at the **chocolate museum**, which chronicles Astorga's centuries-old history as a regional chocolate center, the squat towers of the 15th–16th c. **cathedral** become visible. Uncommonly tall for a relatively small footprint, the building houses the Chapel of San Miguel and Renaissance retablo by Gaspar Becerra, student of Michelangelo and Rafael. Perhaps most prized of all is the 12th c. statue of Nuestra Seíora de la Majestad. Adjacent is the 16th c. **San Esteban**, with its Cell of the Sufferers where women were incarcerated for prayer and penance. Just south is the fairytale **Bishop's Palace and museum**, designed by the famed architect Antoni Gaudí and completed in 1913. The building was so splendid that on completion its ecclesiastical patron and financier decided it was too beautiful to serve as his home. It now houses a museum of pilgrimage relics from the city's many years of service to the Camino. While in Astorga, ask for the *mantecadas* pound cake and *hojaldres* puff pastry desserts.

🔺 Albergue de Siervas de María ◉ ◉ 🔳 🔳 🔳 22/156, €7/-/-/-, Plaza San Francisco 3, www.caminodesantiagoastorga.com, tel 987 616 034

🔺 Albergue San Javier ◉ ◉ 🔳 🔳 🔳 4/110, €10/-/-/-, Calle Portería 6, tel 987 618 532

🔺 Albergue Só Por Hoje 🔳 🔳 🔳 🔳 🔳 🔳 🔳 1/10 & 2/5, €25/-/65/88, Calle Rodríguez de Cela 30, http://alberguesoporhoje.com, tel 690 749 853, Patricia is your host

STAGE 22
Astorga to Foncebadón

Start	Astorga Cathedral
Finish	Foncebadón, parish albergue
Distance	25.7km
Total ascent	770m
Total descent	210m
Difficulty	Moderately hard, due to elevation gain and sometimes difficult footing
Duration	7½hr
Percentage paved	18%
Albergues	Ecce Homo 2.1; Murias de Rechivaldo 4.2; Santa Catalina de Somoza 8.7; El Ganso 13.1; Rabanal del Camino 20.1; Foncebadón 25.7

The Meseta's wide views now fade into memory and are replaced by vistas of mountains and forests. The long and gradual uphill can almost convince you that you are not climbing into the mountains. However, just before Rabanal the path heads more steeply upward, continuing up to Foncebadón and the summit just beyond. The more enticing stage end is charming Rabanal, but an overnight at Foncebadón will make it easier to be at Cruz de Ferro by sunrise.

Leave **Astorga** on a sidewalk alongside the LE-142 highway. Notice low ridges ahead, separating wide and shallow valleys full of grasslands and widely spaced groupings of trees. Continue along the road, coming to **Ecce Homo** ('Behold the Man') hermitage (**2.1km**, rest area, fountain ♠ Ecce Homo 🄳 🆁 🄺 🆆 🆂 4/10, €5/-/-/-, Calle Ecce Homo, www.facebook.com/albergue.ecce.hommo, tel 620 960 060) before crossing the A-6 highway bridge (**0.3km**). Now take up a pathway of crushed rock alongside the roadway to reach

4.2KM MURIAS DE RECHIVALDO (ELEV. 880M, POP. 113) 🄸🄸 🖸 ⦿ (256.6KM)

At Murias the mountain character of the subsequent towns emerges. The mud walls of the Meseta are here replaced by stone walls. Today the local custom of thatched roofs is substituted by durable slate, although window openings remain small to conserve heat in the hard winters. Here the few remaining Maragato mountain people – resident since at least the 10th c. and of either German or Moorish origin – make their homes.

Albergue de Murias de Rechivaldo O D W S 1/18, €9/-/-/-, Carretera de Santa Colomba, **https://alberguemurias.wix.com/home**, tel 638 433 716

Albergue Casa Flor P D R C W S 5/16 & 3/6, €15/40/50/-, Calle Traslosportales 40, **www.facebook.com/alberguecasaflor.caminodesantiago**, tel 644 695 872

Albergue Casa Las Águedas P D R Cr K C W S 2/28 & 5/10, €15/45/55/80, Calle Camino de Santiago 52, **https://lasaguedas.com**, tel 987 691 234

Now walk through a fairly flat area of low, rolling scrubland, noting wind turbines on the right, as well as the town of Castrillo de los Polvazares which the track bypasses. Cross the LE-142 (**2.6km**) and continue uphill gently on the white gravel roadside track of the LE-6304, overlooking views of reddish soil and scrub trees. Pass a rest area (**1.5km**, no fountain) just before reaching

4.5KM SANTA CATALINA DE SOMOZA (ELEV. 983M, POP. 987) (252.1KM)

The town features the modern Church of Santa María with a relic of San Blas.

Albergue Casa Rural El Caminante O P D R Cr W S 2/22 & 12/26, €5/30/45/60, Calle Real 2, **www.elcaminante.es**, tel 987 691 098

Albergue Hospedería San Blas O P D R W S 2/20 & 8/16, €7/30/35/45, Calle Real 11, tel 987 691 411

After town enjoy the 180° view of the surrounding mountainous territory. Back to the roadside pathway, the scrub trees and shrubs begin to space themselves more closely.

4.4KM EL GANSO (ELEV. 1016M, POP. 23) (247.8KM)

A 12th c. hospital once served pilgrims here. The town is now famous among pilgrims for its Cowboy Bar.

Albergue El Gabino D R K W S 3/24, €8/-/-/-, Calle Real 9, **www.facebook.com/hostelgabino**, tel 625 318 585

Pass a picnic area outside of town (**0.9km**, no fountain) and before long see the buildings of Rabanal, nestled in the hillside ahead. Come to an intersection with the

El Ganso's Cowboy bar offers a hint of the American West

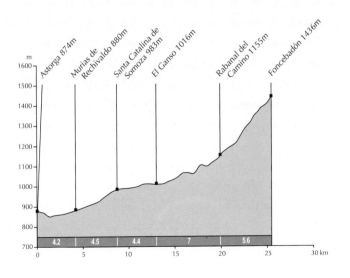

Astorga 874m
Murias de Rechivaldo 880m
Santa Catalina de Somoza 983m
El Ganso 1016m
Rabanal del Camino 1155m
Foncebadón 1436m

m

4.2 | 4.5 | 4.4 | 7 | 5.6

A pilgrim walks the slowly ascending path among undergrowth and purple heather

LE-6302 to Rabanal Viejo (**3.3km**) and with luck a food van (**0.2km**) will greet you with drinks and snacks. Now begin a true uphill climb on loose shale and bedrock, the first steep climb of the day. Soon the path flattens to a pleasant woodland track, eventually returning to the roadside among cow and horse pastures and momentarily rejoining the LE-142 roadway before arriving in

7.0KM RABANAL DEL CAMINO (ELEV. 1155M, POP. 74) ▯ ⊕ ◪ (240.7KM)

Long a natural Camino end-of-stage beyond Astorga, the town of Rabanal del Camino has a colorful pilgrim history that includes an overnight stay by Aymeric Picaud recorded in the *Codex Calixtinus*. The Knights Templar of Ponferrada maintained a garrison here in the 12th c. to protect pilgrims crossing the mountains toward Santiago. At its height Rabanal was site of two hermitages and a pilgrim hospital, **Hospital de San Gregorio** – linked to the noted hermit Gaucelmo – which now houses Refugio Gaucelmo, a much-loved albergue run by the British Confraternity of St James. The adjacent 12th c. **Church of Santa María** (remodeled in the 19th c.) is linked to a small monastic community with services conducted by monks. The building has architectural features from its Romanesque origins and contains a 12th c. image of San Blas, patron saint of wool combers.

🛖 Albergue La Senda ▯ ▯ ▯ ▯ ▯ 4/22, €10/-/-/-, Calle Real, http://hostel-caminodesantiago.com, tel 620 542 247, space to set up a tent

🛖 Albergue Municipal Rabanal del Camino ▯ ▯ ▯ ▯ ▯ ▯ 2/36, €5/-/-/-, Calle Gandana, www.facebook.com/alberguemunicipalrabanaldelcamino, tel 655 274 613

🛖 Refugio Gaucelmo ▯ ▯ 3/36, €Donation, Plaza del Peregrino Julián Campo, www.csj.org.uk/about-us/hospitality-our-refuges, tel 987 631 647, next to the Benedictine Monastery

🛖 Albergue Nuestra Señora del Pilar ▯ ▯ ▯ ▯ ▯ ▯ ▯ 2/76 & 2/4, €10/-/40/-, Plaza de Jerónimo Morán, https://albergueelpilar.com, tel 987 631 621

The concrete road out of town narrows to a wide gravel trail heading uphill, following the trajectory of the nearby LE-142 road. Very wide views now open to the left, with wind turbines atop low green mountains. In season, the path blooms with purple heather and wildflowers of yellow and white, not to mention the omnipresent yellow scotch broom. The track begins to climb steeply, choosing one side then the other of the LE-142 road, interspersed by a fountain (**1.9km**) and rest area (**0.8km**, fountain). Coming to a treeless portion of the climb, enjoy an outlook back to Astorga and the flat plains of the Meseta behind it. Nearing the top, the rocks become more jagged and each footfall more difficult until you finally cross the LE-142 to the foot of **Foncebadón**.

5.6KM FONCEBADÓN (ELEV. 1436M, POP. 18) 🔟 🔼 (235.2KM)

Although historical records note Foncebadón in a monastery donation as early as 946, the town seems first to have been inhabited in the 11th c., when the hermit Gaucelmo built a pilgrim hospital here and received approval from Alfonso VI to populate the village. Sheltered on the east side of a ridge, the town is a natural last stop before summiting the pass. In the mid 18th c. an alternate route over the Montes de León was constructed, leading it eventually to the eerie ghost-town vibe described in Paulo Coelho's *The Pilgrimage*. The modern Camino has brought new life and in the last 10 years several accommodations have sprouted up, while Foncebadón's main street was paved in jarringly modern concrete in 2019.

🔺 Albergue Casa Chelo 🇩 🇷 🇼 🇸 1/10, €10/-/-/-, Calle Real 23, www.facebook.com/AlbergueCasaCheloFoncebadon, tel 619 165 384

🔺 Albergue Parroquial Domus Dei 🇩 🇧 🇨 🇼 1/18, €Donation, Calle Real, www.facebook.com/alberguefoncebadon, community breakfast and dinner, evening prayers

🔺 Albergue La Posada del Druida 🇵 🇩 🇷 🇬 🇧 🇨 🇼 🇸 3/20 & 6/12, €10/32/45/60, Calle Real, www.facebook.com/LaPosadadelDruida, tel 696 820 136

🔺 Convento de Foncebadón 🇵 🇩 🇷 🇬 🇼 🇸 4/24 & 14/28, €10/34/45/63, Calle Real, www.facebook.com/pg/elconventodefoncebadon, tel 987 053 934

STAGE 23

Foncebadón to Ponferrada

Start	Foncebadón, parish albergue
Finish	Ponferrada, Plaza Virgen de la Encina
Distance	26.9km
Total ascent	475m
Total descent	1375m
Difficulty	Hard, due to sometimes slippery and steep mountain paths
Duration	7¼hr
Percentage paved	46%
Albergues	Manjarín 4.3; El Acebo 11.3; Riego de Ambrós 14.8; Molinaseca 19.4; Ponferrada 26.9

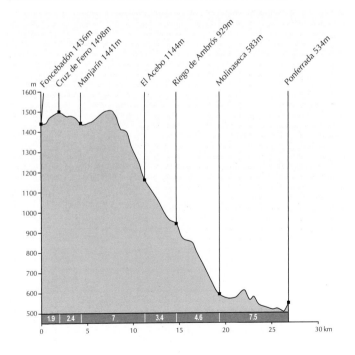

The walk includes some of the Camino's most beautiful mountain vistas on paths that are often very pleasant, particularly with wildflowers in season. The highlight of the day may be Cruz de Ferro, with its tradition of contemplation and spiritual release. The unstable footing on the long downhill into Molinaseca makes the day's middle half sometimes difficult, and the long, suburban walk after Molinaseca, although uninspiring, has the delightful center city of Ponferrada at its culmination.

In **Foncebadón** walk gradually uphill through scattered, deserted and recently re-inhabited homes. Soon the path levels out as it joins the LE-142 Astorga–Molinaseca road. Continue to the

1.9KM CRUZ DE FERRO (ELEV. 1498M, POP. 0) NO SERVICES (233.3KM)

Ancient Celts often piled stones to mark high places, and that practice may have been the ancient origin of a rock cairn at the site atop a bluff near 1504m Monte Irago. In the 12th c. the hermit monk Gaucelmo erected a cross on the pile of stones. The small adjacent chapel was built in 1982. Pilgrims today place stones, personal effects and memorabilia here as signs of contrition, gratitude or reverence.

After the cross there are more ascents ahead, although the path seems at first to descend. Make your way to

Pilgrims offer a small token or prayer at the foot of the Cruz de Ferro (photo: Rod Hoekstra)

2.4KM MANJARÍN (ELEV. 1441M, POP. 0) ⑪ 🏠 (230.9KM)

The medieval village, long abandoned, was reclaimed beginning in the 1990s, today maintaining a small, off-the-grid hostel in the spirit and occasionally costume of the Knights Templar.

🔺 Refugio de Manjarín ⓄⒹⒸⓈ 1/30, No address, €5/-/-/-, basic lodging without running water or showers

Views of the tall mountain ridge to the left open up while the path now climbs toward the large microwave tower ahead with heather, foxglove and Spanish lavender in season. Cross to the opposite side of the LE-142 road (**1.5km**) and climb to the **microwave tower summit** ('Llabana Peak,' **1.7km**), at 1510m the high point of the Camino Francés.

Now the path begins to descend steeply, alternately on dirt, bedrock, or shale with footing sometimes difficult where the track has eroded into deep gullies. As the path crosses the LE-142 again (**2.6km**) the welcome sight of **El Acebo** becomes visible below.

7.0KM EL ACEBO (ELEV. 1144M, POP. 52) ⑪ ⊕ 🏠 (223.8KM)

El Acebo has welcomed pilgrims for over 1000 years. The town was site of an important church council in 946 and hosted a pilgrim hospital in the 15th c. Today it serves as entry to the Bierzo region, known for fine wines.

🔺 Albergue Apóstol Santiago ⒹⒷⒸⓈ 1/22, €Donation, Plaza de la Iglesia, www.facebook.com/AlbergueParroquialSantiagoApostolDeElAceboBierzo, tel – none

🔺 La Casa del Peregrino ⒫ⒹⓇⒼⓌⓈ 12/96 & 4/8, €12/45/60/85, Calle Real 67-69, www.alberguelacasadelperegrino.es, tel 987 057 793, swimming pool and a small store

🔺 Albergue Mesón El Acebo ⒫ⒹⓇⒼⓌⓈ 2/32 & 2/4, €7/-/24/36, Calle Real 16, tel 987 695 074

Continue downhill, with views now of Ponferrada in the distance below. The track alternates between the road and roadside footpaths and comes to

3.4KM RIEGO DE AMBRÓS (ELEV. 929M, POP. 40) ⑪ 🏠 (220.4KM)

Wooden ornamental balconies overhang the street to give shelter from snow. The heavy stone architecture and slate roofs are typical of this region. The 16th c. **Church of María Magdalena** has a fine baroque retablo. Outside town is a small hermitage to San Sebastián.

🔺 Albergue de Riego de Ambrós ⒹⓇⓀⒸⓌⓈ 6/26, €6/-/-/-, Calle Real, tel 640 376 118

After town, descend steeply on bedrock and shale over a path that sometimes shares its downhill direction with a small rivulet. The shade accompanying this new path, offered by oak trees of some size, is a welcome relief on sunny days. After crossing the road, the path takes its farthest diversion from the LE-142 (**1.4km**), heading northward into the quiet valley of the **Arroyo de la Pretadura** ('Stream of Prettiness'), which you cross in 800m after a steep and challenging downhill. Soon you come out of the valley on a somewhat precipitous traverse of the mountainside with a sweeping view of Molinaseca below. Rejoin the road (**1.8km**), passing the Our Lady of Anguish Shrine (**0.3km**) before crossing a picturesque bridge over the Meruelo River into

4.6KM MOLINASECA (ELEV. 583M, POP. 888) 🍴 ⊕ 🛏 🄲 ◉ ⊕ (215.8KM)

As the western terminus of the mountain pass, Molinaseca's importance is traced to Roman times when it guarded this segment of the gold mine route. In medieval times it hosted four pilgrim hospitals. Walkers arrive first at the 17th–18th c. **Sanctuary of Nuestra Señora de las Angustias**, whose porch sheltered pilgrims. Although often locked, the church has a beautiful baroque altarpiece. The **San Nicolás de Bari** church across the bridge has roots in the 12th c. and contains a 17th c. retablo with a statue of San Roque.

🏠 Albergue Compostela **D R C W S** 7/31, €9/-/-/-, Calle la Iglesia 39, tel 622 317 525

🏠 Albergue de Peregrinos San Roque **O D K W S** 1/19, €6/-/-/-, Travesía Manuel Fraga 26, www.facebook.com/alberguedemolinaseca, tel 615 106 125

🏠 Albergue Señor Oso **O D R G W S** 3/18, €12/-/-/-, Calle Real 43, https://senoroso.es, tel 661 761 970, above the bakery

🏠 Albergue Santa Marina **P D R K C W S** 3/38 & 4/10, €10/-/40/60, Travesía Manuel Fraga 55, tel 615 302 390

The restored Knights Templar castle at Ponferrada offers a view of life inside medieval battlements (photo: Rod Hoekstra)

The charming central pilgrim street of Molinaseca spills onto the sidewalk of the LE-142, which carries you nearly into Ponferrada before diverting onto a long and wide gravel road through the tiny village of **Campo** (**4.0km**, Roman fountain). To the right are ever-closer views of Ponferrada's cathedral and its large housing towers east of the center city. After Campo the gravel road becomes asphalt and soon the path follows sidewalks into the south suburbs of town. Cross a stone pedestrian bridge over the Boeza River (**2.7km**) and make your way uphill, crossing under railroad tracks toward the Templar castle, and just beyond it the city center at Plaza Virgen de la Encina.

7.5KM PONFERRADA (ELEV. 534M, POP. 66,447) 🍴 ⊕ 🛏 🅲 ◉ ⊙ Ⓗ ⊕ ⊕ 🛈 (208.3KM)

Nestled on a steep height above the confluence of the Sil and Boeza Rivers, Ponferrada was already an important settlement by the time it was appropriated into the Roman Empire. Destroyed by the Visigoths in the fifth c. and in the ninth c. by Muslim invaders, this market town with its iron-buttressed bridge (hence its name from the Latin *pons ferrata*, or 'iron bridge') was too big for its medieval walls, pushing across the rivers with vibrant French and Jewish neighborhoods. A dozen hospitals served pilgrims at the high point of the Camino, although all have vanished. The town's prominent **castle**, restored in the late 20th c., had Celtic and Roman precedents before being given in 1178 to the Knights Templar, an order of European knights famed for protecting the Temple in Jerusalem during the Crusades. Between 1218 and 1282 they built the enormous castle, some 16,000m^2 in size, which encompassed stables, churches, dungeons, a palace, fort, grand plaza, and a monastery. Due to the Templars' declining fortunes and reputation, the Vatican dissolved the order in 1312, just 30 years after the castle's completion. With the invention of the cannon, as with many European citadels, this castle's walls and battlements were slowly dismantled and their stones used for other building projects. The castle's history is chronicled in the nearby **Museo del Bierzo**, a former prison. The town's **clock tower**, with its coat of arms of Carlos I, stands above a gate in the medieval walls. The 16th c. **Church of Santa María de la Encina** is on the adjacent plaza and its 1630 altarpiece holds an image of the Virgin said to have been found by the Templars in a holm oak.

🛏 Albergue Alea 🄳 🅁 🅲 🅆 🅂 4/18, €15/-/-/-, Calle Teleno 33, http://albergealea.com, tel 987 404 133

🛏 Albergue San Nicolás de Flüe 🅾 🄳 🅆 🅂 7/186, €Donation, Calle Obispo Camilo Lorenzo 2, https://sannicolasdeflue.com, tel 987 413 381

🛏 Albergue Guiana 🄿 🄳 🅁 🄶 🄺 🅆 🅂 12/53 & 6/16, €15/-/60/-, Avenida del Castillo 112, www.albergueguiana.com, tel 987 409 327

STAGE 24
Ponferrada to Villafranca del Bierzo

Start	Ponferrada, Plaza Virgen de la Encina
Finish	Villafranca del Bierzo, *ayuntamiento* (town hall)
Distance	23.6km
Total ascent	495m
Total descent	520m
Difficulty	Moderate, due to walking alongside the roadway
Duration	6½hr
Percentage paved	74%
Albergues	Columbrianos 5.2; Camponaraya 10.1; Cacabelos 15.5; Pieros, 18.0; Villafranca del Bierzo 23.6

The mostly flat stage can be described in three parts – the pleasant riverfront promenade out of Ponferrada; the walk among homes, gardens, villages and vineyards until Cacabelos, and then the not-so-pleasant walk along the highway until just shy of Villafranca del Bierzo. Wine drinkers will want to order a glass of the internationally famous Bierzo vintages. Plan a relaxing evening exploring the churches, castles, shops, restaurants and bars of lovely Villafranca.

In **Ponferrada**, a block past the charming Plaza de la Encina is the equally charming Plaza Ayuntamiento. Both are atmospheric coffee stops before heading down the hill, crossing the bridge over the Sil River (**0.8km**) and following the pleasant riverside park trail out of town. After the trail ends at a modern white auto bridge overhead (**1.3km**) and glass museum, climb a gravel path then walk on neighborhood streets through the ancient town of **Compostilla**, now an industrial suburb of Ponferrada. Cross under the old N-VI highway (**2.0km**), pass the 18th c. **Church of San Esteban** (**0.5km**, sello) and carefully cross the busy CL-631 highway into one end of the long, slender town of

5.2KM COLUMBRIANOS (ELEV. 524M, POP. 1386) 🏨 ⬜ ◉ ⊕ (203.1KM)

Actually one of Bierzo's oldest settlements, the surrounding hills hold four pre-Roman *castros* (fortresses).

🔺 Albergue San Blas 🅾️🅿️🅳🆁🅶🆆🆂 3/18 & 3/6, €10/-/25/-, Calle San Blas 5, www.alberguesanblas.es, tel 611 614 149

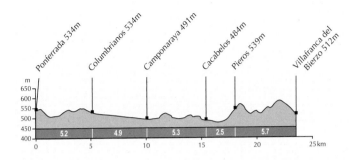

On the way out of town, pass a small hermitage chapel with a mural of pilgrim Saint Roque and follow a long asphalt road among scattered homes on large parcels with hayfields and gardens. As the homes cluster more closely, skirt the northern edge of **Fuentesnuevas** (**2.4km**) and its 15th c. Chapel of the Divine Christ and 17th c. Our Lady of the Assumption. In a few minutes, veer right onto sidewalks of the LE-713 highway (**1.9km**), which serves as the wide main street of **Camponaraya**, populated with a plethora of cafés and restaurants.

4.9KM CAMPONARAYA (ELEV. 491M, POP. 4096) 🍴 🏧 ⊕ ⓒ ⊚ ⊕ (198.2KM)

Originally twin towns of Campo and Naraya that faced each other across the Naraya stream until joining as one in the 15th c. in service to the nearby Carracedo monastery.

🛌 Albergue Naraya 🅳 🆁 🅶 🆆 🆂 5/24, €9/-/-/-, Avenida Galicia 506, www.alberguenaraya.es, tel 987 459 159

🛌 Albergue La Medina 🅾 🅿 🅳 🆁 🅶 🆆 🆂 1/18 & 7/14, €11/38/48/-, Avenida Camino de Santiago 87, tel 667 348 551

The town ends at a roundabout opposite the pleasant Vinas del Bierzo winery (**0.9km**, wine and tapas available) in a neighborhood of scattered warehouses and busy highways. Just after the winery and an adjacent rest area, climb the hill on a gravel track under evergreen trees and then cross a flagstone-paved **pedestrian bridge** (**0.4km**) over the A-6. After rounding the corner, views open to the vineyard-bedecked hills of the Bierzo valley, ringed by green and deep blue mountains. Pass a food truck location (**1.2km**) in a shaded wood, cross the LE-713 highway (**1.1km**), pass the **Bierzo Wine Council** (**0.9km**) and descend into charming and relaxed **Cacabelos** with its trendy bars and eateries.

Vine dressers tend to their subjects in a vineyard after Cacabelos (photo: Rod Hoekstra)

5.3KM CACABELOS (ELEV. 484M, POP. 5152) 🚹 ⊕ 🏠 🄲 ◉ ⊕ ⊕ (192.8KM)

A nearby pre-Roman settlement is chronicled at the **Archaeological Museum of Cacabelos** (http://cacabelos.org/marca), which features artifacts from the nearby *castros* and the Roman city of Bergidum Flavium. The long, narrow town was destroyed in a 12th c. earthquake but soon rebuilt as a center for pilgrim support, ultimately hosting six pilgrim hospitals. In a battle here between the British and French in 1809 at the **Cúa River bridge** the French general Colbert would die by a long-distance shot from Thomas Plunkett, whose feat would make him famous as the 'world's first sniper.'

🛏 Albergue Municipal de Cacabelos ⒹⓌⓈ 35/70, €6/-/-/-, Plaza del Santuario 9, **www.facebook.com/alberguemunicipalcacabelos**, tel 987 547 167, river close by to cool down your feet

🛏 Albergue El Molino ⓄⓅⒹⓇⒼⓌⓈ 4/16 & 4/8, €12/40/40/-, Calle Santa María 10, **www.elmolinoalbergue.com**, tel 987 546 979

🛏 Hostal La Gallega ⓄⓅⒹⓇⒼⓀⓌⓈ 6/26 & 12/23, €12/33/43/50, Calle Santa María 23, **https://hostal-lagallega.webnode.es/**, tel 680 917 109

Now the reverie ends as the central pedestrian street of Cacabelos spits you out onto a sidewalk along the LE-713 highway. Cross the Cúa River bridge (**0.5km**) and follow the sidewalk as it becomes a roadside path. Although the road is quieter since its newer sibling, the A-6, was built, the walk of several kilometers alternates between moments of dreariness and alert concern as cars whiz past. Fortunately, the vineyard-covered hills and blue mountains make for charming companions. Pass the outskirts of tiny

2.5KM PIEROS (ELEV. 539M, POP. 36) ⊞ ⌂ ⊚ **(190.3KM)**

The tiny village includes a tapas bar, albergue/café and bus stop. The town's treasure is the 11th c. Church of San Martín. The Knights Templar once sponsored a pilgrim hospital here, which has since disappeared.

⌂ Albergue El Serbal y La Luna ⊡⊡⊡⊡⊡⊡ 2/18, €10/-/-/-, Calle El Pozo 15, tel 639 888 924

Watch to the right for an unmarked option (**0.4km**) that carries you on quieter backroads north through **Valtuille de Arriba**, adding 1km to the day (see below). Otherwise, to stay on the main route, continue on the road and look on the right for a rest area and turn-off (**1.9km**) leading on gravel uphill to the back of **Villafranca del Bierzo**.

Valtuille de Arriba option
For this more scenic option, turn right and follow the asphalt road for a few hundred meters before veering left onto a wide path among vineyards. Come to central **Valtuille de Arriba (1.5km)** before following arrows back to the southwest through vineyards and rejoining the main route (**2.9km**) just before **Villafranca**, which has also by this time abandoned the highway for the gravel vineyard roads.

Come first to the municipal albergue, then the Church of Santiago (**2.7km**) and its Door of Pardon. Follow the arrows down into town and the outdoor restaurants of the Plaza Mayor.

A quiet street descends to Villafranca del Bierzo's vibrant central square (photo: Rod Hoekstra)

5.7KM VILLAFRANCA DEL BIERZO (ELEV. 512M, POP. 3153)
🏠 ⊕ 🔲 🄲 ⊛ ⊕ ⊕ **ⓘ** (184.7KM)

This ancient town's ascent to prominence is often linked to the 1093 arrival of the Cluniac monks who came to minister to Santiago pilgrims, bringing with them vines for cultivation. Aymeric Picaud speaks highly of Villafranca and includes it as a way-stop in the *Codex Calixtinus*. The international escapades of local nobility allied with the Spanish king brought to Villafranca a flair for Italian architecture, now seen especially on coats of arms in Villafranca's many large homes. A series of disasters hobbled the town's development – a 1589 plague, a destructive flood in 1715 and a series of pillages by Napoléon's army in 1808. Among the survivors are the 12th–13th c. **Church of Santiago**, whose 13th c. north portal was given a 15th c. papal blessing as the **Puerta del Perdón** ('Door of Forgiveness') for sick or injured pilgrims unable to make the final climb up the pass to Santiago. According to tradition, the church was established by St Francis of Assisi during his 1214 visit. Although humble on the outside, its interior contains a fine 1555 Renaissance altarpiece, La Immaculada, and an elaborate 14th c., Mudéjar-style ceiling. The imposing façade of the 17th c. Jesuit **Church of San Nicolás** stands in the center of town while not far away is the **Colegiata de Santa María**, church of the Cluniac monks, one-time pilgrim hospital, and host to the lovely 16th c. plateresque retablo of the Holy Trinity. The 17th c. **Convento de la Anunciada** hosts a series of portraits of hermit saints by the Italian painter Giuseppe Serena. The hulking 15th c. **Castle-Palace of the Marquises** with its squat, round tower, has recently been restored. A walk down the **Calle del Agua** gives a view to the town's best homes and smaller palaces. The star of this show, though, is an outdoor dinner in the **Plaza Mayor**, accompanied of course by a glass of Bierzo's best.

🏠 Albergue Ave Fénix 🄾 🄳 🄲 🅆 🅂 5/80, €6/-/-/-, Calle Santiago 10, tel 987 542 655

🏠 Albergue El Castillo 🄳 🅁 🄶 🄺 🄲 🅆 🅂 2/16, €12/-/-/-, Calle El Castillo 8, tel 987 540 344

🏠 Albergue La Yedra 🄳 🅁 🅆 🅂 1/18, €10/-/-/-, Calle La Yedra 9, www.facebook.com/Albergue-La-Yedra, tel 636 586 872

🏠 Albergue Leo 🄳 🅁 🄺 🅆 🅂 7/24, €12/-/-/-, Calle Ribadeo 10, www.albergueleo.com, tel 987 542 658

🏠 Albergue Municipal Villafranca del Bierzo 🄳 🄺 🅆 🅂 5/58, €6/-/-/-, Campo de la Gallina, www.villafrancadelbierzo.org/albergue, tel 987 542 356

🏠 Albergue de la Piedra 🄿 🄳 🅁 🄶 🄺 🅆 🅂 2/13 & 4/9, €12/24/30/39, Calle Espíritu Santo 14, www.alberguedelapiedra.com, tel 987 540 260, after the bridge by the river

🏠 Albergue Hospedería San Nicolás El Real 🄾 🄿 🄳 🅁 🄶 🄺 🅆 🅂 -/75 & 14/28, €6/25/45/60, Calle Travesía de San Nicolás 4, www.sannicolaselreal.com, tel 696 978 653

STAGE 25
Villafranca del Bierzo to La Faba

Start	Villafranca del Bierzo, *ayuntamiento* (town hall)
Finish	La Faba center
Distance	24.0km (24.8 via Pradela, 29.6 via Dragonte)
Total ascent	1060m (1202m via Pradela, 1855m via Dragonte)
Total descent	660m (800m via Pradela, 1452m via Dragonte)
Difficulty	Moderate, due to pavement and general slow incline (moderately hard via Pradela, hard via Dragonte)
Duration	7¼hr (7¾hr Pradela; 9¾hr Dragonte)
Percentage paved	94%
Albergues	Pereje 5.4; (8.4 Pradela) Trabadelo 9.8; La Portela 13.9; Ambasmestas 15.1; Vega de Valcarce 16.8; Ruitelán 19.1; Las Herrerías 20.4; La Faba 24.0

This long uphill climb is gentle at first, but after La Herrerías becomes quite steep. Although the walk follows the old N-VI (Madrid–A Coruña highway) and shares the narrow valley with the A-6 freeway, the most common sound is the Valcarce River as it makes its way noisily downhill to the accompaniment of songbirds and, well, the occasional belch of a diesel truck groaning up the valley on the freeway above. Planning tip: an overnight at Las Herrerías offers more choice in lodging and meals but pushing the extra 3.6km to La Faba gives a head start on tomorrow's climb.

A concrete barrier near Pereje separates pilgrims from light traffic on the N-VI roadway along the main route

TWO OPTIONAL ROUTES

Besides the not-unpleasant and quite-well-serviced main route, two other paths lead up the Valcarce. The Ruta Pradela or 'Camino Duro' climbs to the top of the ridge north of the main route then quickly descends, landing at Trabadelo. While the views are very pleasant, the added exertion and short duration make it a choice primarily for those eager for a cardio workout. An albergue at Pradela offers an overnight (🔺 Albergue Lamas ⭕ 🅿 🅳 🆁 🅶 🅲 🆆 🆂 🆉 1/6, €10/30/45/-, Calle Principal, tel 677 569 764). The Ruta Dragonte is a wild track that climbs up and down three steep ridges to the south of the main itinerary. While fewer than 1% of pilgrims choose this route, it is perfect for adventurers who are looking for a peek into untouched, rural mountain Spain. The route follows isolated mountain roads and back-country trails through tiny hamlets and was originally a detour chosen by travelers who wanted to bypass the steep tolls of the valley-floor route. People who walk the Dragonte enjoy sweeping views and a day-long taste of solitude. Make certain to take food and water for the day since there are no reliable services along the way. For more information see Facebook group 'Friends of Dragonte'. Kind thanks to TrailSmart app for help in mapping. Of the three available options from Villafranca, only the main Camino route is described below.

From **Villafranca del Bierzo** follow the arrows down and out the main plaza and then up a small rise to the bridge over the Burbia River (**0.4km**). Almost immediately is the 'Y' intersection of the Ruta Pradela 'Camino Duro,' followed by the left turn for the Ruta Dragonte which goes over the Valcarce River. For the main route, however, continue ahead along sidewalks and finally on a walkway separated from the road by concrete barriers until the somewhat rundown and abandoned-looking town of **Pereje** appears just after a double crossing under the elevated A-6 highway.

5.4KM PEREJE (ELEV. 543M, POP. 33) 🏨 ⛲ (179.3KM)

The town's highlight is a carefully manicured pilgrim bar festooned with potted geraniums, petunias and cactuses. A building on the way out of town sports a curved balcony, unique on the Camino for its length.

🔺 Albergue de Pereje ⭕ 🅳 🅺 🆆 🆂 2/30, €5/-/-/-, Calle Camino de Santiago 61A, http://pereje.org/albergue-pereje-leon-bierzo-situacion, tel 987 540 138, tents ok

Continue along the concrete barriers up the hill as you pass the two rest areas (**1.8km, 0.8km**) before reaching **Trabadelo**, nestled along the Valcarce River.

4.4KM TRABADELO (ELEV. 569M, POP. 366) ▣ ▣ (174.9KM)

A town of freeway-exit truck stops, a busy central sawmill and several attractive bars and restaurants. In the Middle Ages Trabadelo boasted a pilgrim hospital and two churches, although all are now vanished. In addition to its lumbermill the town's non-pilgrim industries are beekeeping and the fall harvest of chestnuts.

🔺 Albergue Casa Susi ▣ ▣ ▣ ▣ ▣ ▣ 1/10, €12/-/-/-, Calle Camino de Santiago 25, www.facebook.com/alberguecasasusi, tel 683 278 778

🔺 Albergue Crispeta ▣ ▣ ▣ ▣ ▣ ▣ ▣ ▣ 5/32, €6/25/44/-, Calle Camino de Santiago 1, tel 696 978 653

🔺 Albergue de Trabadelo ▣ ▣ ▣ ▣ ▣ 6/36, €6/-/-/-, Calle Camino de Santiago, www.trabadelo.org, tel 987 566 447

🔺 Albergue Parroquial de Trabadelo ▣ ▣ ▣ ▣ ▣ ▣ ▣ ▣ ▣ 4/26, €5/20/40/-, Calle La Iglesia 2, www.facebook.com/albergueparroquial.trabadelo.7, tel 630 628 130

🔺 Albergue Camino y Leyenda ▣ ▣ ▣ ▣ ▣ ▣ ▣ ▣ 1/2 & 5/12, €25/-/35/45, Calle Camino de Santiago, www.facebook.com/albergcaminoyleyenda, tel 628 921 776

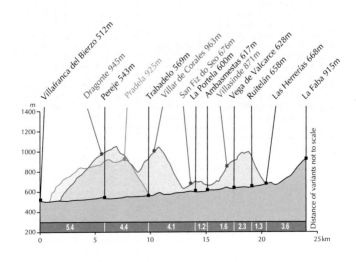

The main street of town turns to a country road that ambles along the valley as a pleasant and quiet walk with the freeway and old highway humming softly across the narrow valley. Drop on a gravel road under the highway bridges and return to the shoulder of the N-VI road (**1.7km**). Cross a series of highway overpasses and continue alongside the road toward tiny **La Portela**, which you find after a thankfully brief wasteland of freeway on-ramps, truck stops, parking lots and roadside hotels.

4.1KM LA PORTELA DE VALCARCE (ELEV. 600M, POP. 22) (170.8KM)

This truck stop town includes the 17th c. Church of San Juan Bautista and a 19th c. blacksmith's shop.

Albergue El Peregrino P D R W S 4/26 & 8/16, €10/28/40/-, Carretera Antigua Nacional VI, **www.laportela.com**, tel 987 543 197

Continue along the old N-VI highway before branching to the left just before the lovely village of **Ambasmestas**, as well tended and charming as La Portela was barren.

1.2KM AMBASMESTAS (ELEV. 617M, POP. 43) (169.5KM)

In Galician the name means 'mixture of waters' and refers to the confluence here of the Valcarce and Balboa rivers. The humble 18th c. **Church of San Pedro Apóstol** sits on the main street.

Albergue Casa del Pescador P D R Cr W S Z 2/24, €10/22/32/-, Carretera Antigua Nacional VI 37, **www.facebook.com/casadelpescadorAmbasmestas**, tel 603 515 868

Albergue Camynos P D R Cr W S 1/10 & 3/6, €12/38/50/-, Carretera Antigua Nacional VI 43, **www.camynos.es/el-albergue**, tel 629 743 124

Albergue El Rincón del Apóstol P D R Cr B C W S 1/7 & 4/8, €17/30/40/60, Carretera Antigua Nacional VI, **www.elrincondelapostol.com**, tel 987 543 099

Continue along the quiet side-road before quickly arriving at the first smatterings of **Vega de Valcarce**, the largest town in the valley. Although rather scattered at first, the town's banks, pharmacy, restaurants, stores and albergues soon cluster together around its squarish, white church steeple.

1.6KM VEGA DE VALCARCE (ELEV. 628M, POP. 652) ⓫ ⊕ 🛏 ◉ ⊕ (167.9KM)

This wide spot (*vega*) in the Valcarce is one of the valley's best places for farming. Here you may see for the first time the *berzas* (tall plants like chard) used in *caldo gallego* (a Galician soup). On March 20, 1520, King Carlos I of Spain spent the night in the **Sarracín Castle** on the adjacent hillside. The castle likely has ancient roots, although its present walls date from its 15th c. rebuilding by the Marquis of Villafranca.

⌂ Albergue de Vega de Valcarce Ⓞ Ⓓ Ⓚ Ⓦ Ⓢ 7/64, €5/-/-/-, Calle Pandelo 91A, www.vegadevalcarce.net/albergue.php, tel 606 792 791

⌂ Albergue do Brasil Ⓓ Ⓡ Ⓒ Ⓦ Ⓢ 1/18, €Donation, Carretera Antigua Nacional VI, www.facebook.com/Alberguedobrasil.Elroble, tel 634 242 642

⌂ Albergue El Paso Ⓟ Ⓓ Ⓡ Ⓚ Ⓦ Ⓢ Ⓩ 6/24, €12/13/26/-, Carretera Antigua Nacional VI, www.albergueelpaso.es, tel 628 104 309, camping possible

⌂ Albergue Santa María Magdalena Ⓞ Ⓟ Ⓓ Ⓡ Ⓒ Ⓦ Ⓢ 1/8 & 4/8, €10/-/30/45, Carretera Antigua Nacional VI 48A, www.facebook.com/alberguesantamagdalena, tel 987 543 230

With the A-6 and N-VI above, the departure from town is full of burbling river sounds and birdsong. Continue on the quiet lane, noting the Sarracín Castle on the ridge above. Soon the slender pillars of the acrobatic freeway bridges appear ahead, looming above **Ruitelán**, a pleasant town of bars and scattered stone homes.

2.3KM RUITELÁN (ELEV. 658M, POP. 31) ⓫ 🛏 (165.6KM)

The town's chapel sits before the entrance to a cave, now behind a vault door, where San Froilán of Lugo (833–905) lived prior to becoming Bishop of León. The saint is said to have converted a wild wolf into a beast of burden that carried the holy man's saddlebags on his journeys.

⌂ El Rincón de Pin Ⓞ Ⓟ Ⓓ Ⓡ Ⓒ Ⓦ Ⓢ 1/10 & 5/10, €10/-/38/55, Carretera Antigua Nacional VI, www.facebook.com/AlbergueElRincondePin, tel 638 704 339

⌂ Refugio Pequeño Potala Ⓞ Ⓟ Ⓓ Ⓡ Ⓑ Ⓒ Ⓦ Ⓢ 2/10 & 2/4, €20/20/40/- Carretera Antigua Nacional VI 20, tel 987 561 322

Continue out of town, calmed by the soothing sound of the Valcarce below. To the left you can now make out Las Herrerías on the opposite side of the river. The track carries you down to the valley floor, across the Lamas River on a 15th c. stone bridge with Roman foundations (**1.0km**), and into laidback **Las Herrerías** whose horse pastures and buildings face each other across the main street.

Las Herrerías is half town, half pasture

1.3KM LAS HERRERÍAS (ELEV. 668M, POP. 39) ⓘ 🏠 (164.3KM)

From Spanish, meaning 'The Ironworks,' the forges of Las Herrerías processed iron ore from the nearby mines of the Sierra del Caurel. The town still includes a smithy, as well as the 18th c. **Church of San Julián** and remains of two fortifications. Project Brigid functions as a welcoming tourist and art center (www.projectbrigid.org). From here pilgrims can also opt to ride up to O Cebreiro on horseback (call Victor at Al Paso, tel 638 041 823).

🔼 Albergue/Refugio Las Herrerías 🅳 🆁 🆆 🆂 3/17, €7/-/-/-, Calle Campo 1, www.facebook.com/alberguelove, tel 654 353 940

🔼 Albergue Casa Lixa 🅿 🅳 🆁 🅶 🆆 🆂 2/18 & 8/25, €15/40/48/62, Calle Camino de Santiago 35, www.casalixa.com, tel 987 134 915

After the bridge at the far end of town the track turns left and continues its long, steep ascent toward O Cebreiro and Alto do Poio beyond. Start steeply uphill on asphalt, then turn left at a pedestrian path (**1.9km**) that proceeds on gentle and fairly flat dirt along the hillside under oak trees. A tiny rivulet is headwater to the Valcarce; cross it, passing a rest area (**0.4km**) and head uphill very steeply on jagged rocks and dirt. The first hints of **La Faba** soon emerge. Enter this tiny, scattered, hip hamlet to enjoy its sparse albergues and restaurants.

3.6KM LA FABA (ELEV. 915M, POP. 28) ⓘ 🏠 (160.7KM)

The penultimate settlement before leaving the Province of León, La Faba holds the 17th–18th c. Church of San Andrés, and little else. Its isolation and youthful population give it a relaxed vibe.

🔼 Albergue de La Faba 🅳 🅺 🆆 🆂 3/66, €8/-/-/-, Calle de la Iglesia, http://lafaba.weebly.com, tel 630 836 865

STAGE 26
La Faba to Triacastela

Start	La Faba center
Finish	Triacastela, Church of Santiago
Distance	25.9km
Total ascent	980m
Total descent	1220m
Difficulty	Moderately hard
Duration	7¾hr
Percentage paved	17%
Albergues	La Laguna 2.5; O Cebreiro 4.7; Liñares 8.0; Hospital da Condesa 10.5; Alto do Poio 13.3; Fonfría 16.8; O Biduedo 19.3; Fillobal 22.2; Triacastela 25.9

A day of sweeping views during steady up- and downhill climbs, almost entirely on paths of dirt and gravel. The climax comes at touristy O Cebreiro, first town of Galicia and an introduction to the unique history of this northwest Spanish region. A steep climb to Alto do Poio is followed by sometimes-steep descents to Triacastela.

Soon after **La Faba** come literally out of the woods and into the midst of open fields among hilltops on what becomes a bright, open-air dirt path. Enjoy sweeping views of the mountainside pastures before **Laguna**. Enter the tiny and loosely gathered town amid cow pastures and barns.

2.5KM LA LAGUNA DE CASTILLA (ELEV. 1164M, POP. 26) ⑪ 🅿 (158.2KM)

The final village in the Province of León, La Laguna de Castilla feels very Galician. Look for low, oval houses known as *pallozas* with thatched roofs and also for the first *hórreos*, elevated grain-storage sheds.

🔺 Albergue La Escuela 🅿 🅳 🆁 🆆 🆂 5/29 & 2/4, €14/-/40/-, Calle Camino de Santiago 10, tel 987 684 786

Continue briefly uphill and then veer left onto a path of dirt, rocks and debris, heading first across and then up the mountainside, which is covered with pastures sloping down to the valley floor far below. Soon come to a landmark **monument**

A painted monument below O Cebreiro marks entry into green Galicia

(**1.1km**) that demarcates the entry into Galicia. Quickly afterward see the first of many distance monuments that count down the kilometers remaining to Santiago. Climbing toward the ridge, the pastures are replaced by treetops on the slopes now too steep for pastures, and views open up to the valley floor back toward distant Bierzo. Come to a stone wall on the right which marks the entry into

2.2KM O CEBREIRO (ELEV. 1297M, POP. 27) 🏠 ⊕ 🖼 (156.0KM)

Since the dawn of the Camino, O Cebreiro has been an important pilgrim stopover – a tradition that continues today, even as it serves dual purpose as a sort of living museum of Galician heritage. Atop the 1293m Cebreiro Pass it is not uncommon to find chilly conditions even in high summer. Even so, the site has been inhabited since pre-Roman times due to its strategic situation between Galicia and the fertile plains to the east. A battle here in 968 stopped Norman invaders from penetrating to León and in 1809 hundreds of British soldiers died here from the cold as they retreated before the French army. The town's pilgrim hospice may date to the ninth c. and a small community of monks served here until 1835. In the 14th c. a pilgrim trudged to mass at the town's **Church of Santa María Real** in a blinding snowstorm, arriving just as the priest was elevating the host. The priest stopped the service and upbraided the man for risking his life for a mere morsel of bread and taste of wine. At that moment, legend has it, the elements turned into flesh and blood. This miracle was confirmed by the Pope in 1487 and the remnants of the eucharist elements, now housed in a silver reliquary, are the object of veneration even today. At the entrance to the church is a bust of Father Elías Valiña Sampedro (1929–1989), the local parish priest, historian and Camino patron who researched the route's ancient roots and then marked the modern trail first with yellow paint and then with the concrete markers that can now be seen all through the Camino's course in Galicia. In O Cebreiro can also be found examples of Celtic *palloza* structures – a style of ancient home/barn with thatched roofs that functioned well in local conditions for thousands of years. Aspects of ancient life in Galicia can be seen at the **Ethnographic Complex of Cebreiro** (http://museos.xunta.gal/en/cebreiro). In town can also be found authentic *caldo gallego* soup as well as the beloved *queso de Cebreiro* raw cow's milk cheese dessert.

🏠 Albergue do Cebreiro Ⓞ Ⓓ Ⓦ Ⓢ 2/106, €8/-/-/-, Rúa Cebreiro, tel 660 396 809

🏠 Albergue Casa Campelo Ⓟ Ⓓ Ⓡ Ⓖ Ⓦ Ⓢ 1/10 & 4/8, €15/-/50/-, Rúa Principal, tel 679 678 458

Find the yellow arrows on the north side of town and take the path of brownish crushed rock above the quiet LU-633 highway. If weather permits, enjoy breathtaking vistas to the right while the path continues on mild undulations to

3.3KM LIÑARES (ELEV. 1226M, POP. 18) 🏔 ⊕ 🏔 (152.6KM)

The name Liñares derives from the fields of flax grown here to provide linens for the pilgrim hospital at O Cebreiro. The hamlet's Church of San Esteban dates prior to the 12th c.

🔺 Albergue Linar do Rei 🅿 🅳 🆁 🅶 🅺 🆆 🆂 🆉 5/20, €12/30/40/-, Liñares, **www.facebook.com/Alberguelinardorei**, tel 616 464 831, small store open 9am

The path continues alongside the north side of the road now, with hints ahead that it will make its way to the saddle between two mountains above. After a brief time, come to **Alto San Roque** (**0.8km**, elev. 1260m) and its windswept bronze pilgrim statue. Continue on the roadside path to

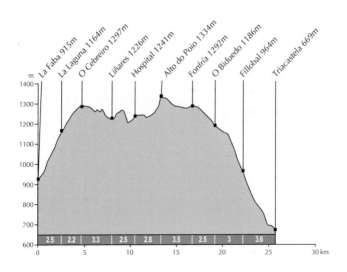

2.5KM HOSPITAL DA CONDESA (ELEV. 1241M, POP. 23) ▣ ▢ (150.1KM)

According to tradition, a large pilgrim hospital, founded by Countess Gatón, served pilgrims here as early as the ninth c. – which if true would make it home to one of the oldest pilgrim hospitals on the Camino.

⌂ Albergue Hospital da Condesa ◉ Ⓓ Ⓦ 2/18, €8/-/-/-, Lugar Hospital 11, tel 660 396 810

Afterward it is right back to the track alongside the highway guard rail, followed soon by an asphalt road. Once you reach a wide dirt path on the left you begin to see high ahead the white buildings of Alto do Poio, the high point of this last range of mountains. Turn onto a narrow asphalt road and reach **Padornelo** (**2.4km**, fountain). The cemetery was site of another pilgrim hospital and the medieval Church of Santa María Magdalena. Come off the asphalt drive and onto a gravel path, now climbing steeply up the ridge to

2.8KM ALTO DO POIO (ELEV. 1334M, POP. 0) ▣ ▢ (147.3KM)

Third highest point on the Camino Francés and the Camino's final mountainous summit, this height once held a hermitage and way station of the Hospitallers of San Juan de Jerusalem.

⌂ Albergue Bar El Puerto ◉ Ⓓ Ⓡ Ⓦ Ⓢ 1/18, €6/-/-/-, Lugar Poio 2, tel 982 367 172

Again a roadside path of brownish-red crushed rock leads the way until you branch off toward the back of

3.5KM FONFRÍA (ELEV. 1292M, POP. 34) ▣ ▢ (143.9KM)

Another pilgrim hospice is recorded here, dedicated to Santa Catalina, open for pilgrims until the 19th c.

⌂ A Reboleira Ⓟ Ⓓ Ⓡ Ⓖ Ⓒ Ⓦ Ⓢ 2/50 & 10/23, €12/35/45/60, Fonfría 15, http://albergueareboleira.blogspot.com/, tel 982 181 271

The concrete road soon becomes a gravel path and then crosses the LU-637 road before descending for a few moments rather steeply. Soon arrive in the tiny settlement of

2.5KM O BIDUEDO (ELEV. 1186M, POP. 31) 🍴🛏🔘 (141.4KM)

Some say the town's church is smallest of any on the Camino Francés. At the height of the medieval Camino, O Biduedo hosted a hospital of the San Juan de Jerusalem knights.

🛏 Casa Quiroga **P R G W S** 9/18, €-/-/40/60, Lugar Biduedo, tel 982 187 299

🛏 Casa Xato Turismo Rural **P R W S** 7/14, €-/25/30/36, Lugar Biduedo 4, tel 982 189 808

Make your way through the village on its concrete alleyway-cum-main-street and note the vast view opening up to the right, with Triacastela nestled into a small valley below and Sarria the first town on what looks to be a vast plain beyond. Now the downhill walk begins in earnest.

3.0KM FILLOBAL (ELEV. 964M, POP. 9) 🍴🛏 (138.4KM)

Originally founded by the order of Hospitallers de San Juan de Jerusalem.

🛏 Albergue Fillobal **O P D R G K W S** 2/18 & 2/4, €10/25/35/-, Fillobal 2, tel 666 826 414

Continue downhill steeply among pastures, arriving soon at a rest area and LU-633 crossing (**1.1km**). The path again descends steeply, this time on broken and jagged rock to **Pasantes** (**0.5km**, no services) where it becomes a shady and cool walk under mature oak trees, with high banks on either side. Come to the carefully and

Centuries-old bells hang from their tower before Triacastela (photo: Rod Hoekstra)

beautiful constructed ancient stone buildings of **Ramil** (**1.5km**) that feature family coats of arms on façades in this quiet and ancient hamlet. Less than a kilometer later are the first buildings of **Triacastela**, snuggled into its valley with the church tower at its heart.

3.6KM TRIACASTELA (ELEV. 669M, POP. 121) ⊞ ⊕ ◪ ☾ ⊙ ⊕ ⊕ (134.7KM)

In the ninth c., after the Reconquista, Count Gatón founded the town as part of his effort to repopulate the region. The three castles once guarding the narrow valley were most likely destroyed in the Norman invasions and not rebuilt. Triacastela is mentioned in royal chronicles as summer home to 13th c. Alfonso IX, King of León, as site of fundraising for the crusading conquests of Fernando III el Santo in 1248, and as the overnight for Prince Felipe II in 1554 as he journeyed to marry his aunt, Mary Tudor. Beginning here, medieval pilgrims would gather the calcium-rich stones of this area and haul them to Castañeda, near Arzúa, to be refined into building materials for the Cathedral of Santiago. The **Casa Pedreira** in the center of town is original site of another hospital of the Countess Gatón, and modern construction here found graves of medieval pilgrims. The apse of the **Church of Santiago** most likely is 600 years older than the rest of the 18th c. church, and its original 15th c. *sagrario* (sanctuary for the consecrated host) is kept at the Museo das Peregrinacións in Santiago. The 1528 **Casa do Concello** building was at various times a jail or a road house for travelers. Today Triacastela is almost completely absorbed in the flow of pilgrims and its sidewalk cafés and lodgings have a distinct and friendly pilgrim vibe.

🛖 Albergue Aitzenea **D R K W S** 4/38, €9/-/-/-, Praza de Vista Alegre 1, www.aitzenea.com, tel 982 548 076

🛖 Albergue Berce do Caminho **D R K W S** 6/28, €8/-/-/-, Calle Camilo José Cela 11, tel 982 548 127

🛖 Albergue Refugio del Oribio **O D R K W S** 2/27, €10/-/-/-, Avenida de Castilla 20, tel 982 548 085

🛖 Albergue Triacastela **O D W** 14/56, €8/-/-/-, Rúa do Peregrino, tel 982 548 087

🛖 Albergue A Horta de Abel **P D R K W S** 2/14 & 3/6, €10/35/40/-, Rúa do Peregrino 5, tel 608 080 556

🛖 Albergue Atrio **P D R Cf K W S** 3/20 & 2/4, €10/-/40/55, Rúa do Peregrino 1, www.xoan65.wixsite.com/albergueatrio, tel 982 548 488

🛖 Albergue Lemos **O P D R Cf K W S** 1/12 & 10/20, €9/40/45/60, Avenida de Castilla 24, www.pensionalberguelemos.com, tel 677 117 238

🛖 Complexo Xacobeo **P D R Cf K W S** 3/36 & 12/24, €11/37/45/57, Rúa Santiago 8, http://complexoxacobeo.com, tel 982 548 037

STAGE 27
Triacastela to Sarria

Start	Triacastela, Church of Santiago
Finish	Sarria, Sarria River bridge
Distance	17.3km (25.0km via Samos variant)
Total ascent	460m (795m with variant)
Total descent	715m (1050m with variant)
Difficulty	Moderate (moderate on variant)
Duration	4¾hr (7¼hr via Samos)
Percentage paved	70% (47% on variant)
Albergues	El Beso 2.0; Pintín 11.0; Aguiada 13.0; San Mamede 14.1; Sarria 17.3. (Variant: Samos 9.9; Aguiada 20.6, San Mamede 21.8, Sarria 25.0)

A short and pretty stage that climbs over a forested ridge before descending into the valley of the Sarria River on a mixture of quiet country roads, sunken paths and forest trails. The Samos variant is an easy and very beautiful option, albeit with some walking alongside a quiet highway. The green, serene and easy track follows the Oribio River and then the Sarria River for a mild and mostly downhill walk under trees to the tune of the joyfully babbling water. The highlight of this variant is the 1500-year-old Samos monastery, the oldest continually inhabited monastery in Spain and a very pleasant visit if the timing is right for a guided tour.

Follow the track west through **Triacastela** and turn right at the T-junction (**0.4km**) marked by twin monuments with distances to Sarria via Samos and via San Xil. A left turn here takes pilgrims onto the Samos variant (see below). Cross the main road and follow the quiet country road, ascending to reach a junction. Pass **El Beso albergue** (**2.0km**) and continue past the unusual square chapel to reach the tiny village of

2.3KM SAN BREIXO/A BALSA (ELEV. 729M, POP. 30) ▯▯ ▱ (132.4KM)

⌂ Albergue El Beso 🄳🅁🄲🅆🅂 1/16, €10/-/-/-, Carretera Da Balsa 3, http://elbeso.org, tel 633 550 558

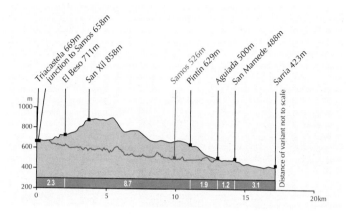

Continue on the gravel track, cross a stream and enter farmland, now walking steeply uphill, the most arduous portion of the day's walk. Pass a fountain (**0.8km**, Fonte dos Lameiros), emerge on a road and turn left to reach the village of **San Xil**. The tiny parish of San Xil de Carballo has a 16th c. chalice. Follow the road as it winds across a plateau, descending steeply through forest. Emerge beside the Santa María de Montán church and fountain (**2.7km**, Romanesque nave) and turn right on pavement

A footbridge of a single stone allows an easy crossing (photo: Mike Wells)

through **Montán**. Leave the village on a narrow lane between two stone barns, following the gravel track steeply downhill. After 45min come to **Furela** (**3.1km**, elev. 668m, chapel has an expressive primitive-style altarpiece). Pass through the village and descend on forested and roadside paths to the town of

8.7KM PINTÍN (ELEV. 629M, POP. 28) 🍴 🛏 (123.7KM)

The town is built on the pre-Roman Castro Astórica. Portions of its eighth c. church remain, although most disappeared in a 19th c. renovation. The baptismal font is of Visigothic, early medieval origin.

⛺ Casa Cines **P** **R** **G** **W** **S** 7/16, €-/-/35/60, Lugar de Pintín 5, http://casacines.com, tel 982 090 837

Leave the village and then descend on a sunken lane to cross the road between arms of a hairpin bend. On a roadside pathway now, pass a roundabout at the Calvor albergue and continue downhill, descending through

1.9KM AGUIADA–CALVOR (ELEV. 500M, POP. 42) 🍴 🛏 (121.8KM)

The town was once host to several pilgrim hospitals. The main route and the Samos variant merge here.

⛺ Albergue de Peregrinos de Calvor **O** **D** **W** 2/22, €8/-/-/-, Antiguas Escuelas, tel 660 396 812

Samos variant

Turn left at the T-junction in Triacastela and head toward the highway, passing a stone Santiago cross memorial on your left. After crossing the bridge, proceed along the quiet LU-633 highway with the exuberant river below and follow it until the yellow arrows lead you to the right (**3.5km**) just before **San Cristovo Real**, home of a 12th c. church with a 17th c. altarpiece and remnants of frescoes on the walls. Enter town and cross the river (here the Oribio) and continue on a soft dirt path under mature trees, with a high bank on the right side.

Return briefly to the highway at **Renche** (**1.9km**, church has statue of Santiago Peregrino) and cross the river (now the Sarria), returning to the lovely valley among pastures. Climb the other side into the small settlement of **Lastres** (**0.5km**) then continue along a delightful and shaded woodland path with the tree-bordered river below. Continue this reverie through another tiny collection of buildings given a name, in this case **Freituxe** (**1.2km**). Not long afterward go downhill on jagged stones and come up on the opposite side of the valley into tiny **San Martiño** (**1.2km**) with its 12th c. white stucco church.

Cross under the road in an oval tunnel (**0.5km**) and continue on the other side, rewarded in five minutes with a view over the Samos monastery. Trace your way down the long walk into the settlement and cross the bridge at the town hall.

9.9KM SAMOS (ELEV. 526M, POP. 151) ▥ ⊕ ⌷ Ⓒ ⊛ ⊕ (132.1KM)

The principle feature of tiny Samos is its sixth c. **Monasterio de San Xulián de Samos**, one of the most important and influential monasteries in the history of Spain. At its height this monastic community controlled over 100 churches, 200 towns and 300 other monasteries as well as many farms, schools, foundries and pharmacies. Its wealth was so well known that it was plundered several times by pirates. In the 10th c. it adopted the Benedictine rule and in the 12th c. joined the Cluniac monastic network. Visits by royalty were common, and the monastery has long maintained a hospital for Santiago pilgrims. The brilliant scientist and scholar, Fr Benito Jerónimo Feijóo y Montenegro (1676–1764), joined as a monk at age 14. Although devastating fires decimated the structures in 1536 and 1951, many treasures remain. The building's 18th c. main façade, with its integral bell towers, is considered a masterpiece of baroque design. Keystones on the archways of the 16th c. Cloister of the Nereidas depict scenes from the life of San Benito (St Benedict). The later Cloister of Feijóo is believed to be the largest in Spain. Pendentives below the church dome depict Benedictine Doctors of the Church. Nearby is a Mozarabic **Ermida do Ciprés chapel** from the 10th c. (Entry to the monastery interior by guided tours only, offered Mon–Sat hourly on the half-hour 9.30am–4.30pm except *siesta*, and Sun afternoons except *siesta*. Public masses in the church daily at 7.30pm; Sun noon and 7.30pm.)

🛏 Albergue de Monasterio de Samos Ⓞ Ⓓ Ⓢ 1/66, €Donation, Calle Monasterio de Samos 1, www.abadiadesamos.com, tel 982 546 046

🛏 Albergue Val de Samos Ⓓ Ⓡ Ⓚ Ⓦ Ⓢ 6/48, €12/-/-/-, Avenida Compostela 16, https://valdesamos.com, tel 982 546 163

🛏 Albergue Tras do Convento Ⓟ Ⓓ Ⓡ Ⓖ Ⓦ Ⓢ 1/6 & 2/4, €12/-/27/-, Rúa do Salvador 1, www.facebook.com/tras.convento.3, tel 631 557 095

Leave town first on sidewalk then on the road's shoulder, passing a monument and rest area on the left. Continue on the road as far as the **Pontenova** restaurant/bar (**2.7km**) and pick up a dirt path that follows the river, leaving the highway behind. Turn left at the **Church of Santa Baia de Pascais** (**1.0km**) onto a rough path leading downhill to the church, house and chicken coop that constitute the town of **Gorolfe** (**1.1km**).

Follow the path through small farms, cornfields and woods, crossing the Sarria River twice more before arriving in **Sivil** (**3.8km**) with its lone but friendly bar/café. (🛏 Pensión A Fonte das Bodas Ⓟ Ⓡ 4/8, €-/-/40/-, Lugar Sivil 1, www.facebook.com/afontedasbodaspension, tel 982 061 910) Continue to follow the quiet road through **Perros** (watching the arrows carefully) and past the Capela de

Nosa Señora do Camiño (**1.5km**). The junction with the official route is just ahead in **Aguiada** (see above for information), beyond the LU-P-560 roadway (**0.5km**).

10.7KM AGUIADA–CALVOR (ELEV. 500M, POP. 42) ⛰ 🏠 (121.8KM)

See above.

To continue on the main route, pass through Aguiada and come to the highway, where soon a dirt path opens on the right side. Continue to

1.2KM SAN MAMEDE (ELEV. 488M, POP. 11) ⛰ 🏠 (120.6KM)

Camino de Santiago pilgrims brought to Spain the veneration of San Mamede (St Mammes of Caesarea), a third c. orphan who was martyred by lions in Rome under Emperor Aurelian. Stately roadside oaks, pride of the village, give shade to pilgrims along the road.

Enjoy views over the rolling, tree-covered hills. At about the 117km marker, crest the hill and see the town of Sarria spread out ahead. Follow the arrows through the tall apartment homes, past the campground (**1.5km**), the pilgrim information center and other pilgrim-oriented shops until you arrive at the Sarria River bridge and riverside promenade of lower **Sarria**.

3.1KM SARRIA (ELEV. 423M, POP. 12,095) ⛰ ⊕ 🏠 🄲 ◉ ◉ ⊕ ⊕ ❶ (117.4KM)

Ample pre-Roman ruins testify to the ancient roots of this prominent Galician town. Destroyed by Muslim invaders in the eighth c., it was soon repopulated and quickly took its place as a major stopover for Santiago pilgrims. At its height the town hosted four pilgrim hospitals, the most famous of which was La Magdalena, founded by Italian monks, which is still maintained at **Monasterio de la Magdalena** as a pilgrim hostel. The old quarters of Sarria hug the hillside upon whose summit once stood a castle of the noble Lemos family, destroyed in an anti-nobility revolt of the 16th c. and finally dismantled in the 19th c. for its stones. A single, reconstructed castle tower, **Tower of the Battalion**, can be seen today. Homes of wealthy merchant families line the Camino route on the Calle Mayor, and family coats of arms are still visible above doorways. Adjacent to the modern **Church of Santa Mariña** is a much-loved mural of medieval pilgrims. The 14th c. **Church of San Salvador** includes a Romanesque apse and medieval metalwork on its doors.

⛰ Albergue A Pedra 🄿 🄳 🅁 🄶 🄺 🄲 🅆 🅂 3/15 & 5/10, €15/-/45/42, Calle Vigo de Sarria 19, https://albergueapedra.com, tel 652 517 199

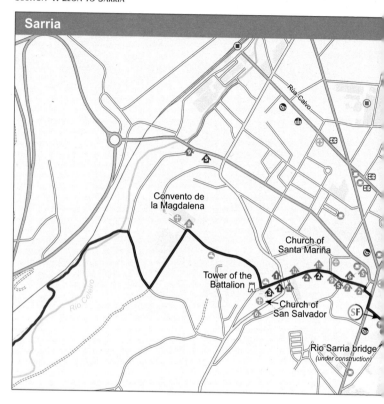

Sarria

🔼 Albergue Alma do Camiño D R G K W S 11/100, €12/-/-/-, Rúa de Calvo Sotelo 199, www.almadelcamino.com, tel 629 822 036, private rooms available for groups or families

🔼 Albergue Casa Peltre D R K W S 3/22, €10/-/-/-, Rúa Escalinata Maior 10, www.alberguecasapeltre.es, tel 606 226 067, private quadruple rooms available

🔼 Albergue Credencial O D R G W S 2/28, €10/-/-/-, Rúa do Peregrino 37, www.alberguecredencial.com, tel 982 876 455

🔼 Albergue de Peregrinos de Sarria O D W 1/40, €8/-/-/-, Rúa Maior 57, tel 660 396 813

🔼 Albergue Dos Oito Marabedís P D R K W S Z 7/22, €10/-/25/-, Rúa Conde de Lemos 23, tel 629 461 770

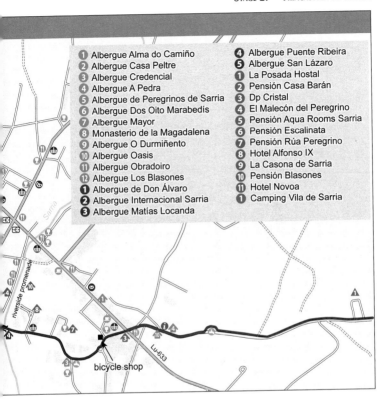

1. Albergue Alma do Camiño
2. Albergue Casa Peltre
3. Albergue Credencial
4. Albergue A Pedra
5. Albergue de Peregrinos de Sarria
6. Albergue Dos Oito Marabedís
7. Albergue Mayor
8. Monasterio de la Magadalena
9. Albergue O Durmiñento
10. Albergue Oasis
11. Albergue Obradoiro
12. Albergue Los Blasones
1. Albergue de Don Álvaro
2. Albergue Internacional Sarria
3. Albergue Matías Locanda

4. Albergue Puente Ribeira
5. Albergue San Lázaro
1. La Posada Hostal
2. Pensión Casa Barán
3. Dp Cristal
4. El Malecón del Peregrino
5. Pensión Aqua Rooms Sarria
6. Pensión Escalinata
7. Pensión Rúa Peregrino
8. Hotel Alfonso IX
9. La Casona de Sarria
10. Pensión Blasones
11. Hotel Novoa
1. Camping Vila de Sarria

bicycle shop

🔺 Albergue Los Blasones D R W S 4/25, €9/-/-/-, Rúa Maior 31, www.alberguelosblasones.com, tel 600 512 565, Pensión at Calle Ameneirizas 8

🔺 Albergue Mayor D R K W S 3/16, €10/-/-/-, Rúa Maior 64, www.alberguemayor.es, tel 671 659 998

🔺 Albergue Monasterio de la Magadalena D R G K W S 3/110, €10/-/-/-, Avenida la Merced 60, www.alberguesdelcamino.com/sarria/albergue-monasterio-de-la-magdalena, tel 982 533 568

🔺 Albergue O Durmiñento P D R G K W S Z 8/41, €10/20/-/-, Rúa Maior 44, tel 982 531 099

⬆ Albergue Oasis ◯ ▣ ▣ ▣ ▣ ▣ ▣ 4/27, €12/-/-/-, Camiño Santiago a Triacastela 12, www.albergueoasis.com, tel 605 948 644

⬆ Albergue Obradoiro ▣ ▣ ▣ ▣ ▣ ▣ 2/38, €10/-/-/-, Rúa Maior 49, www.facebook.com/albergueobradoiro, tel 982 532 442

⬆ Albergue de Don Álvaro ▣ ▣ ▣ ▣ ▣ ▣ ▣ 2/12 & 11/28, €15/35/40/60, Rúa Maior 10, http://alberguedonalvaro.com, 982 531 592

⬆ Albergue Internacional Sarria ▣ ▣ ▣ ▣ ▣ ▣ 4/43 & 3/5, €10/35/50/-, Rúa Maior 57, www.albergueinternacionalsarria.es, tel 982 535 109

⬆ Albergue Matías Locanda ◯ ▣ ▣ ▣ ▣ ▣ ▣ 1/32 & 7/14, €10/36/35/50, Rúa Maior 4, https://matiaslocanda.es, tel 982 886 112, wonderful Italian food in their restaurant too

⬆ Albergue Puente Ribeira ▣ ▣ ▣ ▣ ▣ ▣ 3/28 & 7/14, €12/30/45/-, Rúa do Peregrino 23, www.alberguepuenteribeira.com, tel 982 876 789

⬆ Albergue San Lázaro ▣ ▣ ▣ ▣ ▣ ▣ 3/28 & 6/12, €12/30/40/50, Rúa San Lázaro 7, http://alberguesanlazaro.com, tel 659 185 482

▲ Camping Vila de Sarria €5/-/-/-, Carretera de Pintín km1, www.campingviladesarria.com.es, tel 671 681 333, bungalows and tent camping possible

SECTION 5:
SARRIA TO SANTIAGO
DE COMPOSTELA

A cathedral tower stands high above shops in Santiago de Compostela

SECTION 5:
SARRIA TO SANTIAGO DE COMPOSTELA

Since the *compostela* is awarded only to walkers who've hiked at least the last 100km, Sarria is the point of entry for nearly half of all Camino Francés pilgrims. In high season crowds of local, short-distance walkers flock to the route starting here, their support vans freeing them to walk with just a sweater and a water bottle. Long-distance pilgrims may at first dismiss these 'van-a-grinos,' but their hearts will soften when they meet a Spanish young person who wants to practice her English or walk past a group of developmentally delayed young adults being carefully shepherded by a caregiver.

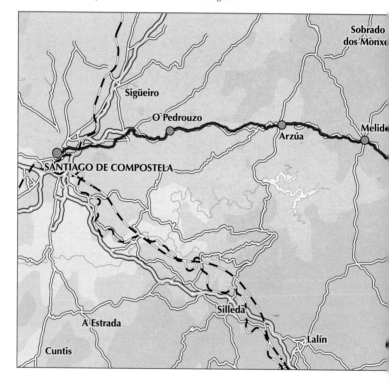

While long-distance pilgrims might yearn for a return to the peaceful stretches of the pre-Sarria Camino, there is still much here to explore and enjoy. At Portomarín an entire town was moved in 1962 from the riverbank up the hillside to make way for a new reservoir, its signature parish church reassembled there, stone by stone. Melide appears at first to be a humdrum modern enclave until you discover its compact and charming old city. While Arzúa and Palas de Rei feel cold and modern, it's just as well, since interest in local landmarks begins to fade as the destination draws near.

In Galicia look for freshly caught scallops, mussels and crabs, although it is Galician *pulpo* (octopus) that is famous around the world. The *tarta de Santiago* almond pastry is a tasty dessert, and see if your waiter will demonstrate a *queimada*, the traditional ritual in which *aguardiente* brandy is set aflame in an earthenware bowl to ward off evil spirits.

And, of course, Santiago is one of the world's enduring spiritual gems.

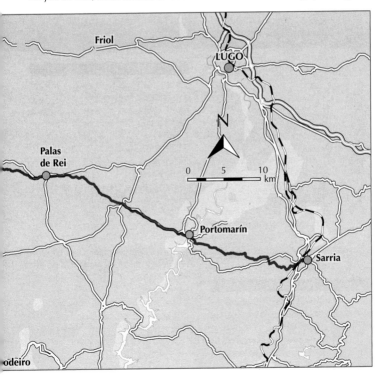

Walls of the castro of Castromaior were built over 2000 years ago by native Celts (Stage 29)

At its center is the tomb of St James the Greater, Apostle of Jesus Christ, his bones said to be contained in a silver reliquary in the cathedral crypt. A reverent or tearful pause at the shining container morphs into smiles and laughter as the smoking *botafumeiro* swings across the cathedral transepts at the close of the pilgrim mass above. But the most emotional moment may simply be found in a sense of relief and accomplishment at finally entering Plaza Obradoiro below the cathedral's lacy towers and hugging another sweaty and footsore pilgrim who feels the same overwhelming joy.

PLANNING

High-season pilgrims should either arrive early at their lodging to ensure a bed or book in advance. The abundance of cafés and bars along the way make it possible to keep a minimum of food and water in the backpack.

WHAT NOT TO MISS

The simple church at Barbadelo (Stage 28), all that remains of a once-grand monastery, offers a peek into Galician Romanesque architecture. The ancient Celtic *castro* (fortress) of Castromaior (Stage 29), missed by many destination-driven pilgrims, is mere steps from the Camino trail and is a pause for exploration. The fortress-church at Portomarín is unlike any other Camino edifice, while the *pulpo* (octopus) restaurants of Melide (Stage 30) beckon the hungry pilgrim to sample a simple but tasty Galician specialty. The riverside albergue at Ribadiso (Stage 30) features a cool afternoon splash in its clear river waters. Santiago de Compostela's cathedral, museums, minor churches, restaurants, outdoor market and street life deserve a full day of their own to experience and enjoy.

STAGE 28
Sarria to Portomarín

Start	Sarria, Sarria River bridge
Finish	Portomarín, Praza (Plaza) Conde Fenosa
Distance	23.0km
Total ascent	670m
Total descent	700m
Difficulty	Moderate, due to elevation changes
Duration	6½hr
Percentage paved	66%
Albergues	Vilei 4.0; Albergue Molino 7.8; Morgade 12.5; Ferreiros 13.9; A Pena 14.7; Mercadoiro 17.5; Portomarín 23.0

A mellow day among pastures, stone fences and cornfields, bookended by a tall staircase at the beginning and one at the end. The highlights are the medieval churches along the way, the lowlight is the heavy pilgrim traffic that in high summer begins here.

All three of **Sarria**'s historic churches are along the exit route out of town. After climbing the Escalinata Maior, note first the Church of Santa Mariña on the right, followed

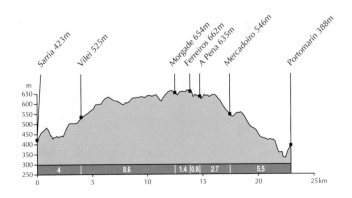

not long after by the Church of San Salvador (**0.6km**). Turn right and soon come to the Magdalena monastery (**0.4km**), which signals a left turn, down and out of town. Cross the stone Ponte de Aspera bridge (**0.5km**) and then a sturdy wooden bridge to come to the first climb of the day – up to the railroad tracks (**0.8km**) followed by the towns of **Vilei** and **Barbadelo**, separated by a few hundred meters.

4.0KM VILEI–BARBADELO (ELEV. 525M, POP. 187, REST AREA AND FOUNTAIN)
🔄 (113.5KM)

A monastery is documented as being here as early as 874, although its only remnant is the small but lovely 12th c. **Church of Santiago Barbadelo**, surrounded in Galician custom by a cemetery. Listed as a national monument in 1976, the church is known for its Romanesque capitals and portals. A volunteer proudly offers *sellos* to pilgrims.

🔺 Albergue de Barbadelo 🅞 🅓 🅦 1/18, €8/-/-/-, Antiguas Escuelas, tel 982 530 412

🔺 Albergue O Pombal 🅓 🅡 🅚 🅦 🅢 1/12, €10/-/-/-, Barbadelo 8, http://alberguoepombal.blogspot.com, tel 686 718 732

🔺 Albergue 108 to Santiago 🅞 🅟 🅓 🅡 🅦 🅢 5/14 & 4/10, €8/25/29/-, Vilei km 108, www.facebook.com/108tosantiago, tel 634 894 524

🔺 Albergue A Casa de Carmen 🅟 🅓 🅡 🅖 🅦 🅢 3/22 & 2/4, €12/-/40/-, Barbadelo 3, www.facebook.com/pg/albergueacasadecarmen, tel 606 156 705, tent space available

🔺 Casa Barbadelo 🅟 🅓 🅡 🅖 🅦 🅢 6/48 & 11/22, €12/40/50/60, Vilei-Barbadelo, www.barbadelo.com, tel 982 531 934

Continue on asphalt through **Rente** (**1.1km** 🔺 Casanova De Rente 🅟 🅡 🅖 🅢 6/12, €-/25/33/-, Lugar Rente 44, www.casanovaderente.com, tel 982 187 854) then cross a road at the **A Serra** café/bar/grocery (**1.1km**). Continue on a dirt path under ancient trees, passing a fountain (**0.7km**). Pass an albergue (**0.7km** 🔺 Albergue Molino de Marzán 🅓 🅡 🅒 🅦 🅢 1/15, €12/-/-/-, Molino de Marzán, www.molinomarzan.com, tel 679 438 077), cross the LU-633 highway (**0.6km**) which we have seen on and off since O Cebreiro, and continue on among small farms and the tiny villages of **A Pena** (**0.4km**), **Peruscallo** (**0.8km**, bakery), **Cortiñas** (**1.0km**), **Lavandeira** (**0.3km**), **O Casal** (**0.2km**) and **A Brea** (**1.0km**, café, rooms) before arriving at

8.6KM MORGADE (ELEV. 654M, POP. 3) 🍴 🔄 (104.9KM)

🔺 Albergue Casa Morgade 🅟 🅓 🅡 🅖 🅦 🅢 1/6 & 14/29, €10/35/46/51, Morgade 2, http://casamorgade.com, tel 982 531 250

Continue along on footpaths to

1.4KM FERREIROS (ELEV. 662M, POP. 116) 🔢 🏠 (103.5KM)

The name means 'blacksmith,' although links to a forge are now gone. The parish church of Santa María includes Romanesque elements.

🔺 Albergue de Ferreiros Ⓞ Ⓓ Ⓦ 1/22, €8/-/-/-, Ferreiros, tel 982 157 496

🔺 Albergue Casa Cruceiro de Ferreiros Ⓟ Ⓓ Ⓡ Ⓖ Ⓦ Ⓢ 2/24 & 2/6, €10/-/40/60, Ferreiros 2, **www.casacruceirodeferreiros.com**, tel 639 020 064

The 100km monument before A Pena receives abundant pilgrim attention

Afterward comes one of the signal moments of the walk – the marker just after Ferreiros that indicates just 100km remain before Santiago, though now somewhat inaccurate. Continue along to **A Pena** first along pathways, then on asphalt.

0.8KM A PENA (ELEV. 635M, POP. 24) ⚏ ⌂ (102.7KM)

🛏 Casa do Rego Ⓟ Ⓓ Ⓡ Ⓒ Ⓦ Ⓢ 1/6 & 2/4, €10/-/40/55, A Pena 4, http://casadorego.com, tel 982 167 812

Note the slate pasture walls, built over centuries. Follow the arrows briefly onto a pathway of flagstones, somewhat slippery when wet, and continue on small roads and pathways, passing the Pilgrim Hospitality Bar (**0.7km**) and arriving at tiny

2.7KM MERCADOIRO (ELEV. 546M, POP. 0) ⚏ ⌂ (100.0KM)

🛏 Albergue Mercadoiro Ⓟ Ⓓ Ⓡ Ⓒ Ⓦ Ⓢ 3/22 & 4/11, €12/-/50/60, Mercadoiro 2, http://mercadoiro.com, tel 982 545 359

One last ridge stands before Portomarín now. Pass a small store (**0.4km**) and come to Descanso café (**1.4km**), with views of Portomarín. Head off the asphalt to a nicely groomed trail of crushed rock and come to **Vilachá** (**1.4km**, vegetarian café, 🛏 Albergue Vilachá Ⓓ Ⓡ Ⓒ Ⓦ Ⓢ 1/10, €13/-/-/-, Vilachá 10, tel 696 004 491 🛏 Casa Banderas Ⓟ Ⓓ Ⓡ Ⓒ Ⓦ Ⓢ Ⓩ 1/8, €13/-/40/-, Lugar Vilachá 4D, www.casabanderas.com, tel 682 179 589), last stop before Portomarín. Back on asphalt now, arrive at a viewpoint where three **options** for entry to the town are

Rain protection keeps a pilgrim dry as she makes her way up a dirt path along a moss-covered stone wall before Portomarín (photo: Rod Hoekstra)

marked on monuments (**0.6km**) – 'Historico' and 'Secondario.' Avoid the 'Historico' option in wet weather. Turn left to go to a historic stone cross or a longer option. For the quickest entry go right on the Secondario which heads steeply downhill before turning briefly onto the highway and then spilling out to the bridge over the Miño River (**1.2km**), here dammed as the Belesar Reservoir. Cross the bridge (in low water look for the old bridge in the waters below), climb into town on the 46-step historic stairway and zigzag up to Rúa Fraga Iribarne, the town's main street, arriving at Plaza Conde Fenosa.

5.5KM PORTOMARÍN (ELEV. 388M, POP. 489) ▥ ⊕ ▧ Ⓒ ◉ ⊕ ⊕ ❶ (94.5KM)

In the 12th c. the Hospitallers of San Juan were given control of this strategic town along the Miño River with the goal of aiding and protecting pilgrims who crossed the important ancient river bridge. Destroyed by Muslim armies in 997 and again in the 12th c. during local upheavals, the bridge was rebuilt by engineer Pedro Peregrino in 1126. Location of a 19th c. highway favored Lugo, 30km north, and the town began a long decline. In the late 1950s, Franco's Belesar hydroelectric dam created a reservoir on the river and in 1962 the entire town was moved up the hill to its present location. The town's most historic buildings were meticulously dismantled then transported stone by stone and reassembled above. Now, when the water level is low, the original bridge and some building foundations can be seen at the lake bottom to the right of the existing bridge. After crossing the long, modern span, pilgrims enter town by climbing a stone stairway over an archway of the reconstructed medieval bridge and at the top of the stairs view the first of the chapels saved from the reservoir. Called the **Virgen de Las Nieves**, here according to tradition prayers against drowning were offered. The squarish Romanesque **Church of San Xoán** (containing the parish of San Nicolás) was built by the Hospitallers as both church and fortress, with an unusual coupling of a lovely rose window below crenellated walls and corner towers. The barrel-vaulted nave makes it the largest Romanesque church of this construction in Galicia. Noteworthy are the sculpted portals from the same period on the north, east and west sides. Adjacent is the 16th c. **Casa del Conde**, also rescued from the river bottom and now serving as the *ayuntamiento* (town hall). Also among rescued buildings is the nearby **Church of San Pedro**, which preserves a reconstructed 12th c. façade similar to that of San Isidoro in León. The town's famous local liquor is *aguardente*, shared especially in the Easter season.

🔼 Albergue Casa Cruz Ⓞ Ⓓ Ⓡ Ⓚ Ⓦ Ⓢ 1/16, €10/-/-/-, Rúa Benigno Quiroga 16, http://casacruzportomarin.com, tel 982 545 140

🔼 Albergue de Peregrinos de Portomarín Ⓞ Ⓓ Ⓦ 6/80, €8/-/-/-, Calle Fraga Iribarne, tel 660 396 816

🔼 Albergue Ferramenteiro Ⓓ Ⓡ Ⓖ Ⓚ Ⓦ Ⓢ 1/130, €12/-/-/-, Avenida de Chantada 3, www.albergueferramenteiro.com, tel 982 545 362, hotel in same building tel 982 545 361

🔼 Albergue Folgueira Ⓞ Ⓓ Ⓡ Ⓖ Ⓚ Ⓦ Ⓢ 1/32, €12/-/-/-, Avenida de Chantada 18, http://alberguefolgueira.com, tel 659 445 651

🔼 Albergue Novo Porto D R K W S 1/22, €12/-/-/-, Rúa Benigno Quiroga 12, http://alberguenovoporto.com, tel 610 436 736

🔼 Albergue Pasiño a Pasiño O D R K W S 6/30, €12/-/-/-, Rúa de Compostela 25, http://pasinapasin.es, tel 665 667 243

🔼 Albergue Villamartín D R K W S 2/22, €10/-/-/-, Rúa dos Peregrinos 11, https://alberguevillamartin.webnode.es, tel 982 545 054

🔼 A Fontana de Luxo O P D R G K B W S 1/10 & 2/4, €15/35/40/-, Fontedagra 2, http://afontanadeluxo.com, tel 645 649 496

🔼 Albergue Aqua Portomarín P D R K W S 1/10 & 3/6, €10/30/35/-, Rúa Barreiros 2, tel 608 921 372

🔼 Albergue Casa do Marabillas P D R K B W S 1/6 & 5/15, €12/30/35/50, Camiño do Monte 3, www.casadomarabillas.com, tel 982 189 086

🔼 Albergue Pons Minea O P D R G K W S 1/24 & 6/12, 12/40/50/65, Avenida de Sarria 11, http://ponsminea.es, tel 982 545 364

🔼 Albergue PortoSantiago O P D R G K W S 2/16 & 4/10, €10/25/35/40, Rúa da Diputación 8, http://albergueportosantiago.com, tel 618 826 515

🔼 Albergue Turístico Huellas O P D R G K W S 1/6 & 4/11, €12/30/40/55, Rúa do Peregrino 15, www.alberguehuellas.com, tel 681 398 278

🔼 Casona da Ponte O D R G K W S 5/47 & 4/9, €12/-/50/75, Camiño da Capela 10, http://casonadaponte.com, tel 686 112 877

🔼 El Caminante P D R G K W S 4/18 & 15/31, €12/30/45/55, Rúa Sánchez Carro 7, http://pensionelcaminante.com, tel 982 545 176

🔼 Ultreia O P D R G K W S 2/14 & 7/21, €12/-/35/45, Rúa Diputación 9, http://ultreiaportomarin.com, tel 982 545 067

STAGE 29
Portomarín to Palas de Rei

Start	Portomarín, Praza Conde Fenosa
Finish	Palas de Rei, Casa do Concello (town hall)
Distance	25.3km
Total ascent	720m
Total descent	560m
Difficulty	Easy
Duration	7¼hr
Percentage paved	58%
Albergues	Gonzar 8.1; Castromaior 9.3; Hospital da Cruz 11.9; Ventas de Narón 13.4; Ligonde 16.7; Airexe 17.6; Portos 19.6; Lestedo 20.3; Xunta albergue 24.2; Palas de Rei 25.3

Although the *Codex Calixtinus* laments that this stretch was the site of open-air brothels serving pilgrim traffic, the only negative today is the smell of an agricultural plant not long after Portomarín. But for a few diversions onto forest paths, today's walk takes a business-like trajectory on roadside pathways and through small dairy-centered villages.

Yellow arrows are sparse leaving **Portomarín**, so follow the Rúa Chantada toward Albergue Folgueira, cross the highway and head over the concrete bridge across the narrow lake inlet. Soon start a long but verdant uphill through the forest of oak, moss and lichen, taking you eventually to a path alongside the familiar LU-633 highway. Pass a now-derelict **brick factory** (**2.9km**). The path continues past an often-odiferous **fertilizer plant** (**1.4km**) then leaves the highway for a time to cross through an eerie forest of burned-out trees. It arrives back at the highway before coming to a rest area (**3.1km**) outside the hamlet of

8.1KM GONZAR (ELEV. 552M, POP. 49) 🚽 ⛲ (86.4KM)

🛏 Albergue de Peregrinos de Gonzar ⓞ Ⓓ Ⓦ 1/30, €8/-/-/-, Lugar Gonzar, tel 982 157 840

🛏 Albergue Casa García Ⓟ Ⓓ Ⓡ Ⓦ Ⓢ 2/26 & 4/8, €10/-/35/-, Gonzar 8, tel 982 157 842

🛏 Hostería de Gonzar Ⓟ Ⓓ Ⓡ Ⓒ Ⓦ Ⓢ 2/10 & 4/10, €12/39/48/68, Lugar de Gonzar 7, https://hosteriadegonzar.com, tel 982 514 878

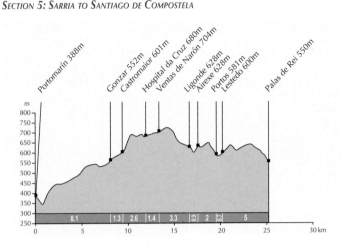

Pick up a path that leads to Albergue Ortiz and then a quiet side-road into

1.3KM CASTROMAIOR (ELEV. 601M, POP. 28) 🔟 ⬜ (85.1KM)

The town includes a small Romanesque church.

🔺 Albergue Ortiz 🅿 🅳 🆁 🅺 🆆 🆂 1/12 & 2/4, €10/25/45/60, Castromaior 2, http://albergueortiz.com, tel 982 099 416

Continue uphill on asphalt until a gravel path branches off on the right side and follow signs toward the **Castro de Castromaior** (1.1km).

Turn just a dozen meters off the route to see a fourth c. BC–AD first c. *castro*, one of the most important archeological sites in northwest Spain and source of the nearby town's name. The **fortress city** was originally encompassed within a 316m stone wall and includes remnants of the dwelling places, moats and defensive battlements of the resident Celts.

Continue toward the LU-633 again before following a side-road into **Hospital da Cruz**, once a hospice for pilgrims.

2.6KM HOSPITAL DA CRUZ (ELEV. 680M, POP. 13) 🔟 ⬜ (82.5KM)

🔺 Albergue de Hospital da Cruz 🅾 🅳 🆆 🆂 2/32, €8/-/-/-, Hospital da Cruz, no phone number

The arrows now send you over the N-540 highway bridge and onto a one-lane asphalt road separated from its shoulder by a narrow row of cobblestones. You'll follow this quiet road, the LU-RX, for much of the rest of the day. Climb the hill, with its tree farm of pines on the right, and continue as the route levels out into wide fields of corn and hay separated by fences of barbed wire. As the fields slowly become gardens, arrive at

1.4KM VENTAS DE NARÓN (ELEV. 704M, POP. 12) 🔼 (81.1KM)

In 820, Christian armies defeated the Muslims in an important battle here. The tiny 13th c. **Capella da Magdalena** is all that remains of a medieval pilgrim hospital.

🛏 Albergue Casa Molar **P D R G W S** 3/28 & 4/10, €10/-/30/40, Ventas de Narón 4, tel 696 794 507

🛏 Albergue O Cruceiro **P D R G W S** 2/22 & 2/4, €10/-/30/-, Ventas de Narón 6, http://albergueocruceiro.blogspot.com, tel 658 064 917

Continue on the cobblestone-curbed road. Through pine trees you can now see wide views of rolling hills to the right. Pines are gradually replaced by farms of imported eucalyptus as you come to a low summit. Continue downhill as views begin to open to the left. After Bar Trisquel (**2.1km**) watch in 700m on the left for the 1672 **Cruceiro de Lameiros** – not just another stone cross but considered by some the most beautifully sculpted of them all. The double-sided cross includes scenes of the Virgin and the Passion.

3.3KM LIGONDE (ELEV. 628M, POP. 5) 🍴 🔼 (FOUNTAIN) (77.8KM)

The first part of the village of Ligonde/Airexe, King Carlos V sojourned here in 1520.

🛏 Albergue Escuela de Ligonde **O D K W S** 1/20, €8/-/-/-, Ligonde 2, tel 679 816 061

🛏 La Fuente del Peregrino **D K S** 2/6, €Donation, Ligonde 4, https://lafuentedelperegrino.com, tel 687 550 527

Continue on the same road as buildings converge once again in

0.9KM AIREXE/EIREXE (ELEV. 628M, POP. 28) 🍴 🔼 (76.9KM)

This is the church neighborhood of its other half village, Ligonde. The 13th c. **Church of Santiago** is just off the pathway to the left. (*Eirexe* is Galician for church.)

🛏 Albergue de Eirexe-Ligonde **O D W S** 1/20, €8/-/-/-, Eirexe 17, tel 982 153 483

🛏 Pensión Eirexe **P D R W S** 1/4 & 5/8, €10/20/30/-, Eirexe de Ligonde 18, tel 982 153 475

Continue on the familiar cobblestone-lined path going uphill, and at the summit – with wide views of the surrounding countryside – cross a narrow one-lane road (**0.9km**), walking along cornfields on the opposite side and soon arriving at

2.0KM PORTOS (ELEV. 581M, POP. 4) ◪ (74.9KM)

⬆ A Paso de Formiga D R G C W S 1/10, €13/-/-/-, Portos 4, http://apasodeformiga.com, tel 618 984 605

Soon reach a turn-off for Vilar de Donas (**0.2km**) and the option to pay an out-and-back visit to its church.

Detour to Vilar de Donas church (no services, 2km off track)
Turn right among small farms and homes, then carefully cross the N-547 highway. Continue to the widely spaced homes of **Vilar de Donas**.

A gift by a noble family to the Order of Santiago, the small monastery on this site became the burial place for prominent members of the Order. As the monastery crumbled around it, the 13th c. chapel became the **parish church of Vilar de Donas**. While the portal, sepulchers, altar and baldachin are all of note, the 15th c. apse paintings, most likely of the 10 virgins, are the church's treasure. (The church is open in the summer with guided tours, but in the off season call Jesus on tel 982 153 833 or 669 544 009 for entry.)

After visiting the church, retrace your steps to return to the trail.

To continue on the main route, walk gently uphill out of town under trees and alongside pastures, arriving before long at

0.7KM LESTEDO (ELEV. 600M, POP. 102) ◪ (74.2KM)

The Romanesque Church of Santiago, set amid a cemetery, contains moldering 12th c. paintings. Fireworks and live music mark the Feast Day of Santiago each year here on July 25.

⬆ Rectoral de Lestedo O P R G S 5/10, €-/-/95/-, Lugar de Lestedo, https://rectoraldelestedo.com, tel 982 196 563

Continue on, past the Santiago parish church (**0.3km**) and past a café at Os Valos (**0.5km**), arriving soon at **A Brea** (**1.3km**, restaurant) alongside the N-547 highway. Follow the path beside the highway briefly before dropping on flagstones to a local park, passing the Xunta 'Os Chacotes' albergue (**1.8km**) and very soon arriving in the upper neighborhood of **Palas de Rei**.

5.0KM PALAS DE REI (ELEV. 550M, POP. 863) ⏹ ⊕ ▣ ⓒ ⊛ ⊕ ⊕ ❶ **(69.2KM)**

The plain buildings of the gray and unremarkable modern-day town bely its ancient history. According to tradition the palace of the eighth c. Visigothic King Witiza gave the town its name. It is called out in the *Codex Calixtinus* and other medieval pilgrim records. The **San Tirso church** includes a fairly plain 12th c. Romanesque portal, but otherwise is a modern construction. The most charming portion of town, a one-block-long pedestrian avenue adjacent to the town hall, holds restaurants and shops catering to pilgrims.

🔺 Albergue A Casiña di Marcello ⓄⓅⒹⓇⒼⒸⓌⓈⓏ 2/14, €13/-/-/, Aldea de Abaixo 13, tel 640 723 903

🔺 Albergue Buen Camino ⒹⓇⒼⓀⓌⓈ 7/42, €12/-/-/-, Rúa do Peregrino 3, www.alberguebuencamino.com, tel 982 380 233

🔺 Albergue Castro ⓄⒹⓇⓌⓈ 9/46, €10/-/-/-, Avenida Ourense 24, http://alberguecastro.com, tel 982 380 321

🔺 Albergue de Palas de Rei ⓄⒹⓌⓈ 5/60, €8/-/-/-, Avenida de Compostela 19, tel 660 396 820

🔺 Albergue de Peregrinos Os Chacotes (Xunta) ⓄⒹⓌ 3/112, €8/-/-/-, Rúa As Lagartas, tel 607 481 536

🔺 Albergue Mesón de Benito ⒹⓇⓌⓈ 6/100, €12/-/-/-, Rúa da Paz, http://alberguemesondebenito.com, tel 636 834 065

🔺 Albergue Outeiro ⒹⓇⒼⓀⓌⓈ 6/64, €12/-/-/-, Plaza de Galicia 25, www.albergueouteiro.com, tel 982 380 242

🔺 Albergue San Marcos ⓅⒹⓇⓀⓌⓈ 10/70 & 23/46, €12/-/50/60, Travesía da Igrexa, http://alberguesanmarcos.es, tel 982 380 711

🔺 Zendoira ⓅⒹⓇⒼⓀⓌⓈ 2/50 & 5/11, €12/30/40/60, Rúa Amado Losada 10, www.zendoira.com, tel 608 490 075

STAGE 30
Palas de Rei to Arzúa

Start	Palas de Rei, Casa do Concello
Finish	Arzúa, Church of Santiago de Arzúa
Distance	29.6km
Total ascent	730m
Total descent	890m
Difficulty	Moderate, due to length
Duration	8¼hr
Percentage paved	57%
Albergues	San Xulián 3.6; Ponte Campaña 4.6; Casanova 5.9; O Coto 8.8; O Leboreiro 9.5; Melide 15.1; Boente 20.9; Castañeda 23.2; Ribadiso da Baixo 26.4; Ribadiso da Carretera 27.2; Arzúa 29.6

Although today's route hugs the path of the N-547 highway, the Camino track touches it only near the settlements, allowing for pleasant walking on well-maintained trails among pastures, cornfields and gardens. The walk includes several ridges and valleys, but none too steep or too long. Highlight of the day is the old town of Melide, with its restaurants, bars and shops.

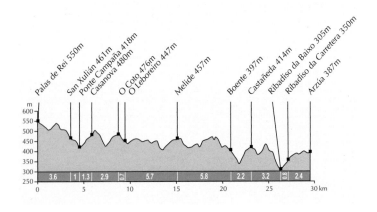

Head down and out of **Palas de Rei** on a flagstone drive, passing a fountain (**0.6km**) then turning right and generally following the highway on sidewalks and nearby pathways before veering to the left to follow a footpath (**1.8km**). The N-547 highway is now left behind for some time as you walk at first under eucalyptus trees and then under a **vacant highway overpass** (**0.8km**) on the way to

3.6KM SAN XULIÁN DO CAMIÑO (ELEV. 461M, POP. 35) 🛏 (65.6KM)

The church has a few 12th c. elements. The setting for Emilia Pardo Bazán's classic novel *The House of Ulloa* is the noble Ulloa family's palace, the remains of which, along with the family's 14th c. Pambre Castle, are a few miles from here.

🛌 Albergue O Abrigadoiro **D R C W S** 3/18, €13/-/-/-, San Xulián Do Camino 15, tel 982 374 117

Continue along a rough asphalt road between corn- and hayfields, then at Graña (no services) descend on a gravel and dirt path under trees. Through gaps in the embankments on either side you can make out fields and ridges rolling off into the distance. Come to a narrow, asphalt road with a bridge over the Pambre River, here a tiny brook, then cross the bridge into

1.0KM PONTE CAMPAÑA (ELEV. 418M, POP. 7) 🛏 (64.6KM)

🛌 Albergue Casa Domingo **D R C W S** 3/21, €12/-/-/-, Ponte Campaña-Mato, https://alberguecasadomingo.com, tel 982 163 226

Head uphill on the gravel path under trees until it turns to asphalt at the village of

1.3KM CASANOVA (ELEV. 480M, POP. 7) 🍽 🛏 (63.3KM)

🛌 Albergue de Mato-Casanova **O D W S** 2/20, €6/-/-/-, Camino de Santiago 61, tel 982 173 483, tents ok

Continue up the hill on the narrow road and then descend on a wide gravel track under stately oak trees. Arrive at the floor of the valley and cross another river on a concrete bridge (**1.5km**) before heading up the hill on the other side to **Campanilla** (**0.7km**, café/bar). Continue again up the hill and come to **O Coto**, visible first with its big green warehouse alongside the N-547.

2.9KM O COTO (ELEV. 476M, POP. 47) 🛏 ◉ (60.5KM)

🛌 Los Dos Alemanes **O P R C W S** 14/28, €-/30/40/-, O Coto-Melide, https://los-dos-alemanes.webnode.es, tel 630 910 803, swimming pool

Departing the highway again, follow the asphalt trail until you reach suburban

0.7KM O LEBOREIRO (ELEV. 447M, POP. 66) 🍴 🛏 (59.8KM)

Mentioned in the *Codex Calixtinus*, the town's 13th c. **Church of Santa María** (rebuilt in the 18th c.) has some interesting and slightly profane architectural elements. Legends say an image of the Virgin was found beneath the local fountain and would return to the fountain in spite of the villagers' efforts to bring it into the church. Finally, they carved the image into the tympanum over the portal and it remained there, although legends say she returns to the fountain on some evenings to comb her hair. Across from the bridge is **Casa de la Enfermería**, in the 12th c. a pilgrim hospital of the nearby Sobrado monastery.

🛏 Casa de los Somoza 🅿 🆁 🅶 🆂 13/20, €-/25/45/60, O Coto/Leboreiro, http://casadelossomoza.com, tel 981 597 372

Leave town on a lovely stone bridge (**0.2km**) over the tiny Seco River while the path nears the N-547, turns to gravel and plays cat and mouse with the N-547 and its roadside car dealerships and factories. Veer away from the highway again and cross the four-arched 13th c. **Furelos stone bridge** (**3.6km**).

The lovely **medieval bridge** across the Furelos River is said to have Roman origins. The old buildings on the opposite side include a one-time pilgrim hospital of the Hospitallers of San Juan. The neighborhood is now a cluster of inviting restaurants.

Follow the gravel-and-flagstone trail, rejoining the N-547 (**1.3km**). With sparse waymarks, turn right at the traffic circle (**0.3km**) to wind your way toward the old part of town, centered at San Pedro de Melide and Praza do Convento.

The medieval bridge at Furelos leads to a small grouping of historic buildings and restaurants

5.7KM MELIDE (ELEV. 457M, POP. 4393) 🏨 ⊕ 🏧 🄲 ◉ ✚ ⊕ ❶ (54.1KM)

Melide's busy modern pilgrim entry, despite being populated by its signature *pulperías* (octopus) restaurants, lacks much warmth or charm. To find some, cross toward the **Church of San Roque/San Pedro**, passing its Renaissance doors and the fine 14th c. **cruceiro** just after, and continue a few steps across the Ronda da Coruña, following rare waymarks to the **Praza do Convento**, center of the old town. Here Melide's medieval roots are evident. The 14th c. **San Pedro de Melide** is what remains of a large and wealthy Franciscan convent that includes tombs of the noble Ulloa family and a baroque altarpiece. Also in the plaza are the 17th c. **Oratorio of San Antonio** and the 17th c. **Casa Consistoriales**, a former palace which is now the town hall. Linger for a few minutes in the **Terre de Melide museum**, housed in a 16th c. building that once served as a pilgrim hospital and now exhibits a diverse display of local artifacts related to Galician ethnography.

🛏 Albergue Alfonso II 🄳 🄡 🄡 🄖 🄦 🄢 3/34, €12/-/-/-, Avenida Toques e Friol 52, http://alberguealfonsoelcasto.com, tel 608 604 850, camping space available

🛏 Albergue Arraigos 🄾 🄳 🄡 🄖 🄦 🄢 1/20, €12/-/-/-, Rúa Cantón San Roque 9, www.facebook.com/albergue.arraigos.58, tel 600 880 769

🛏 Albergue de Peregrinos de Melide 🄾 🄳 🄦 🄢 6/156, €8/-/-/-, Rúa San Antonio 25, tel 660 396 822

🛏 Albergue Ezequiel 🄾 🄳 🄡 🄦 3/18, €10/-/-/-, Rúa Sol 7, www.pulperiaezequiel.com/albergue-melide.html, tel 981 505 291

🛏 Albergue Melide 🄳 🄡 🄖 🄚 🄦 🄢 2/49, €12/-/-/-, Avenida Lugo 92, www.alberguemelide.com, tel 627 901 552, English, Spanish, Gallego, French and Arabic spoken

🛏 Albergue Montoto 🄿 🄳 🄡 🄖 🄚 🄦 🄢 🄩 4/48, €12/-/30/40, Rúa Codeseira 31, www.alberguemontoto.com, tel 646 941 887

🛏 Albergue O Apalpador 🄳 🄡 🄖 🄚 🄒 🄦 🄢 2/26, €12/-/-/-, Rúa San Antonio 23, www.albergueoapalpador.com, tel 981 506 266

🛏 Albergue O Cruceiro 🄳 🄡 🄦 🄢 3/72, €10/-/-/-, Ronda de A Coruña 2, http://albergueocruceiro.es, tel 616 764 896

🛏 Albergue San Antón 🄾 🄳 🄡 🄖 🄚 🄦 🄢 5/36, €12/-/-/-, Rúa San Antonio 6, http://alberguesananton.com, tel 981 506 427

🛏 Albergue Pensión Pereiro 🄾 🄿 🄳 🄡 🄖 🄚 🄦 🄢 4/45 & 4/8, €10/35/45/-, Rúa Progreso 43, www.alberguepereiro.com, tel 981 506 314

Now following ample yellow arrows, wind your way through the streets of the old town and head uphill to the site of Melide's *castro* and castle, now the Capela do Carme and cemetery (**0.4km**). A brisk downhill brings you to **Santa María de Melide** (**0.6km**, no services).

The 12th c. **Church of Santa María de Melide** has two Romanesque portals, including one that depicts Daniel and the lions. The interior frescoes feature images of the Trinity and the Apostles, with Santiago on the left.

Come to an option (**1.0km**) with two monuments pointing in opposite directions. The left option, through Penas, offers a quiet alternative, adding a little less than 400m to the distance. Either choose that way or go right, staying under a canopy of trees, descending to arrive at a **bridge of boulders** (**0.5km**), allowing you to cross the tiny Catasol River. Head immediately uphill toward the N-547, which you join very briefly before veering left into another delightfully shady wood. Descend again on a gravel path, this time steeply. Pass **Parabispo** (**1.5km**, café) and find a rest area (**1.1km**) at the valley floor under birch trees. Soon ascend to the back alleys of

5.8KM BOENTE (ELEV. 397M, POP. 132) 🍴 🛏 ◉ (48.3KM)

Cross the Boente River on a recently rebuilt Roman bridge.

🔼 Albergue El Alemán 🅳 🆁 🅶 🆆 🆂 4/40, €16/-/-/-, Boente de Arriba, www.alberguеelaleman.com, tel 981 501 984

🔼 Albergue Fuente Saleta 🅾 🅳 🆁 🅶 🆆 🆂 7/27, €13/-/-/-, Boente de Abaixo, www.facebook.com/albergue.fuentesaleta, tel 648 836 213

🔼 Albergue Boente 🅾 🅿 🅳 🆁 🅶 🅺 🆆 🆂 4/40 & 7/19, €14/35/50/65, Lugar Boente de Abaixo, https://albergueboente.com, tel 981 501 974, swimming pool

Carefully cross the N-547, passing the Santiago de Boente church and heading downhill under trees on a gravel track. Cross an **underpass** (**0.8km**) and head up the hill on a groomed, gravel trail. At the summit arrive at another option (**0.8km**) where the shorter (main) choice takes you straight ahead, while the green and quiet 1.7km option to the left bypasses Castañeda and adds about 500m to the day. Taking the main route, enter

2.2KM CASTAÑEDA (ELEV. 414M, POP. 157) 🛏 ◉ (46.0KM)

The *Codex Calixtinus* records that pilgrims brought white stones here from Triacastela to be fired in ovens for lime to be used in building the Santiago cathedral.

🔼 Albergue Santiago 🅿 🅳 🆁 🆆 🆂 🆉 1/4, €11/-/35/-, Lugar A Fraga Alta, tel 981 501 711

Continue downhill, walking through a very pleasant valley of fields, homes and orchards. Cross the N-547 on a pleasant **cobblestone bridge** (**2.2km**) with a spindle railing and pick up the gravel path on the other side, going downhill and crossing the Iso River.

Pilgrims relax in the cool waters of the Iso at the Ribadiso da Baixo bridge

3.2KM RIBADISO DA BAIXO (ELEV. 305M, POP. 61) ⬆ (42.9KM)

A bridge over the Iso is recorded here as early as 572, although the current bridge is believed to date to the 13th c. The former San Antón hospital just across the span served pilgrims in the Middle Ages and is now one of the favorite albergues on the Camino Francés. Bathers can be seen in the summertime enjoying a refreshing dip in the river.

🔺 Albergue **Ribadiso da Baixo** 🅞 🅓 🆆 🆂 3/70, €8/-/-/-, Ribadiso, tel 660 396 823, camping possible, river wading

🔺 Albergue Los Caminantes 🅟 🅓 🆁 🅚 🆆 🆂 4/56 & 2/4, €10/-/35/-, Ribadiso da Baixo, https://ribadiso.albergueloscaminantes.com/, 647 020 600, camping possible

Ascend on asphalt, turning left at the top of the hill for the highway underpass (**0.6km**) and coming to

0.8KM RIBADISO DA CARRETERA (ELEV. 350M) 🍴 ⬆ ◉ (42.1KM)

🔺 Albergue Milpes 🅓 🆁 🅖 🆆 🆂 3/24, €12/-/-/-, Ribadiso 7, https://alberguemilpes.com, tel 981 500 425

Continue uphill on sidewalks along the N-547, as **Arzúa**, just scattered buildings along the highway here, begins to form. Continue to the town center, clustered around the Capilla da Madalena.

Hórreo passed on the route toward Arzúa
(photo: Jonathan Williams)

2.4KM ARZÚA (ELEV. 387M, POP. 2728) 🏨 ⊕ 🛏 🄴 🌐 ⊕ ⊕ 🛈 (39.6KM)

The freight trucks that rumble and wheeze up the main street are a living testament to the village's long history as a crossroads – the Roman Via Traiana here crossed regional roads heading to Cantabria. Called 'Villanova' in the *Codex Calixtinus*, the name Arzúa may be linked to later resettlement. Two hospitals served pilgrims at the height of medieval pilgrimage. Although the **Church of Santiago** was built in the 20th c. over older foundations, it contains an 18th c. retablo. Some 20km north of town is the spectacular and haunting 12th c. **Monastery of Sobrado** – one-time capital of the Cistercian presence in Galicia – which retains a grand and empty baroque church of cathedral proportions. It is a final way-stop on the Camino del Norte, which in Arzúa joins the Francés.

🛏 Albergue A Conda 🄳 🅁 🄺 🅆 🅂 1/16, €10/-/-/-, Rúa da Calexa 92, http://pensionvilarino.com, tel 981 500 068, also Hostal Vilariño Moscoso at the same address with private rooms

238

🔺 Albergue Casa del Peregrino 🇩 🇷 🇰 🇼 🇸 1/14, €10/-/-/-, Rúa Cima do Lugar 7, tel 686 708 704

🔺 Albergue de Peregrinos de Arzúa 🇴 🇩 🇼 🇸 1/56, €8/-/-/-, Rúa Cima de Lugar 6, tel 981 500 455

🔺 Albergue Don Quijote 🇴 🇩 🇷 🇼 🇸 4/48, €10/-/-/-, Rúa Lugo 130, http://alberguedonquijote.com, tel 981 500 139

🔺 Albergue Los Caminantes II 🇩 🇷 🇰 🇼 🇸 1/28, €10/-/-/-, Rúa de Santiago 14, www.albergueloscaminantes.com, tel 647 020 600

🔺 Albergue Los Tres Abetos 🇴 🇩 🇷 🇬 🇰 🇼 🇸 5/42, €15/-/-/-, Rúa Lugo 147, www.tres-abetos.com, tel 649 771 142

🔺 Albergue O Botafumeiro 🇵 🇩 🇷 🇰 🇼 🇸 🇿 4/25, €12/-/-/40, Rúa do Carme 18, https://albergue-o-botafumeiro.negocio.site, tel 698 139 402, triple private room available

🔺 Albergue O Santo 🇵 🇩 🇷 🇬 🇰 🇼 🇸 🇿 1/22, €12/36/-/-, Rúa Xosé Neira Vilas 4, www.albergueosanto.com, tel 981 500 957

🔺 Albergue Santiago Apóstol 🇴 🇩 🇷 🇬 🇰 🇼 🇸 3/72, €12/-/-/-, Rúa de Lugo 107, www.alberguesantiagoapostol.com, tel 981 508 132

🔺 Albergue Ultreia 🇴 🇩 🇷 🇬 🇰 🇼 🇸 3/39, €12/-/-/-, Rúa Lugo 126, www.albergueultreia.com, tel 981 500 471

🔺 Albergue Vía Láctea 🇴 🇩 🇷 🇰 🇼 🇸 9/125, €12/-/-/-, Rúa Xosé Neira Vilas 26, www.alberguevialactea.com, tel 981 500 581

🔺 Cruce de Camiños – Arzúa 🇴 🇩 🇷 🇬 🇼 🇸 5/56, €14/-/-/-, Rúa Cima do Lugar 28, www.crucedecaminosarzua.com, tel 604 051 353, Breogan is your host

🔺 De Camino Albergue 🇴 🇩 🇷 🇬 🇼 🇸 4/46, €12/-/-/-, Rúa Lugo 118, http://decaminoalbergue.com, tel 981 500 415

🔺 O Albergue de Selmo 🇩 🇷 🇬 🇰 🇼 🇸 1/46, €10/-/-/-, Rúa Lugo 133, http://oalberguedeselmo.com, tel 981 939 018

🔺 Albergue Arzúa 🇵 🇩 🇷 🇬 🇼 🇸 2/15 & 4/8, €10/-/30/-, Rúa Rosalía de Castro 2, tel 608 380 011

🔺 Albergue Cima do Lugar 🇵 🇩 🇷 🇬 🇼 🇸 1/14 & 8/16, €12/40/50/-, Rúa Cima do Lugar 22, www.facebook.com/cimadolugar, tel 661 633 669

🔺 Albergue San Francisco 🇵 🇩 🇷 🇬 🇼 🇸 2/28 & 2/4, €14/30/45/-, Rúa do Carme 7, https://alberguesanfrancisco.com, tel 881 979 304

🔺 Camping Teiraboa Base Camp €consult website, Teiraboa, www.teiraboabasecamp.com, tel 981 193 102, tent camping, bungalows and pods available

STAGE 31

Arzúa to O Pedrouzo

Start	Arzúa, Church of Santiago de Arzúa
Finish	O Pedrouzo, town hall
Distance	19.7km
Total ascent	520m
Total descent	620m
Difficulty	Easy
Duration	5½hr
Percentage paved	32%
Albergues	A Calle de Ferreiros 8.0; Salceda 11.4; A Brea 13.8; Santa Irene 16.2; A Rúa 18.1; O Pedrouzo 19.7

An easy day of minor climbs and descents through countryside and villages with the ever-present N-547 highway as companion and sometime daunting obstacle. Small dairy farms and tracts of eucalyptus trees cover the low, rolling hills which are dotted with ample rest stops, although there are few villages of interest. Fountains and cafés make for an easy walking day with little preparation necessary. Strong walkers sometimes carry on to Santiago or stop just short at Lavacolla or Monte do Gozo.

In 1863 Rosendo Salvado, a missionary monk, sent **eucalyptus** seeds to his family in Pontevedra, marveling at their ability to grow rapidly. In the early 20th c. the Spanish government began encouraging growth of eucalyptus in order to reforest the countryside that had been cleared by centuries of logging. While the wood was found to be useful for fuel, charcoal, paper and fragrant eucalyptus oil (used by many for coughs, hence the Spanish name *arbre de la salut* – health tree) it is difficult to use in construction except as fiberboard. The plantation monoculture is widely criticized in Spain as being useless for wildlife habitat and thirsty for sometimes-scarce water resources.

In **Arzúa** find what seems to be an alleyway one block south of the Santiago church. Turn right and head downhill on flagstones passing a fountain (**0.5km**), coming to the tiny Vello River at the valley floor and stepping onto a path under trees at the village of **As Barrosas** (**0.4km**). Make your way up the gentle slope and come out to a wide path under tall vine-covered trees. After repeating in a similar valley come to the village of **Pregontoño** (**1.4km**) with its tiny café. Carefully cross the N-547 highway (**0.2km**) and

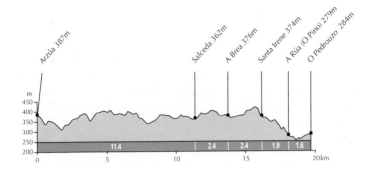

walk among farms, fields and woods to the tiny communities of **A Peroxa** (**1.0km**, restaurant) and then **Tabernavella** (**1.8km**, café ♠ Albergue Taverna Vella 🅿 🄳 🅁 🄶 🄲 🅆 🅂 🅉 1/10, €15/-/70/-, Lugar de Taberna Vella, https://taberna-vella.business.site, tel 687 543 810, tents ok). Just after this tiny settlement, cross by bridge over the wide and unfinished Santiago–Lugo freeway (**0.2km**), pass another tiny village, **A Calzada** (**0.9km**, café), and then come to the back alleys of

8.0KM A CALLE DE FERREIROS (ELEV. 340M, POP 86) 🄷 🄲 (1.9KM)

♠ Albergue A Ponte de Ferreiros 🄾 🄳 🅁 🅆 🅂 2/30, €13/-/-/-, A Ponte de Ferreiros 1, http://albergueaponte.hol.es, tel 665 641 877 (280m from path)

After **Ferreiros** (**0.4km**), **Boavista** (**1.0km**, restaurant) and **Brea** (**1.3km**, café), come to the N-547 at **Salceda**, a roadside town spread out along the highway.

3.4KM SALCEDA (ELEV. 362M, POP. 165) 🄷 🄲 ◉ ⊕ (28.3KM)

♠ El Albergue de Boni 🄳 🅁 🅆 🅂 7/20, €12/-/-/-, Lugar de Salceda 22, tel 618 965 907, pilgrim discounts available

♠ Albergue Alborada 🅿 🄳 🅁 🄶 🄺 🅆 🅂 1/10 & 4/8, €12/-/50/-, Lugar de Salceda, www.facebook.com/pensionalborada.albergue, tel 981 502 956

♠ Albergue Turístico Salceda 🅿 🄳 🅁 🄶 🄲 🅆 🅂 1/8 & 15/30, €13/50/50/70, Lugar Salceda 58, www.albergueturisticosalceda.com, tel 981 502 767, massage and jacuzzi available

Briefly leave the highway and follow a wide gravel path through a forest of oak and eucalyptus before returning to the N-547 and carefully crossing (**0.9km**) to the other side (note the flashing lights activated by the push button). Remain on paths on

Pilgrims fill a roadside path outside A Brea

the south side of the road for a short time before crossing (**1.1km**) the N-547 once again, this time toward another village of **A Brea**.

2.4KM A BREA (ELEV. 376M) 🍴 🛏 (25.9KM)

🛏 Albergue Andaina 🅾 🅳 🆆 🆂 -/15, €12/-/-/-, O Empalme de Santa Irene 11, tel 609 739 404

Afterward, cross to the other side of the N-547 (**1.0km**), enjoying a safe gravel track next to the road before crossing back, once again, at a dangerous curve in **O Empalme** (**1.7km**, two café/bars). Soon come to an option (**0.8km**), with one arrow suggesting a detour under the highway toward adjacent Santa Irene, and another pointing straight ahead for the main route. Both lead to Santa Irene.

2.4KM SANTA IRENE (ELEV. 374M, POP. 9) 🛏 ◉ (23.4KM)

Near the 17th c. **Chapel of Santa Irene** is a fountain with a 1692 image of the saint. Just after Santa Irene the conical summit of Pico Sacro can be seen 20km to the southwest. Here, according to ancient legend (or bedtime stories), the body of Santiago was planned to have been entombed, until it was discovered that dragons lived at the mountaintop. Today a small chapel to San Sebastián guards the Pico Sacro summit.

🛏 Albergue de Peregrinos de Santa Irene 🅾 🅳 🆆 🆂 2/32, €8/-/-/-, Santa Irene, tel 660 396 825

🛏 Albergue Santa Irene 🅳 🆁 🆆 🆂 2/15, €13/-/-/-, Rúa Santa Irene, tel 981 511 000, on the other side of the highway

242

Return to and continue along the north side of the highway, passing a café and albergue, departing briefly through woods before returning to cross the N-547 (**1.2km**) once again before arriving at

1.9KM A RÚA (O PINO) (ELEV. 279M, POP. 207) ⅰⅰ ▣ ◉ (21.6KM)

🔺 Albergue Espíritu Xacobeo ⓞ ℗ ⅅ ℝ ℭ ℍ Ⓦ ⓢ 2/32 & 3/12, €12/-/50/-, A Rúa 49-50, www.espirituxacobeo.com, tel 620 635 284, private double, quadruple and family rooms available

▲ Camping Peregrino O Castiñeiro ⅅ ℝ Ⓦ ⓢ 28/112, €10/-/-/-, A Rúa 28, www.campingperegrino.es, tel 981 197 125, tent sites & bungalows available

At the highway intersection after town (**0.7km**) there is another option: either cross the highway again to bypass the busy and somewhat frenetic O Pedrouzo, or continue along the highway to the center of town with its many shops, restaurants, cafés and lodging options.

1.6KM O PEDROUZO (ELEV. 284M, POP. 618) ⅰⅰ ⊕ ▣ ℭ ◉ ⊕ ⓘ (19.9KM)

The O Pedrouzo urban center sits within the Parish of Arca and is headquarters of the Municipality of O Pino. Services clustered along the highway center on a plain and modern town hall.

🔺 Albergue Cruceiro de Pedrouzo ⅅ ℝ ℍ Ⓦ ⓢ 5/94, €10/-/-/-, Avenida Igrexa 7, www.alberguecruceirodepedrouzo.com, tel 981 511 371

🔺 Albergue de Peregrinos de Arca - O Pino ⓞ ⅅ Ⓦ ⓢ 4/150, €8/-/-/-, Pedrouzo, tel 660 396 826

🔺 Albergue Edreira ℗ ⅅ ℝ Ⓦ ⓢ ℤ 4/40, €12/35/30/-, Rúa da Fonte 19, www.albergue-edreira.com, tel 981 511 365

🔺 Albergue Mirador de Pedrouzo ⅅ ℝ ℭ Ⓦ ⓢ 7/57, €13/-/-/-, Avenida de Lugo, www.alberguemiradordepedrouzo.com, tel 686 871 215

🔺 Albergue O Trisquel ⅅ ℝ ℭ ℍ Ⓦ ⓢ 6/78, €12/-/-/-, Rúa Picón 1, https://albergueotrisquel.es, tel 616 644 740

🔺 Albergue Otero ⅅ ℝ Ⓦ ⓢ 2/34, €12/-/-/-, Rúa Forcarey 2, www.albergueotero.com, tel 671 663 374

🔺 Albergue Porta de Santiago ⅅ Ⓦ ⓢ 2/54, €10/-/-/-, Avenida de Lugo 11, www.portadesantiago.com, tel 607 835 354

🔺 Albergue REM ⅅ ℝ Ⓦ ⓢ 1/40, €10/-/-/-, Avenida Igrexa 7, tel 981 510 407

🔺 Albergue O Burgo ℗ ⅅ ℝ ℭ ℍ Ⓦ ⓢ 1/14 & 5/11, €13/35/40/60, Avenida de Lugo 47, www.albergueoburgo.es, tel 981 511 406

STAGE 32

O Pedrouzo to Santiago de Compostela

Start	O Pedrouzo, town hall
Finish	Santiago de Compostela, Praza do Obradoiro (Cathedral of Santiago)
Distance	20.0km
Total ascent	500m
Total descent	525m
Difficulty	Moderate, due to two tall hills
Duration	5½hr
Percentage paved	68%
Albergues	Amenal 3.2; Lavacolla 9.4; Monte do Gozo 15.0; Santiago de Compostela 19.9

A surprisingly green and peaceful entry into urban Santiago – at least until the final 5km which wind along seemingly never-ending city streets. Two tall hills make the day a moderate workout. The view from Monte do Gozo and the final entry into Praza do Obradoiro can be a deeply emotional climax to a week, a month or season of walking toward this historic pilgrimage destination. The Cathedral of Santiago does not allow backpacks inside so if you plan to attend the noon pilgrim mass leave your rucksack at your accommodation or at the pilgrim office beforehand.

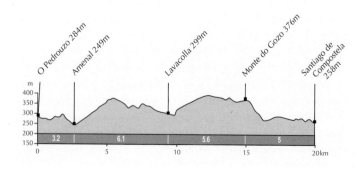

From **O Pedrouzo**, either turn uphill at the town hall (*concello*) or take an easier route by continuing along the N-547 sidewalk out of town toward San Antón (**1.0km**, where the bypass joins the track) with its shops along the highway. Continue to

3.2KM AMENAL (ELEV. 249M, POP. 85) 🅿 ◉ **(16.7KM)**

🛏 Hotel Amenal 🅾 🅿 🆁 🅶 🆆 🆂 13/26, €-/50/52/70, Amenal 12, www.hotelamenal.com, tel 981 540 431

Follow a wooded and dark path uphill, sometimes steeply, increasingly hearing sounds of the nearby Santiago airport. At the summit (**1.9km**) turn right to skirt along the northern border of the airport's runway on a path wedged between the runway and the A-54 freeway. After rounding the runway, capped by a stone **Santiago monument** (**1.2km**), turn right and come very soon to the welcome bar at **San Paio** (**0.9km**, 19th c. church. Site of former monastery. 🛏 Last 12K Guest House 🅿 🆁 🅶 6/12, €-/-/60/75, San Paio 22A, tel 619 904 743). Immediately climb a very steep hill above the tiny village before heading right back down and crossing under the SC-21 airport feeder roadway (**0.5km**). Walk along pathways then on a paved road to the settlement of

6.1KM LAVACOLLA/SABUGUEIRA (ELEV. 299M, POP. 171) 🔢 ⊕ 🅿 ◉ **(10.2KM)**

By tradition the last overnight before Santiago, in Lavacolla pilgrims would purify themselves in the Sionlla River before entering the holy city. Called Lavamentula in the *Codex Calixtinus*, the name (lit. in Latin: 'wash penis') and its successor, Lavacolla (in medieval Romance languages lit. 'wash testicles') suggests a washing ritual of some kind, perhaps one from which women were gratefully excused. Here also merchants advertised pilgrim lodgings and services in Santiago. Today the washing stream is merely a trickle and the town itself is overshadowed by the nearby Santiago airport. The **Church of Benaval** is located on a small hill at its center and the *cruceiro* before it remembers a small miracle – in 1319, Juan Pourón, leader of a peasant revolt, was to be hung. He prayed to the Virgin to be saved from the pain and he died instantly just before his execution.

🛏 Albergue Lavacolla 🅾 🅿 🅳 🆁 🅺 🆆 🆂 🆉 1/40, €13/15/30/-, Lavacolla 35, www.alberguelavacolla.com, tel 654 134 105, pick up from airport possible

Cross the N-634 after the church and find yourself going downhill on asphalt, making a hard right onto a narrow dirt path before crossing on a small wooden bridge the remnant of Lavacolla's Sionlla River (**0.3km**). Climb steeply on asphalt and come to an apparent summit just before the farming town of **Villamaior** (**1.1km**) where you wind your way among barnyards and homes. A long asphalt road leads gradually toward a TV station (**1.6km**) and lumberyard before turning left, passing the **San Marcos campground** (**600m**, café, ⛺ Camping San Marcos tel 662 219 168), then going right past another TV station. At the road's far end is the village of **San Marcos** (**1.2km**, cafés). Follow the

Pilgrim statues at Monte do Gozo point onward to Santiago, just across the valley ahead

arrows toward the left, through the long, narrow town, and then walk uphill to the distinctive sculpture marking the summit of **Monte do Gozo** (0.7km). A careful look through utility towers gives the first view of the Cathedral of Santiago de Compostela.

5.6KM MONTE SAN MARCOS/MONTE DO GOZO (ELEV. 376M, POP. 819)
🎫 🏠 (5.0KM)

Literally 'Mount Joy,' centuries of pilgrims have shared a special celebration atop this small mountain. At the summit stands a curved steel and glass sculpture by Brazilian artist Yolanda D'Augsburg Rodrigues that commemorates the visits of Pope John Paul II in the Holy Year of 1982 and St Francis of Assisi in the 13th c. A more picturesque view is available in the south reaches of the park where two bronze pilgrims eternally point toward the cathedral. Just beyond the brow of the hill is an enormous albergue complex with space for 500 pilgrims.

🔺 Albergue Monte do Gozo 🅞 🅓 🅚 🅦 🆂 3/500, €6/-/-/-, Rúa do Gozo 18, tel 981 558 942

🔺 Albergue del Centro Europeo 🅟 🅓 🆁 🅦 🆂 3/68 & 26/52, €10/22/34/-, Rúa das Estrelas 80, www.facebook.com/polskiealbergue, tel 981 597 222

🔺 Monte do Gozo Albergue 🅞 🅟 🅓 🆁 🅖 🅦 🆂 121/676 & 121/242, €15/55/60/-, Rúa do Gozo 18, www.montedogozo.com, tel 881 255 386

After your visit, follow the roadside gravel path steeply downhill with the enormous, barracks-like albergue to the left. On the right see the many freeways and arterials about to converge into this capital of Galicia. Descend the stairway and cross the AP-9 freeway, railway and SC-20 highway bridges (**1.3km**) into the outskirts of town. In a garden area right after the last bridge you will see the Porta Itineris Santi Jacobi sculpture (fountain) by Cándido Pazos, a symbol of welcome to the city. This first neighborhood of modern Santiago, full of government buildings, is named for the San Lázaro hospital, once a leprosarium outside the medieval city.

Follow the scallop-shell sidewalk medallions and the blue/yellow signs through the modern suburbs, veering onto Rúa do Valiño first, then coming to the Avenida de Lugo (**2.2km**) where you enter the Concheiros neighborhood, named for the stalls where medieval pilgrims could buy their scallop shells. Crossing the road and continuing uphill on Rúa dos Concheiros, now enter the more dense and charming older neighborhood that includes some of Santiago's favorite bars and restaurants.

Enter the old city at the Porta do Camiño by crossing Rúa das Rodas (**0.8km**) and a few blocks later is the imposing Capela de Ánimas. Enjoy the shady, narrow medieval streets as you pass Plaza de Cervantes (**0.2km**) and then the north side of the cathedral. Pass down the tunnel steps under the Gelmírez Palace and turn left into Praza do Obradoiro, facing the imposing baroque façade of the **Cathedral of Santiago de Compostela** – a very welcome sight.

Congratulations. You've made it!

5.0KM SANTIAGO DE COMPOSTELA (ELEV. 258M, POP. 95,966)
🏨 ⊕ 🛏 🅲 ⊛ ◉ ⊞ ⊕ ⊕ ⓘ (0.0KM)

For over 1000 years, pilgrims from throughout Christendom have journeyed to this Galician capital to venerate the remains of the first martyred apostle of Jesus Christ.

Bishop Godescalc of Le Puy-en-Velay, France, made the first documented pilgrimage in 950–951, but it was in the 1100–1140 episcopacy of the industrious Bishop Diego Gelmírez that the city took its current shape. Gelmírez undertook an ambitious new design for the cathedral, built the churches of **Santa Susana**, **San Fructuoso** and **San Benito**, upgraded the city's water supply and built public fountains throughout town. He promoted the Camino around Europe, convinced Pope Callixtus II to proclaim the city an archbishopric, and secured his endorsement of the Camino's famous guidebook, the *Codex Calixtinus*.

By the 17th c., admirers of St Teresa of Avila began to promote her to replace Santiago as Spain's patron saint. A nationwide controversy affirmed Santiago's place in Spanish hearts and led to renewal of the city's antiquated landmarks. At the direction of King Felipe IV a century-long renewal was begun by architect José Vega y Verdugo in 1643. The main altar of the cathedral, its Quintana façade, bell tower and ultimately its Praza Obradoiro façade were completed – all in the grand Spanish baroque style seen today.

High on the central façade of the cathedral stands St James himself, with two of his disciples kneeling at his feet

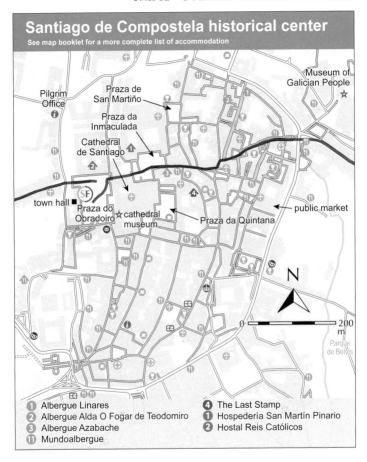

Santiago de Compostela historical center

See map booklet for a more complete list of accommodation

Museum of Galician People

Pilgrim Office

Praza de San Martiño

Praza da Inmaculada

Cathedral de Santiago

town hall

Praza do Obradoiro

cathedral museum

Praza da Quintana

public market

N

0   200 m

Parque de Belvís

1 Albergue Linares
2 Albergue Alda O Fogar de Teodomiro
3 Albergue Azabache
11 Mundoalbergue

4 The Last Stamp
1 Hospedería San Martín Pinario
2 Hostal Reis Católicos

A mere 20min walk from side to side, Santiago's **Zona Monumental** historic center is surrounded by a busy street that once delineated its city walls. The heart of Santiago is **Praza do Obradoiro**, end point of the Camino and gathering place for jubilant pilgrims who've successfully completed their journeys. On the first of four sides of the plaza stands the **Hospital of Catholic Monarchs**, built by Ferdinand and Isabella in 1501 to care for indigent pilgrims and now home of the posh Parador hotel. Just to its left is the 18th c. **Pazo de Raxoi**, town hall of Santiago. Left again is the 16th c. **Pazo de Fonseca**,

249

now library for the University of Santiago, Spain's third oldest institution of higher learning. Left again is the façade of the city's crown jewel – the **Cathedral of Santiago** – one of the most important sites in Christendom and a sight proudly embossed on the one-, two- and five-cent euro coins minted in Spain. The recently refurbished façade is populated by statues of spiritual luminaries, with Santiago Peregrino at its zenith and his disciples Theodorus and Athanasius kneeling below. The traditional entry from Praza do Obradoiro to the cathedral interior is the Portal of Glory, a 12th c. sculptural masterpiece by Maestro Mateo that is now viewed only with a museum ticket. Free entry to the cathedral is from its transept entrances at adjacent Prazas **Praterías** and **Inmaculada**, south and north of the cathedral (before entering, store your backpack at the pilgrim office, Rúa Carretas 33, or drop it at your overnight lodging since packs are not allowed inside the cathedral).

The heavy, surprisingly plain Romanesque interior of the church is adorned by an elaborate high altarpiece and topped by a simple lantern dome. Pilgrims can walk below the altar to the crypt where the bones of the apostle are kept behind glass in a silver reliquary. Highlight of the daily noon mass is the swinging of the smoking *botafumeiro*, a replacement for the original that was stolen by Napoléon's troops. The swinging censer freshened the air around pilgrims who would sleep in the galleries above (consult http://catedraldesantiago.es/en 'Liturgy' for *botafumeiro* schedule).

A worthwhile visit to the **cathedral museum** (€6, https://tickets.catedraldesantiago.es) includes a stop at the Portal of Gloria and entry to Bishop Gelmírez's former palace. **Praza da Quintana**, east of the cathedral, is location of the Jubilee doors, open only in Holy Years, and often hosts outdoor festivals. A stroll through the narrow streets of old Santiago should include a stop at the city's famous market, the **Mercado de Abastos**, to view local cheeses and seafood specialties like *percebes* (barnacles). The **Museo das Peregrinacións** (€2.40, Praza das Praterías, http://museoperegrinacions.xunta.gal) includes an interesting pilgrimage collection, while the **Museum of the Galician People** (€3, near Porto do Camiño, www.museodopobo.gal) hosts local ethnographic exhibits, a peaceful cloister and an amazing triple-spiral staircase. The most relaxing lunch is at the **Café Costa Vella** (Rúa Porta da Pena, 17) while north/south **Rúa do Franco** hosts many of the old city's restaurants. The most memorable meals are the 10 free breakfasts, lunches and dinners offered by the **Santiago Parador** to the first 10 pilgrims at each meal who present their *credencials* and *compostelas*.

🛏 Albergue A Fonte de Compostela 🅾 🅿 🅳 🆁 🅶 🅺 🆆 🆂 🆉 1/30, €14/-/30/-, Rúa de Estocolmo 172, **https://alberguesafonte.com**, tel 604 019 115

🛏 Albergue Alda O Fogar de Teodomiro 🅾 🅳 🆁 🅶 🅺 🆆 🆂 2/18, €12/-/-/-, Rúa Praciña Algalia de Arriba 3, **www.aldahotels.es/alojamientos/albergue-alda-o-fogar-de-teodomiro**, tel 881 092 981

🛏 Albergue Azabache 🅾 🅳 🆁 🅶 🅺 🆆 5/20, €15/-/-/-, Rúa Acibechería 15, **https://albergueazabache.com**, tel 981 071 254

🛏 Albergue Basquiños 45 🅾 🅳 🆁 🅶 🆆 🆂 1/6, €10/-/-/-, Rúa dos Basquiños 45, tel 661 894 536

A priest's assistant gives a first push to the smoking botafumeiro at pilgrim mass in the Cathedral of Santiago de Compostela (photo: Rod Hoekstra)

🔺 Albergue Dream in Santiago 🅳🆁🅺🆆🆂🆉 -/60, €19/-/-/-, Rúa de San Lázaro 81, https://dreaminsantiago.com, tel 981 943 208

🔺 Albergue Fin del Camino 🅳🅺🆆🆂 8/112, €12/-/-/-, Rúa de Moscova 110, https://alberguefindelcamino.com, tel 981 587 324

🔺 Albergue La Credencial 🅳🆁🅶🅺🆆🆂 3/18, €15/-/-/-, Rúa Fonte dos Concheiros 13, www.lacredencial.es, tel 639 966 704

🔺 Albergue La Estación 🅳🆁🅺🆆🆂 2/24, €15/-/-/-, Rúa de Xoana Nogueira 14, www.alberguelaestacion.com, tel 981 594 624

🔺 Albergue La Estrella de Santiago 🅳🆁🅶🆆🆂 7/24, €10/-/-/-, Rúa dos Concheiros 36–38, www.laestrelladesantiago.es, tel 881 973 926

🔺 Albergue Linares 🅾🅿🅳🆁🅶🆆🆂🆉 2/14, €22/70/80/95, Rúa da Algalia de Abaixo 34, www.linaresroomssantiago.com, tel 981 943 253

🔼 Albergue Monterrey **D R G W S** 1/36, €13/-/-/-, Rúa Fontiñas 65, www.alberguemonterrey.es, tel 655 484 299

🔼 Albergue Porta Real **O D R K W S** 6/24, €12/-/-/-, Rúa dos Concheiros 10, http://albergueportareal.es, tel 633 610 114

🔼 Albergue Santiago Km0 **D R G K W S** 10/51, €18/-/-/-, Rúa Carretas 11, https://santiagokm0.es, tel 881 974 992

🔼 Albergue Santo Santiago **D R W S** 3/38, €14/-/-/-, Rúa do Valiño 3, www.elsantosantiago.com, tel 657 402 403

🔼 Albergue Santos **P D R K W Z** 3/24, €15/-/35/-, Rúa dos Concheiros 48, https://albergue-santos.negocio.site, tel 881 169 386

🔼 Albergue SCQ **D R K B W S** 3/24, €17/-/-/-, Rúa da Fonte dos Concheiros 2C, www.alberguescq.com, tel 622 037 300

🔼 Albergue SIXTOS no Caminho **P D R G W Z** 1/40, €15/-/45/-, Rúa da Fonte dos Concheiros 2A, www.sixtosnocaminho.com/albergue-sixtos-0-home, tel 682 721 194

🔼 Meiga Backpackers Hostel **D R G K W S** 5/30, €16/-/-/-, Rúa dos Basquiños 67, www.meiga-backpackers.es, tel 981 570 846

🔼 Mundoalbergue **O D R W S** 1/34, €16/-/-/-, Rúa de San Clemente 26, www.mundoalbergue.es, tel 981 588 625

🔼 Albergue Seminario Menor La Asunción **P D R K W S** 12/173 & 81/81, €17/17/34/-, Avenida Quiroga Palacios, www.alberguesdelcamino.com/santiago, tel 881 031 768

🔼 Blanco Albergue **O P D R G W S** 2/20 & 4/10, €15/-/35/55, Rúa das Galeras 30, www.prblanco.com, tel 699 591 238

🔼 LoopINN Santiago **P D R G W S** 31/73 & -/-, €18/35/58/78, Rúa Tras Santa Clara, https://loopinnhostels.com/santiago, tel 981 585 667

🔼 The Last Stamp **P D R G K W S** 8/62 & 4/8, €15/-/25/-, Rúa do Preguntoiro 10, www.thelaststamp.es, tel 981 563 525

🔺 Camping As Cancelas **O R W** €consult website, Rúa do Vintecinco de Xullo 3, www.campingascancelas.com, tel 981 580 266, bungalows, tent camping, swimming pool

Worth a splurge due to location near the cathedral:
🔼 Hospedería San Martín Pinario **O P R G S** 81/199, €-/48/67/-, Praza da Inmaculada 3, www.hsanmartinpinario.com, tel 981 560 282

Worth a splurge due to its history and grandeur plus location near the cathedral:
🔼 Hostal Reis Católicos **O P R G S** 137/262, €-/140/155/215, Praza do Obradoiro 1, www.parador.es/en, tel 981 582 200

SECTION 6:
CAMINO FINISTERRE/MUXÍA

A red boat bobs in the harbor at Finisterre (photo: Rod Hoekstra)

SECTION 6:
CAMINO FINISTERRE/MUXÍA

Many people believe the ancient Romans or Celts walked a sort of pre-Camino pilgrimage ending not at Santiago but at the colorful sunsets over the Atlantic horizon. Modern archeology has found evidence of Celtic and Roman holy sites at Finisterre and Muxía, and considering the area's natural beauty and ancient identification as the 'end of the earth' it's very possible the ancients did indeed travel great distances to experience the same beauty found today by pilgrims who journey beyond Santiago to the coast.

For pilgrims weary of the crowds between Sarria and Santiago, the green, peaceful and less-well-traveled coastal countryside is a welcome change.

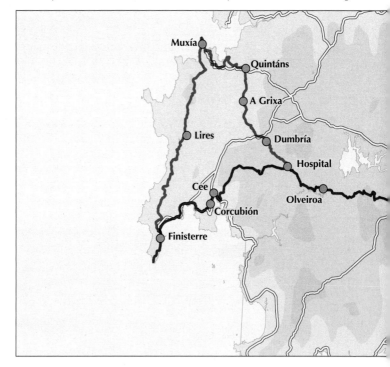

While most of the towns along the way are small or forgettable, on a sun-dappled day the lovely coastal settlements of Cee and Corcubión are a delight of colorful boats bobbing in tiny harbors. The sandy beaches that dot the otherwise rocky coastline lure the pilgrim onward until, finally near either Finisterre or Muxía, the boots come off and the long-suffering feet can be refreshed by a touch of sand and sea.

The region is aptly named Costa da Morte because of its long history of catastrophic shipwrecks. While the combination of rugged coastline and brutal weather may not be optimal for navigators, visitors here find a regenerative energy in the nightly sunset vista, as if the blaze of colors at the daily death of sunlight gives new life for the next day. In the evening, lovers snuggle on the high banks of Cape Finisterre, sharing a bottle of wine as they watch the last lights of the sun fade in the west. Life, death, longing, peace and romance all push to the surface when, finally, the long Camino trail ends at the ocean and all that is left is to stand in awe at the bright and fading sunset colors on the distant horizon.

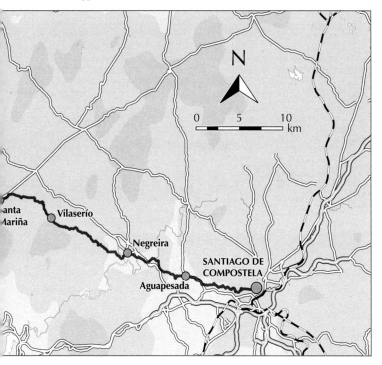

The town of Muxía surrounds its small harbour, and is propelled by its fishing and tourism industries (photo: Mike Wells)

1 At the 'Y' intersection at Hospital (Stage 35A/B), pilgrims must choose between walking to Finisterre or Muxía. Finisterre (Fisterra in Galician) is the larger of the two end-point villages and has the most pilgrim services while Muxía is a quieter village that is just as lovely. An ideal walk would include a visit to both.

2 By walking first to Finisterre a pilgrim can enjoy the scenic villages of Cee and Corcubión, which otherwise would be missed by walking first to Muxía.

3 For pilgrims who want to experience both end points, the walk between the two is a beautiful and very quiet one-day option (Stage 36). In the right weather, bring a sack lunch and plenty of water for an hour's diversion to gorgeous Rostro, Nemiña or Lourido beaches.

Look back toward Santiago at Sarela de Abaixo to see a farewell view of the cathedral. Cross the stone bridge at A Ponte Maceira (Stage 33) and enjoy the charming atmosphere of this former mill town. Gaze down on the Ponte Olveira reservoir after Olveiroa and relish the lovely forest walk between Hospital and Cee (Stage 35A), one of the longest uninterrupted natural stretches on the entire Camino. The cafés of Corcubión beckon for a coffee or an ice cream. Walk the final kilometers to Finisterre with your feet in the waters at Langosteira Beach. An overnight at Finisterre or Muxía demands a splurge at a seafood restaurant before heading out for a sunset refreshment at either cape. At Muxía, look for the 'tipping rock' of Punta da Barca and feel the salt sea spray on your face in the shadow of the Virgen de la Barca church. Because of its height above the water, nothing can compare to Cape Finisterre for its sunset vista as a fitting conclusion to a marvelous Camino Francés.

STAGE 33
Santiago de Compostela to Negreira

Start	Santiago de Compostela, Praza do Obradoiro
Finish	Negreira, town hall
Distance	21.2km
Total ascent	690m
Total descent	780m
Difficulty	Easy
Duration	6¼hr
Percentage paved	77%
Albergues	Negreira 21.2

A pleasant and sometimes serene day's walk among leafy suburbs, forests, ridges and valleys. One serious hill stands in the way, and a few highway crossings are the only negatives, while sparse but sufficient cafés and bars ease the way. The pilgrim community shrinks after Santiago, so the new-found solitude adds to the charm. Municipality information from here on refers to distance remaining to Finisterre.

With the **Cathedral of Santiago** behind you, carefully follow the yellow arrows to the outskirts of town, arriving at the San Lorenzo park, home to the first waymark

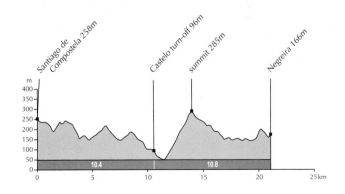

Santiago's streets are quiet during an early morning departure for the coast

monument (**0.9km**), which reads: 'Finisterre km 89.6, Muxía km 86.5.' Walk through the park and downhill, crossing the tiny Sarela River (**0.4km**) and then climbing beneath oak and eucalyptus. Descend to the small suburban neighborhood of **Sarela de Abaixo** (**0.9km**), and after walking past the first three homes a quick look behind offers a splendid western view of the cathedral.

Continue downhill through woods and then the loosely gathered neighborhoods of **As Moas** (**1.5km**) and **O Carballal** (**1.0km**). Climb a wooded ridge to enter a pleasant and green valley where you cross the DP-7802 highway (**2.3km**, note the Os Arcos café hidden to the right). Continue downhill and cross the narrow Roxos River (**0.6km**, rest area) on a concrete bridge. Come to the AC-453 highway (**1.2km**) and a welcome bar/café. Partway down the long descending trajectory, pass at the turn-off for **Castelo** (**1.6km**, café).

Continue past the Parillada o Cruceiro café and cross the Rego dos Pasos (stream) at **Aguapesada** (**2.7km**, restaurant, pharmacy). Turn left, off the sidewalk, onto a flagstone path leading downhill past a stone bridge. Cross the CP-0203 road and immediately begin a sometimes-steep uphill through eucalyptus on the day's longest sustained climb. The wide gravel path meets a companion asphalt road twice before finally joining it near the summit. At the top, pass a rest area (**2.4km**, fountain) and enter the towns of **Carballo** (**0.5km**) and **Trasmonte** (**0.9km**) with its Casa Poncho café. Gradually walking downhill, pass through the town of **Burgueiros** (**1.0km**) and, continuing downhill among stately, moss-covered oaks to the floor of the valley, cross the noisy Tambre River at the lovely bridge of **Ponte Maceira** (**0.9km**).

It is believed that the picturesque, five-arched **stone bridge** over the Tambre was first built by the Romans. Legend holds that Roman soldiers were pursuing Santiago's disciples as they sought to bury his body. After they crossed the bridge it miraculously fell down, trapping the Romans on the other side. The existing bridge of ashlar masonry was built in the 13th–14th c. on order of the Archbishop of Santiago and reconstructed in the 18th c. A 12th c. battle was fought at this site between Diego Gelmírez, Archbishop of Santiago, and the forces of Pedro Fróilaz da Traba. Below the bridge are two former mills (one is the Ponte Maceira restaurant) and across the bridge is the historic town of A Ponte Maceira, with its small 18th c. chapel to San Blas and its Romanesque **Church of Santa María de Portor** whose 12th c. tower is still intact.

Turn left after the bridge to follow the asphalt road out of town. After a short time, catch a dirt path at a fork to the left, following the **Ruta dos Tres Pasos** (**0.8km**), at first a gentle dirt path along the river. Walk under the northern arch of the **Ponte Nova bridge** (**0.1km**) across the Tambre and then under the high-tech, modern bridge of the AC-544 highway (**0.3km**) among small cornfields. Soon arrive at the AC-447 highway (**0.5km**), crossing back and forth among suburban car dealerships and small factories until finally shortcutting left on a quiet side-street to enter **Negreira**. Walk uphill past the pilgrim statue to find the town center.

21.2KM NEGREIRA (ELEV. 166M, POP. 3788) ⬛ ⊕ ◨ Ⓒ ⊙ ⊕ ⊕ (70.2KM)

Mentioned as early as the Roman era, Negreira (Latin: Nicraria Tamara) sits on a hillside above the Barcala and Tambre Rivers where in the Roman era its fortifications protected

An archway of the Pazo do Cotón, which served both as a palace for Negreira's nobility and as a fortress

silver mined in the nearby mountains. The town was destroyed in a Norman incursion in 979 and finally rebuilt in 1113. Its main monument is the **Pazo do Cotón**, a medieval fortress/palace that includes some of the city's former walls and is connected to the 18th c. **Chapel of San Mauro**, both viewable on the way out of town. Prehistoric megaliths can be found west of town at nearby Mt Corzán. Negreira serves today as a regional economic center and bedroom community of nearby Santiago, which can be reached in 10min on the freeway by car.

🔺 Albergue Alecrín **D R G K W S** 2/42, €14/-/-/-, Avenida Santiago 53, www.albergueennegreira.com, tel 981 818 286

🔺 Albergue Anjana **D R G W S** 3/20, €12/-/-/-, Chancela 39, https://albergueanjana.es/, tel 607 387 229

🔺 Albergue de Negreira **O D K** 3/20, €8/-/-/-, Rúa do Patrocinio 10, www.concellodenegreira.gal ('Turismo'), tel 664 081 498

🔺 Albergue El Carmen **D R W S** 2/30, €12/-/-/-, Rúa do Carmen 2, www.alberguehostalmezquita.com/albergue/en/, tel 636 129 691, Pensión La Mezquita with private rooms at same address

🔺 Albergue Lua **D R K W S** 1/40, €12/-/-/-, Avenida de Santiago 22, tel 698 128 883

🔺 Albergue Bergando **O P D R G K W S** 1/28 & 5/10, €17/-/60/-, Monte Bergando, www.facebook.com/alberguebergando, tel 649 466 390

🔺 Albergue San José **O P D R G K W S** 3/50 & 15/30, €12/20/30/45, Rúa Castelao 20, www.alberguesanjose.es, tel 881 976 934

STAGE 34
Negreira to Olveiroa

Start	Negreira, town hall
Finish	Olveiroa, Albergue de Olveiroa
Distance	34.5km
Total ascent	980m
Total descent	870m
Difficulty	Moderately hard, due to length
Duration	9¾hr
Percentage paved	61%
Albergues	Piaxe/A Pena 8.5; Vilaserío 13.1; Santa Mariña 21.4; Lago 28.1; Ponte Olveira 32.3; Olveiroa 34.5

A beautiful, quiet and green day among forests and farms as signs of the nearby ocean begin to pervade. Highway walking is balanced with footpaths under forests and between fields. Either make an early start in preparation for a long day's walk or break up the distance with an overnight at one of the intervening villages.

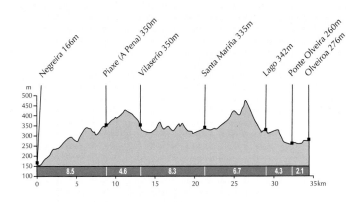

An hórreo stands in the mist after Negreira (photo: Rod Hoekstra)

From **Negreira** walk downhill on Carreira de San Mauro and cross under the archway at Plaza Cotón (**0.3km**) with its chapel, noting the statue to the emigrant to the side. Cross over the Barcala River and see a sign for an option (**0.5km**) with an additional 0.5km mostly along the river. Choosing the shorter (main) route, go uphill on asphalt and come to tiny Upper Negreira and its moldering late-18th c. **Church of San Xulián** (**0.5km**). Slowly ascend on the tranquil forested path, accompanied sometimes by sounds of autos from the adjacent DP-5603. Walk briefly on the highway's narrow shoulder and then cross it at **Zas** (**2.1km**, grocery store, café). Soon come to a beautiful forest of eucalyptus and oak as you continue uphill. Turn left through cornfields, passing a rest area and fountain just before **O Rapote** (**4.2km**). Return to the woods and skirt to the north of the high ridge of Monte Pena (493m), before long arriving at the welcome signs for **Piaxe (A Pena)**.

8.5KM PIAXE (A PENA) (ELEV. 350M, POP. 164) 🍴 🛏 (61.7KM)

🏠 Albergue Alto da Pena ⓄⓅⒹⓇⒼⓀⓌⓈ 4/20 & 3/9, €15/-/50/75, Piaxe 5, tel 609 853 486, double, triple & quadruple rooms available

🏠 Albergue Rectoral San Mamede da Pena ⓄⓅⒹⓇⒼⓀⓌⓈ 7/24 & 4/10, €15/35/60/75, Piaxe 8, tel 649 948 014

After visiting the café, pass the 19th c. San Mamede church and its cemetery just on the outskirts of town. Walk along the road, turning left to follow the 1m shoulder of the DP-5603 roadway (**0.7km**). Turn right from the highway (**0.5km**) and find a somewhat misleading sign bearing information about an 'official' and 'alternative' option, neither of which is a bad choice, although the official route spends more time on the pavement of the quiet highway. Sticking to the official route, continue as the path becomes a single track through the sparse forest of eucalyptus, crossing an odd bridge of short, round logs (**0.6km**) and continuing uneventfully uphill through the forest until you rejoin the DP-5603 (**0.5km**). Follow the road until the alternative track rejoins you at the km 57.032 marker (**2.0km**), just before turning left off the highway and descending on a dirt path to

4.6KM VILASERÍO (ELEV. 350M, POP. 66) 🍴 🛏 ◉ (57.1KM)

🔺 Albergue Municipal de Vilaserío ◯ 🄳 🅂 1/14, €Donation, Vilaserío 37, tel 648 792 029

🔺 Albergue O Rueiro ◯ 🄳 🅁 🄶 🆆 🅂 3/30, €12/-/-/-, Vilaserío 28, www.restaurantealbergueorueiro.com, tel 981 893 561

🔺 Albergue Casa Vella 🄿 🄳 🅁 🄺 🄲 🆆 🅂 2/14 & 3/7, €12/25/35/65, Vilaserío 23, https://casavellavilaserioblog.wordpress.com, tel 981 893 516

Continue along the DP-5603, enjoying the wide cornfields, passing the municipal albergue (**0.5km**) and finally biding *adieu* to the highway at the sign for Cornado (**1.4km**). Turn left out of this collection of farm homes and barns and then come to the DP-5604 highway, which you join briefly until you turn off to the left on a gravel road (**0.3km**) leading gradually downhill. Continue as the road becomes asphalt and crosses through the villages of **As Maroñas** (**3.5km**) and

8.3KM SANTA MARIÑA (ELEV. 335M, POP. 15) 🍴 🛏 (48.8KM)

🔺 Albergue Santa Mariña 🄳 🅁 🄶 🄺 🆆 🅂 3/34, €10/-/-/-, Lamelas-Maroñas Mazaricos, tel 655 806 800

🔺 Albergue Casa Pepa ◯ 🄿 🄳 🅁 🆆 🅂 5/38 & 4/8, €12/-/45/-, Santa Mariña 4, https://alberguecasapepa.wordpress.com, tel 981 852 881

Afterwards, briefly walk along the provincial AC-400 highway through **Lamelas** (**0.6km**, café) before turning right on a gravel road that climbs slowly among cornfields. Pass through the hamlets of **Bom Xesús** (**1.9km**) and **Gueima** (**0.4km**) before turning off toward **Vilar do Castro** (**0.7km**). Afterwards come out into an open space of broad hayfields and cornfields. Continue to the paved road and soon come to an option: turn left on the 'official' route to climb 40m steeply to a **lookout** (**0.4km**) or, if the weather is foggy, continue ahead on the 'old route' along the paved road until a left turn rejoins the two paths and brings you to

6.7KM LAGO (ELEV. 342M, POP. <50) 🍴 ⊕ 🛏 (42.1KM)

🔺 Albergue Monte Aro 🄿 🄳 🅁 🄶 🆆 🅂 🅉 1/28, €12/-/52/-, Lago 12, https://alberguemontearo.com/en/road-to-fisterra, tel 682 586 157

Leave Lago on a mauve-painted road among barns, ripe with the smells of agriculture, turning right at **Abeleiroas (0.9km)** toward Corzón and then weaving on asphalt through an odd terrain of small boulders, pine trees and low shrubs, finally arriving at

3.2KM CORZÓN (ELEV. 286M, POP. 244) ⑪ (39.0KM)

The red-roofed Church of San Cristóbal sits in a cemetery opposite a well-preserved *cruceiro*. The church has baroque and neoclassical altarpieces.

Soon turn right onto the DP-3404 highway, entering **Ponte Olveira** with its understated bridge.

1.1KM PONTE OLVEIRA (ELEV. 260M, POP. 26) ⑪ ⬛ (37.9KM)

The eponymous bridge crosses the Xallas River here. Citizens led by Fr. Xoán Pispieiro, a local priest, bravely battled the Napoleonic army here on April 12, 1809. The French could not be stopped and decimated the area as far as Cee and Corcubión.

🛖 Albergue Ponte Olveira 🅿 🅳 🆁 🅺 🆆 🆂 3/20 & 4/8, €12/-/40/-, Ponte Olveira 3, www.ponteolveira.com, tel 981 852 135

Afterward continue on the wide shoulder of the DP-3404 highway before finally veering left at the large Olveiroa sign to enter

2.1KM OLVEIROA (ELEV. 276M, POP. 109) ⑪ ⬛ (35.7KM)

The tiny village retains much of its medieval character. The Albergue de Olveiroa – the Xunta albergue – sits astride a village street, inhabiting a community of low farm buildings. The **Santiago de Olveiroa church** and cemetery are a maze of tiny spires in pure Galician fashion.

🛖 Albergue de Olveiroa 🅾 🅳 🆆 🆂 6/40, €8/-/-/-, Olveiroa, tel 658 045 242

🛖 Albergue Hórreo 🅳 🆁 🅶 🅺 🆆 🆂 7/58, €14/-/-/-, Olveiroa 25, http://casaloncho.com, tel 617 026 005, next to Casa Loncho which has private rooms

🛖 Albergue O Peregrino 🅾 🅳 🆁 🆆 🆂 1/12, €10/-/-/-, Olveiroa, tel 981 741 682

🛖 Albergue Santa Lucía de Olveiroa 🅾 🅿 🅳 🆁 🅺 🆆 🆂 🆉 3/16, €12/25/35/-, Olveiroa, www.alberguedeolveiroa.com, tel 683 190 767

🛖 Albergue Casa Manola 🅿 🅳 🆁 🅶 🆆 🆂 3/18 & 7/14, €12/-/49/-, Olveiroa 24, http://casamanola.com, tel 981 741 745

STAGE 35A
Olveiroa to Finisterre

Start	Olveiroa, Albergue de Olveiroa
Finish	Cape Finisterre
Distance	35.7km
Total ascent	980m
Total descent	1145m
Difficulty	Moderately hard, due to duration
Duration	10hr
Percentage paved	37%
Albergues	O Logoso 3.7; Hospital 5.1; Cee 19.7; Corcubión 21.7; Sardiñeiro de Abaixo 26.6; Finisterre 32.4

There are lovely views over the Xallas River dam, but some stiff, forested uphills until O Logoso make for a hard start. After Hospital the quiet forest is followed by spectacular views overlooking Cee, Corcubión and Finisterre, making this an unforgettable walk. In good weather the day has two extraordinary endings – a stroll in the surf along Langosteira Beach and a walk to Cape Finisterre for a sunset celebration. After Hospital, the forest hike of 15km with no services requires some advance planning for food and water.

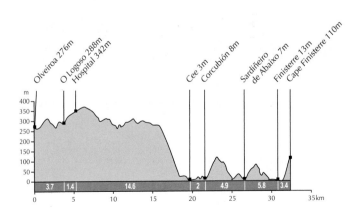

Leave **Olveiroa** by walking down to the gentle river and then uphill on a moderately steep path below wind turbines. Note, in the gorge far below, the dam on the Xallas River and enjoy the sounds of local tributaries splashing their way down the mountainside to join their larger neighbor. Cross the **crenellated bridge** (**2.7km**) over the Hospital River and head uphill steeply before coming to the small settlement of

3.7KM O LOGOSO (ELEV. 288M, POP. 30) 🏨 🛏 (32.1KM)

⛰ Albergue O Logoso Ⓞ Ⓟ Ⓓ Ⓡ Ⓖ Ⓚ Ⓦ Ⓢ 4/40 & 6/12, €12/30/35/-, Camino a Santiago-Finisterra km 28, www.facebook.com/albergueologoso, tel 659 505 399

Continue down and out of town, then uphill on gravel again, this time under pines. As you come to a building that looks like a gas station discover instead it is the pilgrim information office at

1.4KM HOSPITAL (ELEV. 342M, POP. 42) 🏨 🛏 ❶ (30.7KM)

⛰ Albergue O Casteliño Ⓞ Ⓟ Ⓓ Ⓡ Ⓚ Ⓦ Ⓢ Ⓩ 3/18, €12/20/40/-, Rúa Hospital, tel 981 747 387

After the office, continue to the highway, passing the albergue/bar at **Casteliño** (**0.4km**) and continuing to a traffic circle across from a carbide plant where two monuments show an important option (**0.6km**) – one right to Muxía, the other left to Finisterre (to walk to Muxía, follow Stage 35B).

Make certain you stock up on provisions at the Casteliño bar before continuing onto the unserviced 15km forest path. To continue towards Finisterre, briefly join the DP-2302 highway until the signs point you to a gravel road (**0.6km**) on the right. Follow this long, pleasant road through a beautiful forest, passing an **historic cross** (**1.8km**), the **Our Lady of Snows chapel** (**2.0km**, picnic area) and **San Pedro Mártir chapel** (**3.4km**, fountain). Continue along until you are interrupted by stunning views of the towns of Cee and Corcubión as well as vistas of Finisterre in the far distance. After a steep downhill, arrive at the AC-550 highway on the outskirts of Cee (**4.4km**) where you have the option of following the waymarks along the highway and through the shopping district of town or heading downhill to the park at the head of the inlet to walk on Concha Beach and shave off an extra kilometer or two.

14.6KM CEE (ELEV. 3M, POP. 4411) 🏨 ⊕ 🛏 Ⓒ ⊚ Ⓗ ⊕ ⊕ (16.0KM)

Largest town on the Costa da Morte, Cee traces its name to the Latin word *cetus* for large sea animal, pointing to the town's historic roots in the fishing economy. The 12th c. Romanesque **Church of San Adrián de Toba**, just north of town, and the Gothic main chapel of the **Church of Santa María da Xunqueira** are its primary medieval monuments.

April 1809 saw the devastating French invasion which, coupled with a decline in the local fishery, led to a century of emigration to the Western Hemisphere. One local emigrant, Fernando Blanco de Lema (1796–1875) who became rich in Cuba, donated a school to the community. The town's museum now bears his name. The official Camino route follows the **Rúa Magdalena**, which maintains some of the town's former medieval charm, while the area around the **Praza da Constitución** is site of many of the town's fine 19th c. buildings. The **Virxe da Xunqueira hospital** is the largest medical center on the Costa da Morte.

🔺 Albergue A Casa da Fonte 🅳 🆁 🅺 🅲 🆆 🆂 2/42, €13/-/-/-, Rúa de Arriba 36, http://alberguecasadafonte.blogspot.com, tel 981 746 663. Pilgrims run this albergue!

🔺 Albergue O Bordón 🅞 🅳 🆁 🅺 🆆 🆂 1/24, €15/-/-/-, Calle Camiños Chans-Brens-Cee-La Coruña, www.facebook.com/ObordonAlbergue, tel 655 903 932

🔺 Albergue Tequerón 🅞 🅟 🅳 🆁 🅶 🅺 🅱 🆆 🆂 🆉 3/16, €12/-/41/-, Rúa de Arriba 31, tel 666 119 594

🔺 Albergue Moreira 🅟 🅳 🆁 🅺 🆆 🆂 2/14 & 4/8, €12/-/30/-, Rúa Rosalía de Castro 75, www.alberguemoreira.es, tel 981 746 282

Continue through Cee, walking along the Avenida Fisterra and very shortly finding yourself in its posher next-door neighbor

2.0KM CORCUBIÓN (ELEV. 8M, POP. 1442) 🍴 🛏 🏠 🅲 🄰 ⊕ 🛈 (14.1KM)

This charming and photogenic village most likely received its name by combining the ancient Celtic or archaic Galician words *corcu* (circle) and *-bion* (lake), which perhaps described the shape of the harbor in ancient times. Ancient historians suggest the town belonged to the Nerios tribe, who placed the town center further up the hill where it could be protected from marauding pirates. With the ebb of piracy in the 13th c. the town began to spread downhill toward the waterfront site of its fishing trade. The **San Marcos parish church** includes a 14th c. chapel and 15th c. nave with a 600-year-old sculpture of San Marcos da Cadeira the centerpiece of its interior.

🔺 Albergue San Roque 🅞 🅳 🅱 🅲 🆂 1/14, €Donation, Campo de San Pedro, www.amigosdelcamino.com ('Hospitalidad'), tel 679 460 942, 1 km after Corcubión, breakfast & dinner by donation

🔺 Praia de Quenxe 🅞 🅟 🅳 🆁 🅶 🅺 🆆 🆂 4/18 & 9/18, €15/50/50/-, Rúa Editor Francisco Porrúa 3, www.playadequenxe.com, tel 881 084 053

The signs direct you up and onto a rough and narrow path between walls, climbing the mountain behind town. After passing through Vilar (**1.0km**) begin a series of eight somewhat harrowing road crossings of the AC-445 that will bring you through the settlements of San Roque (**0.5km**, fountain) with its albergue (see above),

Amarela (**0.7km**) and **Estorda** (1.1km). The noisy whir of nearby autos is offset by enticing views to the left of sandy beaches with an occasional glimpse of the day's goal. Continue to

4.9KM SARDIÑEIRO DE ABAIXO (ELEV. 7M, POP. 490) 🍽 ⊕ 🛏 (9.1KM)

Full of vacation homes and restaurants for seasonal tourists, this seaside town makes for a welcome pause and rest before Finisterre.

▲ Camping Ruta Finisterre D R G W S -/-, €7/-/-/-, Playa Estorde 216, www.rutafinisterre.com, tel 981 746 302

Climb behind town through woods of eucalyptus and pine before heading down one final time across the AC-445 (**2.0km**). A steep path carries you downhill toward tiny, secluded **Talon Beach** (**0.2km**), then returns you to the highway before a drive-way brings you downhill onto justifiably the most popular beach of the area, beautiful **Langosteira** (**0.8km**). Here you can either walk at the water's edge for your final steps into Finisterre or take the path among dunes just to the right. At the end of the beach (**2.0km**), follow the signs up the stairs and into the heart of town.

The beach at Langosteira makes a pleasant walk as Finisterre sits across the bay

5.8KM FINISTERRE (ELEV. 13M, POP. 3034) 🚉 ⊕ 🛏 ⓒ ◉ ⊕ ⊕ ❶ (3.4KM)

In ancient times the lack of a suitable harbor undoubtedly limited the town's development, and Roman artifacts at Dugium – in the Duio neighborhood of Finisterre above **Langosteira Beach** – suggest it as the original site of the village. The town's historic importance comes from its proximity to majestic and mysterious Cape Finisterre. The town's most ancient monument is **Santa María das Arenas** (Our Lady of the Sands) which hearkens from the 12th c. A long relationship with pilgrimage is demonstrated in the 1469 pilgrim hospital founded by the church's priest, Fr. Alonso García. The 17th c. **Castillo de San Carlos** was built to protect the bay from foreign attack and now houses the local fishing museum. A modern breakwater shelters a small harbor of fishing boats and is site of the 1993 **Monument to the Emigrant**, which remembers the loss of men and women through emigration forced by desperate economic conditions. South of the main harbor, along the Paseo Ribeira is the **Lonja de Finisterre**, a large fish market where the latest catches are auctioned. Finisterre's most charming neighborhood is undoubtedly the stretch of **Rúa Real** between the harbor and the **Praza da Constitución**. In the immediate vicinity of Finisterre are three sandy beaches – Langosteira at its entrance, as well as tiny **Ribeira** below the Castillo de San Carlos and **Corveiro** below the Santa María church. On the opposite side of the cape from the village is the **Mar de Fora**, considered by some the most beautiful beach on the Costa da Morte.

🔺 Albergue A Pedra Santa 🅿 🄳 🅁 🄺 🅆 🅂 🅉 3/20, €13/22/-/-, Travesía de Arriba 6, www.facebook.com/apedrasantafis, tel 615 170 488

🔺 Albergue Arasolis 🄾 🄳 🅁 🄶 🄺 🅆 🅂 2/16, €12/-/-/-, Rúa Ara Solís 3, tel 638 326 869

🔺 Albergue de Sonia Buen Camino 🄾 🅿 🄳 🅁 🄶 🄺 🄲 🅆 🅂 🅉 7/50, €15/25/40/-, Rúa Atalaya 11, www.buencaminofinisterre.com, tel 981 740 771

🔺 Albergue Mar de Rostro 🄳 🅁 🄺 🅆 🅂 2/23, €10/-/-/-, Rúa Alcalde Fernández 45, www.facebook.com/pg/alberguemarde.rostroenfisterra, tel 637 107 765

🔺 Albergue Municipal de Fisterra 🄾 🄳 🄺 🅆 🅂 2/26, €8/-/-/-, Rúa Real 2, www.concellofisterra.com ('Turismo'), tel 981 740 781

🔺 Albergue Oceanus Finisterre 🅿 🄳 🅁 🄶 🄺 🅆 🅂 🅉 1/36, €15/25/35/-, Avenida A Coruña 33, http://oceanusfinisterre.es, tel 609 821 302

🔺 Albergue Por Fin 🅿 🄳 🅁 🄺 🅆 🅂 🅉 2/11, €15/-/34/-, Rúa Federico Ávila 23, tel 636 764 726

🔺 Albergue Cabo da Vila 🄾 🅿 🄳 🅁 🄶 🄺 🅆 🅂 1/28 & 9/18, €12/30/40/50, Avenida A Coruña 13, www.alberguecabodavila.com, tel 981 740 454

🔺 Albergue de Paz 🄾 🅿 🄳 🅁 🅆 🅂 5/28 & 2/4, €12/20/30/-, Rúa Víctor Cardalda 11, tel 981 740 332

🔺 Albergue do Sol e da Lúa 🄾 🅿 🄳 🅁 🄲 🅆 🅂 3/18 & 3/6, €11/20/27/-, Rúa Atalaya 7, http://alberguedosol.blogspot.com.es, tel 617 568 648

🔺 Albergue Fin da Terra e do Camiño P D R K W S 3/12 & 7/14, €10/20/40/-, Rúa Alfredo Saralegui 15, www.facebook.com/findaterraedocamino, tel 687 155 215

🔺 Albergue Finistellae P D R Gr K W S 2/20 & 6/15, €12/30/35/50, Rúa Manuel Lago País 7, www.finistellae.com, tel 637 821 296, pensión located 100 meters from albergue

🔺 Albergue La Espiral O P D R K B W 2/12 & 2/4, €12/-/30/-, Rúa Fonte Vella 19, www.facebook.com/alberguelaespiral, tel 607 684 248

🔺 Albergue Mar de Fora P D R K W S 5/34 & 2/5, €12/-/35/-, Rúa Potiña 14, www.alberguemardefora.com, tel 981 740 298

🔺 Albergue O Encontro O P D R Gr W S 2/14 & 4/8, €12/-/40/-, Rúa Fonte Vella 22, tel 981 740 369

Follow waymarks back up to the AC-445 highway, which you follow along the left shoulder uphill past a rest area and fountain (**2.0km**) to **Cape Finisterre**, the 0.0km monument (**1.2km**) and lovely the Finisterre lighthouse and viewpoint.

3.4KM CAPE FINISTERRE (ELEV. 110M, POP. 0) 🏨 🏞 (0.0KM)

There are many suggestions of a long tradition of pre-Christian pilgrimage to the Cape, and some suggest that the Camino de Santiago itself is a Christianization of a more ancient tradition of pilgrimage toward the setting of the sun, culminating at this rocky promontory at what was thought to be the westernmost tip of Europe. The name derives from the Latin *finis terrae* (end of the earth). The **Vilar Vello** mountaintop above the Cape (accessible by footpath) in ancient days held an altar to the sun – Ara Solis – built by pre-Roman inhabitants of the area. Some say a monolith there had fertility powers and that women wanting to conceive would rub their bodies against the stone. In medieval times the stone was replaced by a hermitage to San Guillermo. The **Finisterre lighthouse**, built in 1868 and critical to safe navigation around the tip of the coast, is the second most visited place in Galicia after the Cathedral of Santiago.

Worth a splurge for location near the lighthouse at the Cape:

🔺 Hotel O Semáforo de Fisterra P R Gr B 7/14, €-/95/280/-, Carretera del Faro, www.hotelsemaforodefisterra.com, tel 981 110 210

The lighthouse at Cape Finisterre signals to passing ships.

STAGE 35B
Olveiroa to Muxía

Start	Olveiroa, Albergue de Peregrinos
Finish	Muxía, Punta da Barca
Distance	31.6km
Total ascent	615m
Total descent	970m
Difficulty	Moderately hard, due to duration
Duration	9hr
Percentage paved	47%
Albergues	O Logoso 3.7; Hospital 5.1; Dumbría 8.8; A Grixa 16.1; Quintáns 20.4; Moraime 27.1; Muxía 30.8

After Hospital the stage undulates through the coastal hills of Galicia to reach the quiet seaside resort town of Muxía. Much of the route is covered with forestry plantations of eucalyptus and pine, interspersed with pastoral fields surrounding scattered dairy farming villages. Municipality information from here on refers to distance remaining to Muxia.

Follow the directions in Stage 35A to **Hospital**. At the roundabout above town, bear right at the twin monuments (a left turn takes you to Finisterre on Stage 35A). Follow the road downhill and turn left on a path (**1.1km**) that descends through forest. Cross the DP-3404 road (**0.5km**) and continue through forest before rejoining the highway (**0.7km**) for a short distance. Turn left on a forest path (**0.2km**), descending on switchbacks to **Carizas** (**0.3km**) and then the long string of homes, shops and businesses that is

3.7KM DUMBRÍA (ELEV. 189M, POP. 496) Ⅲ ⊕ ◪ ⓒ ⊕ ⊕ (22.9KM)

Although the region includes many prehistoric links, the first formal mention of Dumbría is in 868. Its 16th–18th c. **Church of Santa Eulalia** has a fine baroque altar reminiscent of the Cathedral of Santiago.

⌂ Albergue de Dumbría ◯ ◻ ◻ ⓢ 4/26, €8/-/-/-, Dumbría, tel 981 744 001

At the end of the village by its large health center (**1.2km**), fork left and follow the road out of town. Cross the **Fragoso River** (**0.6km**) then the AC-552 highway (**0.2km**)

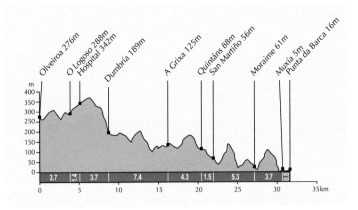

onto a forest track. This ascends over a low ridge then descends to **Trasufre** (**1.8km**), which you skirt to the north. After passing the last house turn right into the forest (**0.8km**) and follow a series of asphalt roads winding through forest before emerging into fields surrounding **Senande** (**1.8km**, bar, café, grocery, bakery). Turn left in the village and follow the road downhill, passing a *cruceiro* wayside cross before the tiny hamlet of

7.4KM A GRIXA (ELEV. 125M, POP. 50) 🛏 (15.5KM)

Here the route passes between the tiny Church of San Cibrán and its separate bell tower on the opposite side of the road. The bell ropes hang over a wall and can be rung from the road.

🔼 Albergue O Cabanel 🅞🅟🅓🅡🅖🅚🅒🅦🅢🅩 2/12, €14/-/40/-, A Grixa,
http://alberguecabanel.com, tel 600 644 879

Follow the waymarks to a forest road that climbs steadily before descending to

4.3KM QUINTÁNS (ELEV. 88M, POP. 178) 🍴🛏◉⊕ (11.2KM)

🔼 Albergue Et Suseia 🅓🅡 1/10, €15/-/-/-, Lugar Pedragas 1,
www.facebook.com/etsuseiaalbergue, tel 689 946 840

Cross the AC-440 and bear left through the village following a track that winds through fields before turning uphill into nearby San Martiño de Ozón **1.5km**.

The **Church of San Martiño** was originally part of a Benedictine monastery. Two of three original Romanesque apses are preserved at the rear of the building. The *hórreo* (granary) behind the church has 22 pairs of legs, making it one of the longest in Galicia.

Continue uphill through this spread-out village, turning sharply left then sharply right at **Vilar de Sobremonte** (**0.8km**) onto a forest track. Reach a summit (**0.2km**) and afterward enjoy the first views of the Atlantic ahead. At the beginning of **Merexo** (**1.2km**) turn left and follow the road winding above the ocean through forest, coming to **Os Muíños** (**1.9km**, restaurant, pharmacy). Turn right onto the AC-440 through the village then cross the Negro River, climbing to cross the AC-440 again to reach the tiny hamlet of

6.7KM MORAIME (ELEV. 61M, POP. 25) ⬛ (4.5KM)

The complex of buildings at Moraime include traces of a Roman villa, part of a Benedictine monastery (now an albergue), and the Romanesque Church of San Xiao (San Xulián) built in 1119 by King Alfonso VII of León to replace an earlier church destroyed by Norman pirates.

🛏 Monasterio de Moraime ⓞ Ⓟ Ⓓ Ⓡ Ⓖ Ⓑ Ⓦ Ⓢ 2/38 & 4/24, €14/-/41/-, Lugar de Moraime 2, **www.hostelmonasteriodemoraime.com**, tel 881 076 055

Follow the road climbing over forested headland past the chapel of San Roque (**0.8km**). Descend through Chorente (**0.6km**), passing the Dunes of Espinerido (**0.9km**, public bath) then walking alongside the AC-440 highway to reach the center of **Muxía**.

3.7KM MUXÍA (ELEV. 5M, POP. 1527) 🏧 ⊕ ⬛ Ⓔ ◉ ⊕ ⊕ ❶ (0.8KM)

Muxía's roots as a fishing village likely go back to prehistory, and the 'rocking stone' of **Pedra da Barca** (Pedra Abalar) is believed to have been a Celtic holy place. The long beach and harbor have made it a prime fishing village for centuries but also opened it up to successive attacks by pirates. Emperor Charles V purchased the town in the 16th c. so he could ensure a good harbor to the northwest of his lands. In the 19th c. Muxía was destroyed by French armies under Napoléon. Spain's worst environmental catastrophe occurred on November 19, 2002 when the leaking Greek oil tanker *Prestige* split in half off the nearby coast, spilling 60,000 metric tons of oil into the Atlantic. Today Muxía is a laidback and pleasant resort town where many pilgrims choose to relax in the sun and surf after their long pilgrimage.

🔺 Albergue de Muxía **O** **D** **K** **S** 2/32, €8/-/-/-, Rúa Enfesto 22, tel 610 264 325

🔺 Albergue@Muxía **O** **P** **D** **R** **G** **K** **W** **S** 2/40 & 2/6, €13/-/40/-, Rúa Enfesto 12, www.alberguemuxia.com, tel 981 742 118

🔺 Albergue Arribada **P** **D** **R** **G** **K** **W** **S** 4/40 & 2/4, €15/48/64/80, Rúa José María del Río 30, www.arribadaalbergue.com, tel 981 742 516

🔺 Albergue da Costa **P** **D** **R** **G** **K** **W** **S** 1/8 & 3/6, €15/-/35/-, Avenida Doctor Toba 33, www.dacostamuxia.com, tel 676 363 820

🔺 Albergue Muxía Mare **O** **P** **D** **R** **G** **K** **W** **S** 2/16 & 2/4, €15/45/45/-, Rúa Castelao 14, www.alberguemuxiamare.es, tel 981 742 423

🔺 Bela Muxía **P** **D** **R** **G** **K** **W** **S** 6/52 & 9/18, €15/50/55/75, Rúa da Encarnación 30, www.facebook.com/alberguebelamuxia, tel 687 798 222

Continue past the harbor on Rúa Virxe da Barca to reach the dramatic end of the route.

The A Ferida sculpture and the Santuario de Nosa Señora da Barca share the cape at Muxía (photo: Mike Wells)

0.8KM PUNTA DA BARCA (ELEV. 16M, POP. 0) (NO SERVICES) (0.0KM)

The 17th c. **Santuario de Nosa Señora da Barca**, which holds a 14th c. Gothic carving of the Virgin Mary, was originally a Celtic shrine and holy place. Some believe the Virgin Mary landed here in a stone boat when she appeared in Galicia to give encouragement to Santiago in his missionary efforts. The lonely church stands on the tip of the headland just beyond reach of the crashing surf. The roof of the sanctuary burned after a lightning strike on Christmas Day 2013 and was quickly replaced. Nearby is '**A Ferida,**' an 11m-high sculpture of a 400-ton rock cleft by a lightning bolt, marking the catastrophic sinking of the *Prestige* in 2002.

Kilometer 0.0 at Punta da Barca outside Muxía (photo: Mike Wells)

STAGE 36
Finisterre to Muxía

Start	Finisterre, Plaza Santa Catalina (variant starts from Muxía)
Finish	Muxía, Punta da Barca (variant ends at Finisterre)
Distance	29.5km
Total ascent	910m
Total descent	915m
Difficulty	Moderately hard, due to distance
Duration	8½hr
Percentage paved	63%
Albergues	Lires 14.0; Muxía 28.4. (Lires 14.5 from Muxía)

A walk with precious few views of the beach, but with many kilometers of quiet paths among forests and villages. Except for a café at Buxán and a vending machine at Frixe, the only pilgrim service is midway at Lires. A few steep hills make for healthy exercise while the climax at the opposite end of this two-way stage affords a quiet setting for reflection.. (To begin at Muxía, follow directions at the end of the stage.)

Retrace your steps from **Finisterre**'s Plaza Santa Catalina toward Langosteira Beach, staying on the AC-445 by keeping left just before Hotel Mar Fisterra (**0.7km**). Turn left again after Hotel Arenal (**0.4km**) in the direction of San Martiño going uphill, noting here the first monument (**0.8km**) marked 'A Muxía.' Traverse the ridge ahead,

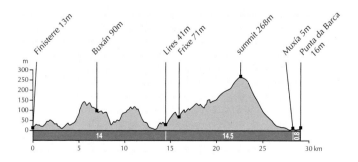

277

The trail nears the beach at Castrexe

enjoying views of Langosteira. Soon turn left (**1.2km**) on a long asphalt road leading uphill, leaving views of the beach behind. Walk among forests and farms first through **Hormedesuxo** (**0.7km**) and then San Salvador de Duio (**0.5km**), site of archeological digs where Roman ruins were unearthed. Walk through woods to **Buxán** (**2.8km**) with its must-find but easily missed, low-key café. After town, enjoy views of **Rostro Beach** (**0.4km**) on the left.

Pass through **Castrexe** (**1.3km**) and then briefly join the road at Padrís (**1.0km**). The path soon becomes a pleasant and flat track among pine trees, although a 2018 logging operation reduced the forest here. Come to an **option** (**1.7km**) that gives you the choice of heading downhill for a long and scenic 'Beach Option' to Muxía. Continue on the primary trail to the town of **Canosa** (**0.5km**, picnic area, non-potable fountain). Here watch carefully for the suddenly scarce waymark monuments. Follow a road to the left of the highway, cross the Lires River (**1.2km**) and find yourself at the foot of **Lires** itself, at the 17th c. Church of Santo Estevo (**0.4km**). Walk up through town to find the main road and the town's services.

14.0KM LIRES (ELEV. 41M, POP. 149) 🍴 🏔 (15.5KM)

Lires sits on an estuary at the mouth of the Castro River and is birthplace of the famous Galician author, Concha Blanco.

🛏 Albergue As Eiras ⓞⓟ ⒹⓇⒼⓦⓢ 4/30 & 20/40, €15/-/40/-, Lires 82, https://ruralaseiras.com, tel 981 748 180

Retrace your steps northward from the town center, veering right through woods and crossing a bridge over the Castro River (**0.5km**) then heading through woods and fields to the tiny village of **Frixe** (**1.7km**). Just before leaving town, look left and find a community center with a bathroom, vending machine and swimming pool. The road climbs slowly in a forest of tall pines and the occasional cornfield. Continue through **Guisamonde** (**2.5km**) and then cross the first ridge of wind turbines toward **Morquitián** (**1.8km**). Here head uphill on flagstone pavers for the day's major climb. After the **summit** (**2.2km**, elev. 268m) come to the town of **Xurarantes** (**2.6km**), where the spectacular Parador (♦ **Parador Costa da Morte** 🅿 🆁 63/126, €-/-/110/-, Lugar de Lourido, www.parador.es/en/paradores/parador-costa-da-morte-muxia, tel 881 161 111) offers an enticing luxury splurge. After Xurarantes go directly to the DP-5201 highway (**0.7km**) along the opposite hillside and turn left there, passing along the **beach** and following the pedestrian lane of this seaside highway beyond the sea-sprayed football field (**1.2km**) all the way into

14.5KM MUXÍA (ELEV. 5M, POP. 1527) 🄷 ⊕ 🄴 🄲 ◉ ⊕ ⊕ ❶ (1.1KM)

See the description of Muxía in Stage 35B.

Once at the large triangular sculpture plaza along the highway, either stay on the highway to arrive after five blocks at the town center or veer left onto the Rúa Coldo/ Rúa Atalaia that skirts the west edge of town heading directly to

1.1KM PUNTA DA BARCA (ELEV. 16M, POP. 0) NO SERVICES (0.0KM)

See the description of Punta da Barca in Stage 35B.

From Muxía to Finisterre
From **Muxía** follow Avenida Doctor Toba south, passing the football pitch then **Lourido Beach**. Fork right on a road that leads toward the Parador luxury hotel, which can be seen on the headland beyond. Turn on a quiet road, climbing steadily through eucalyptus forest to pass through the edge of **Xurarantes** (**3.2km**). Continue ascending on a track winding through forest to reach the **summit** (**2.6km**, elev. 268m) and then continue downhill into **Morquintián** (**2.2km**) and through forest to **Guisamonde** (**1.8km**). Come to **Frixe** (**2.5km**, vending machines) then cross the Castro River (**1.7km**) into

14.5KM LIRES (ELEV. 41M, POP. 149) 🄷 🄲 (14.0KM)

For services in Lires, see above.

The scale of the wind turbines becomes clear as a pilgrim approaches a tower below Morquitián

Large beaches dot the coastline between Muxía and Finisterre

Follow the road winding downhill through the village and turn left beside the Santo Estevo church (**0.3km**). Just before the last house, turn right onto a track that crosses the river and winds through fields. When this track returns to the riverside, turn right along a walled lane that climbs gently into forest and continues uphill past **Canosa** (**1.5km**). Follow the delightful sunken lane winding through mixed eucalyptus and pine forest before descending to Padrís (**2.2km**) and then **Castrexe** (**1.3km**). Pass a large sawmill and turn left into **Buxán** (**1.7km**, café). Fork right in the village and continue ascending through forest. Cross a road at the summit and descend on a broad track to San Salvador de Duio (**2.8km**). Follow the road through the village and continue into **Hormedesuxo** (**0.7km**). After 700m, follow a winding road past a series of small farms to San Martíño de Duio (**1.7km**). Turn right at the AC-445 main road into

14.0KM FINISTERRE (ELEV. 13M, POP. 3034) 🚌 ⊕ 🛏 🄲 🅟 ⊕ ⊕ 🅘 (3.4KM)

For information on Finisterre see the end of Stage 35A.

Continue as at the end of Stage 35A to **Cape Finisterre**.

APPENDIX A
Stage planning tables

Distances between accommodation intervals are given below. For simplicity, only the primary routes are shown, rather than options and variants (eg Valcarlos, Roman road, Samos, etc). Sample itineraries are shown for 20km, 25km and 30km per day, or you can use this planning table to set your own itinerary and stages.

Saint-Jean-Pied-de-Port to Santiago de Compostela

Stage No.	Name	Distance from origin (km)	Distance from previous place (km)	Itinerary at 20km stage average (km)	Guidebook itinerary: 25km stage average (km)	Itinerary at 30km stage average (km)	My itinerary
	Saint-Jean-Pied-de-Port	0.0					
	Gîte Huntto	5.3	5.3				
	Refuge Orisson	7.7	2.4	7.7			
	Roncesvalles	24.7	17.0		24.7		
	Burguete	27.6	2.9	19.9		27.6	
	Espinal	31.2	3.6				
	Viscarret	36.4	5.2				
	Linzoain	38.4	2.0				
	Zubiri	46.5	8.2	18.9	21.8		
	Ilárraz/Urdániz	49.5	3.0				
	Larrasoaña	52.2	2.7				
	Zuriaín	56.0	3.9				
	Zabaldika	59.2	3.2			31.6	
	Trinidad de Arre	63.0	3.8				
	Villava/Burlada	64.3	1.3				
	Pamplona	67.6	3.3	21.1	21.1		
	Cizur Menor	72.8	5.1				
	Zariquiegui	78.9	6.2				
	Uterga	84.8	5.9				
	Muruzábal	87.5	2.7	19.9			
	Obanos	89.3	1.8			30.1	
	Puente la Reina	92.1	2.8		24.4		
	Mañeru	96.9	4.8				

Stage No.	Name	Distance from origin (km)	Distance from previous place (km)	Itinerary at 20km stage average (km)	Guidebook itinerary: 25km stage average (km)	Itinerary at 30km stage average (km)	My itinerary
	Cirauqui	99.5	2.6				
	Lorca	105.1	5.6				
	Villatuerta	109.4	4.2	21.8			
	Estella	113.7	4.3		21.6		
	Ayegui	114.4	0.7				
	Irache Urbanización	117.8	3.2				
	Azqueta	121.1	3.4			31.8	
	Villamayor de Monjardín	122.9	1.8				
	Los Arcos	135.2	12.3	25.9	21.6		
	Sansol	142.1	6.9				
	Torres del Río	142.9	0.8				
	Viana	153.5	10.6	18.3		32.4	
	Logroño	163.4	9.9		28.2		
	Navarrete	175.9	12.5	22.4			
	Sotés (turn-off)	179.9	4.0				
	Ventosa (turn-off)	181.4	1.5			27.9	
	Nájera	191.9	10.4		28.5		
	Azofra	198.1	6.2	22.2			
	Cirueña	207.6	9.5				
	Santo Domingo de la Calzada	214.0	6.4		22.1	32.5	
	Grañón	220.4	6.5	22.4			
	Redecilla del Camino	224.6	4.1				
	Castildelgado	226.2	1.6				
	Viloria de Rioja	228.1	1.9				
	Villamayor del Río	231.4	3.4				
	Belorado	236.4	5.0		22.5		
	Tosantos	241.2	4.8	20.8			
	Villambistia	243.1	1.9			29.2	

Stage No.	Name	Distance from origin (km)	Distance from previous place (km)	Itinerary at 20km stage average (km)	Guidebook itinerary: 25km stage average (km)	Itinerary at 30km stage average (km)	My itinerary
	Espinosa del Camino	244.8	1.6				
	Villafranca Montes de Oca	248.3	3.5				
	San Juan de Ortega	260.4	12.1	19.3	24.0		
	Agés	264.1	3.6				
	Atapuerca	266.7	2.6				
	Cardeñuela Riopico	273.0	6.4			29.9	
	Orbañeja Riopico	275.1	2.1	14.7			
	Burgos	287.3	12.2		26.8		
	Tardajos	298.0	10.7				
	Rabé de las Calzadas	300.3	2.3	25.2		27.3	
	Hornillos del Camino	308.2	7.9				
	Arroyo San Bol	313.9	5.7				
	Hontanas	318.9	5.0	18.6	31.7		
	Monasterio de San Antón	324.6	5.7				
	Castrojeríz	328.3	3.6			28.0	
	Ermita de San Nicolás	337.4	9.2	18.5			
	Itero de la Vega	339.4	2.0				
	Boadilla del Camino	347.7	8.3		28.8		
	Frómista	353.7	6.0				
	Población de Campos	357.3	3.7	19.9		29.1	
	Villarmentero de Campos	363.0	5.7				
	Villalcázar de Sirga	367.1	4.1				
	Carrión de los Condes	373.0	5.8	15.6	25.3		

Stage No.	Name	Distance from origin (km)	Distance from previous place (km)	Itinerary at 20km stage average (km)	Guidebook itinerary: 25km stage average (km)	Itinerary at 30km stage average (km)	My itinerary
	Calzadilla de la Cueza	390.2	17.3	17.3		32.9	
	Ledigos	396.3	6.1				
	Terradillos de los Templarios	399.4	3.1		26.4		
	Moratinos	402.8	3.4				
	San Nicolás del Real Camino	405.6	2.8				
	Sahagún	413.9	8.2	23.6			
	Bercianos del Real Camino	423.8	10.0		24.5	33.6	
	El Burgo Ranero	431.5	7.7	17.7			
	Reliegos	444.6	13.0				
	Mansilla de las Mulas	450.7	6.1	19.2	26.8	26.8	
	Puente Villarente	456.8	6.1				
	Arcahueja	461.4	4.6				
	León	469.7	8.4	19.1	19.1		
	Trobajo del Camino	473.6	3.9				
	La Virgen del Camino	477.1	3.5			26.4	
	Oncina de la Valdoncina	481.0	3.9				
	Villar de Mazarife	490.9	10.0	21.2			
	Villavante	500.9	9.9				
	Hospital de Órbigo	505.4	4.6		35.7		
	Villares de Órbigo	508.0	2.6			30.9	
	Santibáñez de Valdeiglesias	510.8	2.7	19.8			
	San Justo de la Vega	518.7	7.9				
	Astorga	522.8	4.1		17.4		
	Murias de Rechivaldo	527.0	4.2				

Stage No.	Name	Distance from origin (km)	Distance from previous place (km)	Itinerary at 20km stage average (km)	Guidebook itinerary: 25km stage average (km)	Itinerary at 30km stage average (km)	My itinerary
	Santa Catalina de Somoza	531.5	4.5	20.7			
	El Ganso	535.9	4.4			27.8	
	Rabanal del Camino	542.8	6.9				
	Foncebadón	548.4	5.6	16.9	25.6		
	Manjarín	552.7	4.3				
	El Acebo	559.7	7.1				
	Riego de Ambrós	563.1	3.4				
	Molinaseca	567.8	4.6	19.4		31.9	
	Ponferrada	575.2	7.5		26.9		
	Columbrianos	580.4	5.2				
	Camponaraya	585.4	5.0	17.6			
	Cacabelos	590.7	5.3				
	Pieros	593.3	2.6				
	Villafranca del Bierzo	598.9	5.6		23.6	31.1	
	Pereje	604.3	5.4	18.9			
	Trabadelo	608.7	4.4				
	La Portela	612.8	4.1				
	Ambasmestas	614.1	1.3				
	Vega de Valcarce	615.6	1.5				
	Ruitelán	618.0	2.3				
	Las Herrerías	619.3	1.3				
	La Faba	622.9	3.6	18.7	24.0		
	La Laguna	625.4	2.4				
	O Cebreiro	627.6	2.3			28.8	
	Liñares	631.0	3.4				
	Hospital	633.5	2.5				
	Alto do Poio	636.3	2.8				
	Fonfría	639.7	3.4				
	O Biduedo	642.2	2.5	19.3			
	Fillobal	645.2	3.0				

Stage No.	Name	Distance from origin (km)	Distance from previous place (km)	Itinerary at 20km stage average (km)	Guidebook itinerary: 25km stage average (km)	Itinerary at 30km stage average (km)	My itinerary
	Triacastela	648.8	3.7		25.9		
	El Beso (San Breixo/A Balsa)	650.8	2.0				
	Pintín	659.9	9.1			32.2	
	Aguiada	661.9	2.0				
	San Mamede	663.1	1.2				
	Sarria	666.2	3.1	24.0	17.4		
	Vilei/Barbadelo	670.1	3.9				
	Morgade	678.7	8.6				
	Ferreiros	680.1	1.4				
	A Pena	680.9	0.8				
	Mercadoiro	683.6	2.7				
	Portomarín	689.2	5.5	23.0	23.0	29.3	
	Gonzar	697.2	8.1				
	Castromaior	698.5	1.3				
	Hospital da Cruz	701.1	2.6				
	Ventas de Narón	702.5	1.4				
	Ligonde	705.8	3.3				
	Airexe	706.7	0.9				
	Portos	708.8	2.0				
	Lestedo	709.4	0.6	20.3			
	Xunta Albergue	713.3	3.9				
	Palas de Rei	714.4	1.1		25.3		
	San Xulián do Camiño	718.0	3.6				
	Ponte Campaña	719.0	1.0			29.9	
	Casanova	720.3	1.3				
	O Coto	723.2	2.9				
	O Leboreiro	723.9	0.7				
	Melide	729.5	5.7	20.1			
	Boente	735.4	5.8				
	Castañeda	737.6	2.2				
	Ribadiso da Baixo	740.8	3.2				

Stage No.	Name	Distance from origin (km)	Distance from previous place (km)	Itinerary at 20km stage average (km)	Guidebook itinerary: 25km stage average (km)	Itinerary at 30km stage average (km)	My itinerary
	Ribadiso da Carretera	741.6	0.8				
	Arzúa	744.0	2.4		29.6		
	A Calle	751.9	8.0				
	Salceda	755.4	3.4	25.8		36.4	
	A Brea	757.7	2.4				
	Santa Irene	760.2	2.5				
	A Rúa (O Pino)	762.1	1.9				
	O Pedrouzo	763.7	1.6		19.7		
	Amenal	767.0	3.2	11.6			
	Lavacolla	773.1	6.1				
	Camping San Marcos	776.8	3.7				
	Monte do Gozo	778.7	1.9				
	Santiago de Compostela	783.6	5.0	16.7	19.9	28.3	
	Total distance			**783.6**	**783.6**	**783.6**	
	Total stages			**40**	**32**	**26**	

Santiago to Finisterre

Stage No.	Name	Distance from origin (km)	Distance from previous place (km)	Itinerary at 18km stage average (km)	Itinerary at 22km stage average (km)	Itinerary at 29km stage average (km)	My itinerary
	Santiago	0.0					
	Castelo	10.4	10.4				
	Negreira	21.2	10.8	21.2	21.2		
	Piaxe/A Pena	29.7	8.5			29.7	
	Vilaserío	34.3	4.6				
	Santa Mariña	42.6	8.3	21.4			
	Lago	49.3	6.7		28.1		
	Corzón	52.4	3.2				
	Ponte Olveira	53.5	1.1				

Stage No.	Name	Distance from origin (km)	Distance from previous place (km)	Itinerary at 18km stage average (km)	Itinerary at 22km stage average (km)	Itinerary at 29km stage average (km)	My itinerary
	Olveiroa	55.7	2.1				
	O Logoso	59.3	3.7			29.6	
	Hospital	60.7	1.4	18.2			
	Cee	75.4	14.6		26.1		
	Corcubión	77.3	2.0	16.6			
	Sardiñeiro de Abaixo	82.3	4.9				
	Finisterre	88.0	5.8	10.7	12.7	28.7	
	Total distance		**88.0**	**88.0**	**88.0**	**88.0**	
	Number of stages			**5**	**4**	**3**	

Santiago to Muxía

Stage No.	Name	Distance from origin (km)	Distance from previous place (km)	Itinerary at 20km stage average (km)	Guidebook itinerary: 25km stage average (km)	Itinerary at 30km stage average (km)	My itinerary
	Santiago	0.0					
	Negreira	21.2	21.2	21.2	21.2		
	Piaxe/A Pena	29.7	8.5			29.7	
	Vilaserío	34.3	4.6	13.1			
	Santa Mariña	42.6	8.3		21.4		
	Lago	49.3	6.7				
	Corzón	52.4	3.2				
	Ponte Olveiroa	53.5	1.1				
	Olveiroa	55.7	2.1	21.4			
	O Logoso	59.3	3.7				
	Hospital	60.7	1.4			31.0	
	Dumbría	64.4	3.7		21.8		
	A Grixa	71.8	7.4				
	Quintáns	76.1	4.3	20.4			

Stage No.	Name	Distance from origin (km)	Distance from previous place (km)	Itinerary at 20km stage average (km)	Guidebook itinerary: 25km stage average (km)	Itinerary at 30km stage average (km)	My itinerary
	Moraime	82.8	6.7				
	Muxía	86.4	3.7	10.4	22.0	25.7	
	Total distance		**86.4**	**86.4**	**86.4**	**86.4**	
	Number of stages			**5**	**4**	**3**	

APPENDIX B
Major local festivals

Date – Festival	Location
January	
1 – New Year's Day	Throughout Spain
6 – Epiphany	Throughout Spain
9 – Festival of Holy Martyrs	Samos
Mid month – Festival of San Antón	Astorga
22 – San Vicente festival	O Pedrouzo
25 – Our Lady of Bethlehem	Belorado
28 – Festival of Santo Tirso	Villafranca del Bierzo
30 – Santa Eugenia festival	Mansilla de las Mulas
30 – Celtic pork stew fair	Sarria
February	
3 – Festival of San Blas	Los Arcos, Carrión de los Condes, O Pedrouzo
5 – Festival of San Águeda	Frómista, Carrión de los Condes
Mid month – Festival of San Pedro	Astorga
Last weekend – Festival of Slaughter	Burgos
March	
1 – Labor Day	Closures throughout Spain
First weekend – Cheese festival	Arzúa
7 – Esmorga Fest	Sarria
Second Sunday – Melindre festival	Melide
21 – Equinox light phenomenon	San Juan de Ortega
25 – Conger festival	Muxía
Month-end – Virgin of Perales procession	Bercianos del Real Camino
Variable, spring – Holy Week, Easter, Ascension, Pentecost, Corpus Christi	Throughout Spain
April	
Good Friday – Cheese fair	O Cebreiro
Holy Saturday – Craft fair	Triacastela
Easter Sunday – Festival of Brandy	Portomarín
Monday after Easter – San Telmo, El Olé procession	Frómista
4–5 – antiquities fair, San Lázaro Fair	Sarria
Mid month – Festival of Santo Toribio	Astorga

Date – Festival	Location
25 – Bagpipe and tamboril festival	Santo Domingo de la Calzada
25 – Festival of San Marcos	Corcubión
28 – Festival of San Prudencio	Nájera
Last Sunday – Celebration of Las Cabezadas	León
May	
Start of month – May festival	Villafranca del Bierzo
1 – Festival of King Fernando II and medieval market opens	Nájera
1 – Muiñeira celebration	Cee
8 – Christ of San Miguel	Boadilla del Camino
10–15 – Festival of Santo Domingo	Santo Domingo de la Calzada
12 – Patron festival	El Burgo Ranero
15 – Brotherhood of San Isidro Labrador	Boadilla del Camino, Terradillos de los Templarios, Berciano del Real Camino
15 – Festival of San Isidro	Frómista
25 – Pilgrimage of Virgen del Puy	Estella
June	
2 – Market celebration	San Juan de Ortega
First weekend – Celebration of the Horse	Arzúa
7 – Corpus Christi	Carrión de los Condes
11 – Festival of San Bernabé	Logroño
13 – Festival of San Antonio de Padua	Boadilla del Camino, Melide
Second Sunday – San Antonio de Padua	Cee
Mid month – Corpus Christi	Astorga
16–17 – Festival of San Adrián	Cee
19–21 – Celebration of the Pilar	Muxía
20–21 – Festival of San Juan de Covelo	Palas de Rei
Week of 23rd – Festival of San Juan	Castrojeríz
23 – Celebration of the Pilgrim	Arzúa
24 – Festival of John the Baptist	Throughout Spain
24 – Pilgrimage of San Juan de Cestillos	Carrión de los Condes
24 – Festival of San Juan	León, Corcubión
24–29 – Festival of San Juan and San Pedro	Nájera
26 – Youth festival	Palas de Rei
29 – Festival of San Pedro Apóstol	Terradillos de los Templarios, El Burgo Ranero, Melide, O Pedrouzo, Corcubión
30 – Feast of San Pedro	León

Date – Festival	Location
July	
First week – Templars Night	Ponferrada
6–14 – San Fermin (Running of the Bulls)	Pamplona
10 – Costa da Morte Race	Muxía
Second weekend – medieval festival; Festival of Cherry	Burgos
Mid month – San Bieto gastronomic festival (pilgrim party)	Samos
Mid month – Pilgrim party	Negreira
Mid month – Festival of San Cristóbal	Cee
Mid month through end of August – Ajo fair	Castrojeríz
16 – Virgen del Carmen	Triacastela, Melide, Arzúa, Cee, Corcubión
Third weekend – Medieval weekend	Corcubión
25 – Feast Day of Santiago	Nationwide, but especially in Puente la Reina, Nájera, Frómista, Carrión de los Condes, Santiago de Compostela, Olveiroa, Cee
25 – Medieval Convocation	Mansilla de las Mulas
Last week – Medieval week	Estella
Last weekend – Virgen del Carmen	Muxía
Month-end – Festival of the Rooster	Hornillos del Camino
Month-end – Festival of Asturians and Romans	Astorga
Month-end – Langosteira beach party	Finisterre
August	
First weekend – San Esteban	Zubiri, Pamplona
First Sunday – Longueirón Party	Finisterre
First weeks – Melgareña orchard festival	Burgos
Early month – Festival of the Rooster, Fiesta of the Cabalar	O Pedrouzo
9 – Old Patron Party	Berciano del Real Camino
13–16 – Celebration of Virgen de la Xunqueira	Cee
14 – Camino de Santiago fair	Los Arcos
Mid month – Boat festival	Arzúa
15–21 – Festival of San Roque	Melide
17 – Pilgrimage of San Mamede	Triacastela
17 – Ponte de Lóuzara fair	Samos
20–23 – Festival of Magic	Sarria
Third weekend – End of Camino festival	Finisterre

Date – Festival	Location
25–26 – Sea Routes Market celebration	Muxía
26 – Beast of San Vitores	Belorado
Last Monday – San Zoilo festival (celebrated second half of August)	Carrión de los Condes
Last weekend – Tomato fair	Mansilla de las Mulas
End of month – Celebration of the Cockle	Cee
September	
First week – Festival of La Virgen de la Encina	Ponferrada
First weekend – Thanksgiving	Belorado
First weekend – Patron festival	Portomarín
First Sunday – Pilgrim's day	Frómista
First Sunday – Virgen de la Gracia	Mansilla de las Mulas
First week – Festival of El Sejo	Castrojeríz
8 – Virgin of Roncesvalles	Roncesvalles
8 – Our Lady of Bethlehem	Carrión de los Condes
8 – Virgin of Perales	Bercianos del Real Camino
8–10 – Fiesta del Carmen	Finisterre
Second weekend – Feast of the Virgin of the Boat	Muxía
14 – Holiest Christ of Hope	Villafranca del Bierzo
Mid month – Fiesta de Gracias and San Jerónimo Hermosilla	Santo Domingo de la Calzada
Mid month – San Caralampio festival	Melide
20 – Festival of Garitosis	Sarria
21 – Festival of San Mateo	Logroño
22 – Equinox light phenomenon	San Juan de Ortega
26 – Fiesta de Garazi	Saint-Jean-Pied-de-Port
October	
5 – Festival of San Froilán	León
12 – Spanish National Day	Throughout Spain
November	
1 – All Saints Day	Throughout Spain
11 – San Martín fair	Mansilla de las Mulas
18 – Festival of San Román	Hornillos del Camino
28–30 – Festival of San Andrés	Estella
December	
6 – San Nicolás de Bari	San Juan de Ortega
Year-end – Chocolate festival	Astorga

APPENDIX C
Useful contacts, links and apps

Useful phone numbers

All emergencies
112

Fire department
080 (or 112)

Local police
092 (or 112)

Civil guard (rural areas)
062

Tourist helpline
902 102 112
(English, French, German, Italian)

Domestic violence
900 100 009

Non-emergency medical
1003

Emergency dentist
961 496 199

Local information
010

Lost or stolen credit cards
902 375 637 – American Express
900 971 231 – Master Card
900 991 124 – Visa

Pilgrim offices and other useful pilgrim info

Saint-Jean-Pied-de-Port
www.aucoeurduchemin.org

Santiago de Compostela
https://oficinadelperegrino.com/en

Cathedral of Santiago
(includes *botafumeiro* schedule)
http://catedraldesantiago.es/en

Mass times in churches on the Camino
https://oficinadelperegrino.com/en/
preparation/mass-on-the-way/

Transportation

Bus
www.alsa.com

Trains in Spain
www.renfe.com

Trains in France
www.sncf.com/en

Major cell phone providers in Spain

Movistar
www.movistar.es

Orange
https://en.orange.es

Vodafone
www.vodafone.es

Yoigo
www.yoigo.com

Camino forums and social media resources

Ivar's Forum
www.caminodesantiago.me

Leslie's Forum
www.caminodesantiago.org.uk

Confraternity of St James
www.facebook.com/groups/
confraternitysaintjames

American Pilgrims
www.facebook.com/groups/
AmericanPilgrims

Spanish-language Camino resources

Gronze pilgrim guide
www.gronze.com

Consumer Eroski guide
http://caminodessantiago.consumer.es

Useful smartphone apps (iPhone and Android)

Accommodation

Booking.com Travel Deals

My Camino Bed

Bus

Alsa, Busbud

Cities/regions

Auritz-Burguete

León El Camino de Santiago

Santiago

Cathedral of Santiago de Compostela

Muxía

Money exchange rate

XE

Spanish language

Google Translate

Collins Spanish-English Translation
Dictionary and Verbs

Spanish weather

AEMET

Transit

Omio: Train, Bus, Flight in Europe

Train

Renfe Ticket (buy tickets on Spanish
trains)

Renfe Horarios (long- and medium-
distance Spanish trains)

Renfe Cercanías (Spanish urban train
schedules)

OUI.sncf: Train Travel (France)

Unit converter

Converter (unit conversions)

Vegetarian/vegan

HappyCow: Find Vegan Food &
Restaurants

APPENDIX D
Bibliography and further reading

Reference works used in this book and suggested further reading

Bahrami, Beebe, *The Spiritual Traveler: Spain, A Guide to Sacred Sites and Pilgrim Routes*, Mahwah, New Jersey: Hidden Spring, 2009. Bahrami shares tales of sites on the Camino and other sacred Spanish places.

Cousineau, Phil, *The Art of Pilgrimage: The Seeker's Guide to Making Travel Sacred*, San Francisco: Conari, 2012. Cousineau helps the reader understand mythic aspects of modern pilgrimage in this book that has quickly become a classic.

Dennett, Laurie, '2000 Years of the Pilgrimage,' www.csj.org.uk. Initially a lecture, this is an excellent short summary of Camino history.

Gitlitz, David M. & Linda Kay Davidson, *The Pilgrimage Road to Santiago: The Complete Cultural Handbook*, New York: Saint Martin's Griffin, 2000.

Melczer, William, *The Pilgrim's Guide to Santiago de Compostela*, New York: Italica Press, 1993. The authoritative English translation of the *Liber Jacobi* or *Codex Calixtinus*.

O'Callaghan, Joseph P., *A History of Medieval Spain*, Ithaca NY: Cornell Paperback, 1983. Now a classic, this book covers the 8th-15th centuries of Spanish history and is an excellent reference work for sorting out royalty and their realms.

Ruiz, Federico & Gustavo Lopez, 'Review of Cultivation, History and Uses of Eucalyptus in Spain,' conference paper, Eucalyptus Species Management Conference, Addis Ababa, 2010. A helpful review of how Eucalyptus has dominated the forests of northwest Spain.

Steves, Rick, *Rick Steves Spain 2019*, New York: Avalon. The chapters on the Camino and on Santiago de Compostela itself include excellent information and helpful self-guided walking tours.

Tremlett, Giles, *Ghosts of Spain: Travels through Spain and its Silent Past*, New York: Bloomsbury USA, 2008. An ex-pat describes how to scratch the surface of modern Spain to understand the influences that made it what it is today.

Webb, Diana, *Medieval European Pilgrimage, c. 700-c.1500*, London: Palgrave, 2002. Important background for understanding the role of pilgrimage in medieval life.

Yates, S., *Pilgrim Tips & Packing List Camino de Santiago: What you need to know*, Scotts Valley, California: CreateSpace, 2013. The most detailed guide to Camino packing and prep.

Selected Camino Francés travelogues

Bennett, Bill, *The Way, My Way: A Camino Memoir*, Scotts Valley, California: CreateSpace, 2014. Bennett is humorous and self-deprecating, with an introspective voice.

Choquette, Sonia, *Walking Home: A Pilgrimage from Humbled to Healed*, Carlsbad, California: Hay House, 2015. After some setbacks, this spiritual teacher and guide walks the Camino and finds healing.

Codd, Kevin, *To the Field of Stars: A Pilgrim's Journey to Santiago de Compostela*, Grand Rapids: Eerdmans, 2008. Codd, a Catholic priest, shares his joys and disappointments as he yearns for sincerity and meaning in the religious aspects of the walk.

Coelho, Paulo, *The Pilgrimage*, New York: Harper Collins, 2006. Originally published in 1987, Coelho's magical book has launched many *caminos*.

Eagan, Kerry, *Fumbling: A Pilgrimage Tale of Love, Grief, and Spiritual Renewal on the Camino de Santiago*, New York: Broadway, 2006. An accessible and humble book that describes the varied emotions of a pilgrimage.

Gray, Patrick, *I'll Push You: A Journey of 500 Miles, Two Best Friends, and One Wheelchair*, Carol Stream, Illinois: Tyndale House, 2017. An emotional story of the love and friendship between friends.

Hitt, Jack, *Off the Road: A Modern-Day Walk Down the Pilgrim's Route in Spain*, New York: Simon & Schuster, 2005. Irreverent, funny and engaging, the author enjoys the places and people of the Camino.

Jusino, Beth, *Walking to the End of the World: A Thousand Miles on the Camino de Santiago*, Seattle: Mountaineers Books, 2018. The author begins at Le Puy and recounts her journey with humor and humility.

Kerkeling, Hape, *I'm Off Then: Losing and Finding Myself on the Camino de Santiago*, New York: Free Press, 2009. This German comedian's book was a longtime bestseller in his native Germany and the English translation does not disappoint.

Rupp, Joyce, *Walk in a Relaxed Manner: Life Lessons from the Camino*, Ossining, New York: Orbis, 2005. This well-written story of the author-nun's walk with a retired priest is organized in lesson-chapters like 'Savor Solitude' and 'Deal with Disappointments.'

Soper, Katharine B., *Steps Out of Time: One Woman's Journey on the Camino*, Ann Arbor: Stellaire Press, 2013. Carefully descriptive, this book recounts the journey of a secular pilgrim and mother.

Astorga City hall
(Stages 21/22)

DOWNLOAD THE ROUTES
IN GPX FORMAT

All the routes in this guide are available for download from:

www.cicerone.co.uk/1004/GPX

as standard format GPX files. You should be able to load them into most online GPX systems and mobile devices, whether GPS or smartphone. You may need to convert the file into your preferred format using a conversion programme such as gpsvisualizer.com or one of the many other such websites and programmes.

When you follow this link, you will be asked for your email address and where you purchased the guidebook, and have the option to subscribe to the Cicerone e-newsletter.

www.cicerone.co.uk

LISTING OF CICERONE GUIDES

Ski Touring and Snowshoeing in
  the Dolomites
The Way of St Francis
Trekking in the Apennines
Trekking in the Dolomites
Trekking the Giants' Trail: Alta Via 1
  through the Italian Pennine Alps
Via Ferratas of the Italian Dolomites
  Vols 1&2
Walking and Trekking in the
  Gran Paradiso
Walking in Abruzzo
Walking in Italy's Cinque Terre
Walking in Italy's Stelvio
  National Park
Walking in Sicily
Walking in the Dolomites
Walking in Tuscany
Walking in Umbria
Walking Lake Como and Maggiore
Walking Lake Garda and Iseo
Walking on the Amalfi Coast
Walking the Via Francigena
  pilgrim route – Parts 2&3
Walks and Treks in the
  Maritime Alps

MEDITERRANEAN
The High Mountains of Crete
Trekking in Greece
Treks and Climbs in Wadi Rum,
  Jordan
Walking and Trekking in Zagori
Walking and Trekking on Corfu
Walking in Cyprus
Walking on Malta
Walking on the Greek Islands –
  the Cyclades

**NEW ZEALAND
AND AUSTRALIA**
Hiking the Overland Track

NORTH AMERICA
The John Muir Trail
The Pacific Crest Trail

SOUTH AMERICA
Aconcagua and the Southern Andes
Hiking and Biking Peru's Inca Trails
Torres del Paine

**SCANDINAVIA, ICELAND
AND GREENLAND**
Hiking in Norway – South
Trekking in Greenland – The Arctic
  Circle Trail
Trekking the Kungsleden
Walking and Trekking in Iceland

**SLOVENIA, CROATIA,
MONTENEGRO AND ALBANIA**
Mountain Biking in Slovenia
The Islands of Croatia
The Julian Alps of Slovenia
The Mountains of Montenegro
The Peaks of the Balkans Trail
The Slovene Mountain Trail
Walking in Slovenia: The Karavanke
Walks and Treks in Croatia

SPAIN AND PORTUGAL
Camino de Santiago:
  Camino Frances
Coastal Walks in Andalucia
Cycling the Camino de Santiago
Cycling the Ruta Via de la Plata
Mountain Walking in Mallorca
Mountain Walking in
  Southern Catalunya
Portugal's Rota Vicentina
Spain's Sendero Historico: The GR1
The Andalucian Coast to Coast Walk
The Camino del Norte and
  Camino Primitivo
The Camino Ingles and Ruta do Mar
The Camino Portugues
The Mountains of Nerja
The Mountains of Ronda
  and Grazalema
The Sierras of Extremadura
Trekking in Mallorca
Trekking in the Canary Islands
Trekking the GR7 in Andalucia
Walking and Trekking in the
  Sierra Nevada
Walking in Andalucia
Walking in Menorca
Walking in Portugal
Walking in the Algarve
Walking on the Azores
Walking in the Cordillera Cantabrica
Walking on Gran Canaria
Walking on La Gomera and El Hierro
Walking on La Palma
Walking on Lanzarote
  and Fuerteventura
Walking on Madeira
Walking on Tenerife
Walking on the Costa Blanca
Walking the Camino dos Faros

SWITZERLAND
Switzerland's Jura Crest Trail
The Swiss Alpine Pass Route –
  Via Alpina Route 1
The Swiss Alps
Tour of the Jungfrau Region
Walking in the Bernese Oberland

Walking in the Engadine – Switzerland
Walking in the Valais
Walking in Zermatt and Saas-Fee

JAPAN AND ASIA
Hiking and Trekking in the Japan Alps
  and Mount Fuji
Japan's Kumano Kodo Pilgrimage
Trekking in Tajikistan

HIMALAYA
Annapurna
Everest: A Trekker's Guide
Trekking in the Himalaya
Trekking in Bhutan
Trekking in Ladakh

MOUNTAIN LITERATURE
8000 metres
A Walk in the Clouds
Abode of the Gods
Fifty Years of Adventure
The Pennine Way – the Path,
  the People, the Journey
Unjustifiable Risk?

TECHNIQUES
Fastpacking
Geocaching in the UK
Map and Compass
Outdoor Photography
Polar Exploration
The Mountain Hut Book

MINI GUIDES
Alpine Flowers
Navigation
Pocket First Aid and
  Wilderness Medicine
Snow

For full information on all our guides,
books and eBooks, visit our website:
www.cicerone.co.uk